ROBIN HOOD

Recent Titles in
Contributions to the Study of World Literature

ROBIN HOOD

The Shaping of the Legend

cz

JEFFREY L. SINGMAN

Contributions to the Study of World Literature, Number 92

Greenwood Press
Westport, Connecticut • London

APR 0 8 1999

Library of Congress Cataloging-in-Publication Data

Singman, Jeffrey L.
    Robin Hood : the shaping of the legend / Jeffrey L. Singman.
        p.   cm.—(Contributions to the study of world literature,
    ISSN 0738–9345 ; no. 92)
    Includes bibliographical references (p.   ) and index.
    ISBN 0–313–30101–8 (alk. paper)
    1. Robin Hood (Legendary character) in literature.   2. Ballads,
English—England—History and criticism.   3. Folk drama, English—
History and criticism.   4. English literature—History and
criticism.   5. Middle Ages in literature.   6. Outlaws—England—
Legends.   7. Outlaws in literature.   8. Legends in literature.
9. Medievalism.   I. Title.   II. Series.
PR2129.S56   1998
820.9′351—dc21   97–48565

British Library Cataloguing in Publication Data is available.

Library of Congress Catalog Card Number: 97–48565
ISBN: 0–313–30101–8
ISSN: 0738–9345

First published in 1998

Greenwood Press, 88 Post Road West, Westport, CT 06881
An imprint of Greenwood Publishing Group, Inc.

Printed in the United States of America

The paper used in this book complies with the
Permanent Paper Standard issued by the National
Information Standards Organization (Z39.48–1984).

10 9 8 7 6 5 4 3 2 1

Contents

Maps

Acknowledgments

This work has been many years in the making, and a number of hands have played some part in it. Thanks are due first to David Underdown, who suggested Robin Hood as a topic worth pursuing. I would also like to express my gratitude to the editors and staff involved in the Records of Early English Drama project, who have been unfailingly helpful in sharing their time and rich stores of information on the Robin Hood games: among these are Alexandra Johnston, director of REED, and the source of information on the games in Berkshire, Buckinghamshire, Oxfordshire; Sally-Beth MacLean, executive editor of REED, to whom I am also indebted for information on the games in Surrey; James Stokes, whose researches on Somerset have turned up some of the most noteworthy details on the games to date; Peter Greenfield for his information on the games in Hertfordshire; Evelyn Newlyn and Sally L. Joyce for their information on the games in Cornwall; and Rosalind C. Hays and C. E. McGee for their information on the games in Dorset. I would also like to thank Douglas Moffat, who plowed through an early version of this book, and Jean and Joan Mitchell for their introduction to the Robin Hood country. Finally, thanks are due to my wife, Victoria Hadfield, who has doubtless found life with Robin Hood to be extremely cramped quarters over the years.

Abbreviations

CPR	*Calendar of Patent Rolls*
EE	The English Experience
EHR	*English Historical Review*
EETS	Early English Texts Society
HMSO	His/Her Majesty's Stationery Office
MED	*Middle English Dictionary*
MLR	*Modern Language Review*
REED	Records of Early English Drama
REED: Devon	John M. Wasson, *Records of Early English Drama: Devon*
REED: Lancashire	David George, *Records of Early English Drama: Lancashire*
REED: Shropshire	Alan B. Somerset, *Records of Early English Drama: Shropshire*
REED: Somerset	James Stokes, *Records of Early English Drama: Somerset*
REED: Worcester	David Klausner, *Records of Early English Drama: Herefordshire and Worcestershire*
RS	Rolls Series
SR(A)	Edward Arber, *A Transcript of the Registers of the Company of Stationers of London, 1554–1640*
SR(B)	G.E.B. Eyre, *A Transcript of the Registers of the Worshipful Company of Stationers from 1640–1708*
STC	A. W. Pollard and G. R. Redgrave, *A Short-Title Catalogue . . . 1475–1640*
STS	Scottish Texts Society
Wing	Donald Wing, *A Short-Title Catalogue . . . 1641–1700*

Introduction

Among the narrative traditions of the Middle Ages, the Robin Hood legend occupies a position unique, important, and all too often overlooked. Robin Hood's uniqueness and importance begin with his status as the only English contribution to world mythology. King Arthur is ultimately a British rather than an English figure; a few tales of English origin, such as the romance of Guy of Warwick, have enjoyed some limited popularity outside of England; but no English hero can claim anything like the widespread and enduring mythic stature of the Outlaw of Sherwood. Nor is Robin's importance simply as an English legend. His is also the only lasting myth to arise from the High Middle Ages and the last Western legend to achieve a sustained international appeal. Never again would any European figure be the center of so truly living and vibrant a mythology.

The vitality and importance of the Robin Hood legend is attested by his numberless appearances in an extraordinary diversity of contexts. There survive some five Robin Hood ballads of known medieval origin, a unique corpus in a literature from which relatively few native heroes survive. From the fifteenth to the seventeenth centuries Robin Hood also featured in folk drama and other forms of playacting known to scholars as Robin Hood games. During his long career he has figured in broadside ballads and in chapbooks, in proverbs and place-names, in operas and in farces, in the names of clubs and the names of taverns, and even as the name of a brand of flour. Since 1980 there have appeared well over a half-dozen novels based on the legend, and while the Arthurian legend has also been fertile ground for novelists, Arthur cannot begin to compete with the plethora of children's stories, films, and television series inspired by Robin Hood during this century.[1]

A tale so often told must be profoundly significant to the society that retells it. It would not be revisited so frequently if it did not answer some deep need, nor can it be so many times repeated without having substantial cultural impact. Yet in spite of its importance, the Robin Hood legend has received surprisingly little study. The volume of Robin Hood scholarship has grown significantly in recent decades, but it remains small for a figure who has been a household name and the subject of a diverse and extensive tradition for the past seven centuries, and the legend's history still languishes at the margins of scholarly awareness. Most well-read English speakers have heard of Sir Thomas Malory and his version of the Arthurian legend; many know of Geoffrey of Monmouth, Chrétien de Troyes, and *Sir Gawain and the Green Knight*; but scarcely any can name the defining texts of the Robin Hood tradition, and even among scholars who specialize in medieval literature, few have heard of the *Gest of Robin Hood*.

The history of Robin Hood scholarship begins in 1795 with the publication of Joseph Ritson's impressive if eccentric *Robin Hood: A Collection of All the Ancient Poems, Songs and Ballads Now Extant*. Ritson was a notable antiquary and political radical in his day. His anthology included all the Robin Hood ballads he was able to find: the collection is extensive, and subsequent scholarship has found little to add to his corpus of early Robin Hood balladry. The book begins with an elaborate (and fanciful) biography of the outlaw; in his annotations to this biography Ritson amasses an enormous and perennially valuable body of early references to the legend. Although Ritson's work was eventually overtaken in the nineteenth century by the new critical approaches to sources, he left subsequent scholars a rich legacy upon which to build.

Most work on Robin Hood during the following century was largely dependent on Ritson.[2] Only toward the end of the nineteenth century was the study of Robin Hood placed on a new footing by the American philologist Francis James Child, whose *English and Scottish Ballads* re-edited the entire corpus of early Robin Hood ballads, with an apparatus reflecting the highest standards of nineteenth-century scholarship. His account of the legend, although brief, is meticulous and well reasoned, and it continues to repay study to this day. In particular, Child rejected both the historicizing and mythologizing interpretations of the outlaw: in his opinion, Robin Hood was "entirely a creation of the ballad muse."[3]

The question of whether Robin Hood was originally a historical, mythological, or literary figure, along with the search for the "real" Robin Hood, continued to dominate Robin Hood studies throughout the nineteenth and early twentieth centuries.[4] A pair of articles by Rodney Hilton and Maurice Keen in 1958 began to shift the emphasis from the genesis of the legend toward its social context by associating the early Robin Hood ballads with peasant discontent, specifically that of the fourteenth century which erupted in the Peasants' Revolt of 1381.[5] Their views were not especially controversial in light of the received view of Robin Hood as a figure of populist social protest, but they prompted a vigorous and groundbreaking response by J. C. Holt in an article published in 1960. Holt argued that "the Robin Hood ballads were originally the literature, not of a discontented peasantry, but of the gentry."[6] He drew attention to the ballads' lack of agrarian social complaint, and the presence of aristocratic cultural values: "the original audience was not concerned with alleged or actual class conflicts, of which the ballads are remarkably free, but with hospitality and its formalities, and with the precedence which arose from service and status."[7] A brief but lively flurry of articles ensued, testimony to Holt's service in waking the study of Robin Hood from its somnolence.[8]

The response to Holt's reinterpretation of the legend has been mixed. Keen reiterated his stance in *The Outlaws of Medieval Legend* (1961), but retracted his position in the introduction to the revised edition in 1977. Hilton on the other hand has continued to interpret the legend as an expression of popular discontent.[9] Holt offered a slightly modified version of his own perspective in his monograph *Robin Hood* (1982, rev. ed. 1989), suggesting that the origins of the legend lie among the "yeomen in service" in aristocratic households.[10] Even more recently, Richard Tardif has proposed quite a different view, associating the legend with urban wage artisans.[11]

The "origins and audience" debate initiated by Holt has done much to improve the critical standards of Robin Hood scholarship, but the relative lack of scholarly attention to the outlaw hero remains evident in the underdeveloped state of the field. At a basic level, the linguistic analyses, source studies, and other background work that underpin the study of other major medieval literature are generally lacking or lamentably out of date. On a more theoretical plane, there has been little of what Clifford Geertz would call "refinement of debate": the sophistication of Robin Hood studies, while greatly improved by the past forty years' work, has hardly kept up with that of comparable fields.

Most contributions to Robin Hood scholarship in the past forty years have come from historians. Since the early 1960s, a few historians have uncovered possible thirteenth-century evidence of the legend;[12] others have examined the relationship between the Robin Hood legend and social conditions in the later Middle Ages;[13] several have devoted their energies to the age-old quest for the "real" Robin Hood.[14] The principal critical anthology of Robin Hood texts in this century is the work of the historians R. B. Dobson and J. Taylor, whose *Rymes of Robin Hood* (1976; 2nd ed. 1989) ranges from medieval ballads to nineteenth-century poetry and drama; the introduction to the anthology constitutes one of the best brief histories of the legend written to date.

During the same period, comparatively few literary scholars have devoted attention to Robin Hood, and new trends in literary theory in recent decades have been slow to permeate the discussion of the legend.[15] David Fowler's *A Literary History of the Popular Ballad* (1968) devotes a chapter to the medieval Robin Hood ballads, which he sees as a critical point of contact at which "the metrical romance tradition of the later Middle Ages joined the mainstream of folksong to create a type of narrative song which we now call the ballad."[16] Dean A. Hoffman has emphasized the narrative and symbolic significance of archery in the Robin Hood ballads over its use for practical ends.[17] Douglas Gray's *explication de texte* of the medieval ballads firmly establishes their amenability to analysis as literary creations.[18] P. R. Coss has drawn attention to the subversiveness of the class relations depicted in *The Gest of Robin Hood*, suggesting that the aristocratic elements of that ballad reflect cultural diffusion to a lower stratum of society.[19] Peter Stallybrass has shown something of the applicability of semiotic analysis to the Robin Hood legend, offering some valuable ideas as to the systemic relationships between Robin Hood and the dominant culture.[20]

The only substantial literary study of the legend as a whole is Stephen Knight's *Robin Hood. A Complete Study of the English Outlaw* (1994). Knight departs forcefully from the historicist approach that has dominated the study of Robin Hood, offering an emphatically literary version of the legend: the study is only partially chronologized, relying heavily on distinctions of theme and genre to divide the material. Bringing to the material a postmodernist sense of the plurality of voices in a text, Knight finds in the Robin Hood tradition "a discourse which can represent aspects of dissent to established power and yet can also be complicit with such institutions of authority."[21] More recently, Knight, in cooperation with Thomas Ohlgren, has produced a new anthology of Robin Hood texts which, it is to be hoped, will help make the surviving materials of the early legend more accessible to students unacquainted with the tradition.[22]

One aspect of the legend especially in need of elucidation is the Robin Hood games. The principal study of the subject to date is David Wiles's *The Early Plays of Robin Hood* (1981). Wiles's book is valuable, but all too brief, and has since been overtaken by the work of the Records of Early English Drama project (REED) at the University of Toronto. Since its inception in 1975, REED has greatly augmented the body of available information on the games and challenged many traditional beliefs about their character and history; yet Robin Hood scholars have been slow to absorb the new data, and almost no reference to the work of REED can be found in the mainstream of Robin Hood scholarship. A few articles relating to the Robin Hood games have been offered by editors involved in the project,[23] but the subject remains in desperate need of a full-length study—an undertaking that will probably have to wait until the intense period of discoveries brought about by REED has at last wound down.

This present study of the outlaw hero has been brewing for almost two decades. It was initially undertaken in response to the paucity of scholarship on the subject of Robin Hood; as the foregoing survey of Robin Hood scholarship suggests, there has been a fair bit of interest in the outlaw in the interim, but much work remains to be done to bring Robin Hood studies in line with the state of other medieval literature. The principal focus of this book is the interaction between fictive text and social context. It takes the story of the legend as far as 1700, divided into two stages: first the period in which the legend was generated, when the relationship between text and context was extremely intimate, and then a period of transition in which that relationship became increasingly attentuated. As is appropriate to a work attempting to bridge the divide between the worlds of fiction and history, this study strives to incorporate the strengths of both the historical and literary approaches, respecting both the circumstances of the historic setting and the legend's status as a fictive creation within the semiautonomous domain of language.

One general problem in the study of Robin Hood has been the lack of a viable chronological framework for interpreting the evolution of the tradition. There has been a tendency to adhere to the traditional division between medieval and modern, extending to the legend the political historian's watershed at the end of the fifteenth century. Such a distinction does not well reflect the realities of the tradition. While events of the late fifteenth and early sixteenth centuries did influence the Robin Hood legend, their effect was delayed: many of the stories recorded in sixteenth- or seventeenth-century sources are not obviously different in form or content from the earlier ones, while texts composed in the Middle Ages can be shown to have remained in circulation until at least the late sixteenth century. Changes in the modes of transmission begin around 1500, but they are not complete before the latter part of the seventeenth century, with the demise of the Robin Hood games. Substantive changes in content cannot be documented until after 1550, and in the case of the games, there is no evidence to suggest any fundamental difference between fifteenth- and sixteenth-century versions.

A more useful distinction, albeit more subtle and challenging, would be one based on socioeconomic contexts of transmission, contrasting the "modern" with the "premodern" legend. The early or premodern Robin Hood legend was circulated orally in a milieu dominated by folk performers and itinerant entertainers; the modes of transmission involved limited economic specialization, with the economic transaction highly integrated into social relationships. The modern Robin Hood tradition was (and is) transmitted in a context shaped primarily by commercial media, most especially printed texts and professional drama, which involve impersonalized economic transactions and a high degree of economic specialization. The process of modernization begins some time around 1500, with the appearance of the first printed Robin Hood text; it is more or less complete by the latter part of the seventeenth century, by which date the traditional Robin Hood games had died out and the oral ballads had been supplanted by printed versions. Between these two dates both modern and premodern elements existed simultaneously and must be distinguished from each other on the basis of context and content rather than chronology.

Robin Hood scholarship has also been hindered by too close a reliance on the surviving texts as a means of understanding the premodern Robin Hood tradition. Holt explicitly characterizes the five surviving "medieval" ballads as "a typical and perhaps considerable part of the whole"; and other scholars implicitly assume that the stories known to us are more or less representative of the legend in general.[24] Yet medieval sources allude frequently to "rimes," "tales," or "romances" of Robin Hood, suggesting a corpus more extensive than a mere five stories. There were very possibly prose tales as well. No examples survive in medieval sources, but vernacular prose tales are rare in Middle English, particularly when the matter in question is on the level of a folktale, even though folktales surely existed.[25] Contemporary evidence associates the legend with oral rather than written culture, making it all the more likely that the written survivals represent only a fraction of the original tradition. Even the survival of five stories is unique for any native English folk hero in this period, most of whom are known to us only as names. It is probably the sheer volume and ubiquity of the Robin Hood legend that has ensured the survival of at least a few tales. Moreover, narratives were only a part of the tradition: place-names, proverbs, and iconography also played a part in its transmission. Finally, the surviving Robin Hood narratives, as written texts, are by definition weighted toward the interests of the tiny literate subset of the original audience. Close reading of the texts is in itself a valid exercise, but to understand the whole tradition—and hence the literary context in which the surviving texts were read—we need to see the forest as well as the trees, allowing space in our reckoning for material lost to the record, but nonetheless integral to the legend as a whole.

Partly for this reason, this study will focus on the structures of the tradition. The Robin Hood legend was expressed by manifold voices in diverse media. To the degree that it can be identified as a unitary phenomenon, this unity is manifested at the structural level. As far as possible, the principal constituents of this structural unity must be identified on the basis of evidence internal to the tradition. Any interpretive act is necessarily shaped by the interpreter, so that in an absolute sense no text truly speaks for itself, yet in practical terms we can interrogate the legend to yield a kind of dialogue, looking for the legend's priorities in those consistently recurring elements that determine its distinctive shape.

This book will attempt to shed new light on the shapes and structures of the Robin Hood legend in relation to the society that formed it. The first two chapters examine the early Robin Hood tradition. Chapter 1 considers nondramatic manifestations of the legend, while Chapter 2 looks at the Robin Hood games; each offers a survey of the evidence and a provisional exposition of the key structures that defined these forms of the legend. Chapter 3 turns to the period of transition in the sixteenth and seventeenth centuries, examining the various transformations at work and the ways in which they affected the underlying structures. The final chapter examines how the structures of the legend interacted with each other and with the exterior world to create a network of significances, and how this network was altered by the process of modernization.

One major aspect of traditional Robin Hood scholarship that will be wholly ignored here is the search for a historical Robin Hood. This pursuit has been the perennial will-o'-the-wisp of Robin Hood studies; even Knight, avowed anti-historicist though he is, cannot wholly resist its allure, offering a displaced version of the "real" Robin Hood in what amounts to his candidate for the "real" Barnsdale.[26] The doggedness with which this quarry has been pursued has been in inverse proportion to the usefulness of the hunt. No widely accepted candidate has been found, and it may be questioned whether such a discovery is at all possible. If Robin Hood did exist, he was a commoner, and as such belonged to a class of people whose individual activities are not well documented in medieval texts. We have little reason to hope that we would recognize the original Robin Hood even if we did find him. The medieval tales of Robin Hood are fictions, and cannot be trusted to provide a positive identification, especially after centuries of oral transmission. Nor is it certain that Robin Hood existed at all. As a name for a medieval highwayman, "Robin Hood" has a suspiciously pseudonymic ring; it may well be that the only forests this outlaw ever prowled were those of the imagination. Ultimately, the most significant discoveries to be made about Robin Hood lie not in the domain of history, but in that of legend: the myth, as we shall see, is much more interesting than the man could ever have been.

Since Robin Hood is a prominent part of our common cultural heritage, I have tried to ensure that this book will be accessible to the educated lay reader as well as the academic specialist. For this reason, primary sources cited in the body of the text are given translations or glosses as necessary. The use of *i* and *j* as well as *u* and *v* has been regularized according to modern orthography; the character þ has been rendered as *th*, but ʒ has been left as is, since it can represent Modern English *y* or *gh*, depending on the context. Punctuation, capitalization, and word division have been altered as necessary to clarify the sense, since in most cases the original conventions are substantially different from those of Modern English; abbreviations have been expanded on a similar basis. Emendations in texts are given in square brackets; angled brackets indicate gaps in the original.

Dates are always given in New Style: in English usage of the period, the number of the year changed on March 25, but for simplicity and clarity all dates are given as they would have been numbered according to modern practice. Dates of publication are given in parentheses; square brackets indicate dates of composition and of manuscripts. Dates of account entries are often given as a two-year span—the accounting year did not generally correspond to the calendar year, so unless a month or day is specified, the entry could refer to an event in either year.

The task of assigning names to Robin Hood tales is in some cases complex. The earliest sources do not generally offer titles, while later ones often assign multiple names to the same story, or the same name to different stories. In most cases, I have used the names assigned by Child; where multiple versions of a single story exist, they are given a name indicative of the content and distinguished as A, B, or C versions. Stories not existing as independent texts are named in quotation marks rather than italics.

Appendix A offers a compilation of references to the Robin Hood games. Such a document has some disadvantages, notably the fact that the ongoing efforts of the Records of Early English Drama project have made it outdated even as it was being written. However, it serves two useful purposes that justify its inclusion. On a practical level, it replaces what would otherwise have been an extremely cumbersome body of footnotes in Chapter 2. At a more general level, there has been no such compilation of information on the games since the rather laconic appendices to David Wiles's study in 1981. The present compilation can serve as a working corpus until such time as the completion of the REED project allows for a full reassessment of the games. Appendix B reproduces a series of texts relating to the riots resulting from the Robin Hood games in Edinburgh in 1561. These disturbances constitute a particularly revealing moment in the history of the Robin Hood games and merit full and accessible documentation for students of the legend.

NOTES

1. Recent novels include Gary L. Blackwood, *The Lion and the Unicorn* (Rolla, Mo.: Eagle Books, 1982); Nicholas Chase, *Locksley* (New York: St. Martin's/Marek, 1983); Parke Godwin, *Robin and the King* (New York: Morrow, 1993); B. Green, *Marion's Christmas Rose* (Braunton, Devon: Merlin, 1984); Richard Kluger, *The Sheriff of Nottingham* (New York: Viking, 1992); Robin McKinley, *The Outlaws of Sherwood* (New York: Greenwillow Books, 1988); David Stuart Ryan, *The Lost Journal of Robyn Hood, Outlaw* (London and New York: Kozmik Press, 1989); Peter Vansittart, *The Death of Robin Hood: A Novel* (London: Owen, 1981); for a collection of short stories see Martin H. Greenberg, ed., *The Fantastic Adventures of Robin Hood* (New York: Penguin, 1991). For a recent study of other twentieth-century versions of the legend in print and on film, see Stephen Knight, *Robin Hood. A Complete Study of the English Outlaw* (Oxford and Cambridge, Mass.: Blackwell, 1994), ch. 6.

2. The only major addition to Ritson's collection has been the fifteenth-century ballad of *Robin Hood and the Monk*, known to Ritson only in a fragmentary version. It was published in full for the first time in John Matthew Gutch's *A Lyttel Geste of Robin Hood* (London: Longman, Brown, Green and Longmans, 1847).

3. F. J. Child, *The English and Scottish Popular Ballads* (Boston: Little, Brown and Co., 1882-98; rpt. New York: Cooper Square, 1962), 3.39–233.

4. For a bibliography of early Robin Hood studies, see J. Harris Gable, *Bibliography of Robin Hood*, University of Nebraska Studies in Language, Literature, and Criticism 17 (Lincoln, Neb.: University of Nebraska, 1939).

5. Rodney H. Hilton, "The Origins of Robin Hood," *Past and Present* 14 (1958), 30–44; Maurice Keen, "Robin Hood, a Peasant Hero," *History Today* 8 (1958), 684–89.

6. J. C. Holt, "The Origins and Audience of the Ballads of Robin Hood," *Past and Present* 18 (1960), 90.

7. *Ibid.*, 100.

8. Maurice Keen, "Robin Hood—Peasant or Gentleman?" *Past and Present* 19 (1961), 7–15; J. C. Holt, "Robin Hood: Some Comments," *Past and Present* 19 (1961), 16–18; T. H. Aston, "Robin Hood. Communication," *Past and Present* 20 (1962), 7–9.

9. Rodney H. Hilton, *Class Conflict and the Crisis of Feudalism*, 2nd. ed. (London and New York: Verso, 1990).

10. J. C. Holt, *Robin Hood*, 2nd ed. (London: Thames and Hudson, 1989), 110.

11. Richard Tardif, "The 'Mistery' of Robin Hood: A New Social Context for the Texts," in *Words and Worlds. Studies in the Social Role of Verbal Culture*, ed. Stephen Knight and S. N. Mukherjee, Sydney Studies in Society and Culture 1 (Sydney: Sydney Association for Studies in Society and Culture, 1983), 130–45.

12. David Crook, "Some Further Evidence Concerning the Dating of the Origins of the Legend of Robin Hood," *EHR* 99 (1984), 530–34.

13. Barbara A. Hanawalt, "Ballads and Bandits: Fourteenth-Century Outlaws and the Robin Hood Poems," in Barbara A. Hanawalt, ed., *Chaucer's England. Literature in Historical Context*, Medieval Studies at Minnesota 4 (Minneapolis: University of Minnesota Press, 1992), 154–75; J. R. Maddicott, "The Birth and Setting of the Ballads of Robin Hood," *EHR* 93 (1978), 276–99; John Bellamy, *Robin Hood: An Historical Enquiry* (London: Croom Helm, 1985); Andrew Ayton, "Military Service and the Development of the Robin Hood Legend in the Fourteenth Century," *Nottingham Medieval Studies* 36 (1992), 126–47. Colin Richmond's "An Outlaw and Some Peasants: The Possible Significance of Robin Hood" [*Nottingham Medieval Studies* 37 (1993), 90–101] is particularly noteworthy for mediating between the legend and its social context without losing sight of the former's fictive character.

14. See Maddicott, "The Birth and Setting of the Ballads of Robin Hood"; Bellamy, *Robin Hood*; David Crook, "The Sheriff of Nottingham and Robin Hood: The Genesis of the Legend?" in *Thirteenth-Century England 2. Proceedings of the Newcastle upon Tyne Conference 1987*, ed. P. R. Coss and S. D. Lloyd (Woodbridge, Suffolk: Boydell, 1988), 59–68; Richard de Vries, *On the Trail of Robin Hood* (rev. ed. Hightown: Crossbow Books, 1988).

15. For literary-historical approaches, see Malcolm Nelson, *The Robin Hood Tradition in the English Renaissance*, Salzburg Studies in English Literature (Salzburg: Institut für Englische Sprache und Literatur, 1973); J. B. Bessinger, "The Gest of Robin Hood Revisited," in *The Learned and the Lewed: Studies in Chaucer and Medieval Literature* (Cambridge, Mass.: Harvard University Press, 1974).

16. D. C. Fowler, *A Literary History of the Popular Ballad* (Durham, N.C.: Duke University Press, 1968), 18; also 10, 65 ff.

17. Dean A. Hoffman, "'With the Shot Y Wyll/ Alle Thy Lustes to Full-Fyl': Archery as Symbol in the Early Ballads of Robin Hood," *Neuphilologische Mitteilungen* 86 (1985), 494–505.

18. Douglas Gray, "The Robin Hood Poems," *Poetica: An International Journal of Linguistic and Literary Studies* (Tokyo) 18 (1984), 1–39.

19. P. R. Coss, "Aspects of Cultural Diffusion in Medieval England: The Early Romances, Local Society, and Robin Hood," *Past and Present* 108 (1985), 35–79.

20. Peter Stallybrass, "'Drunk with the Cup of Liberty': Robin Hood, the Carnivalesque and the Rhetoric of Violence in Early Modern England," *Semiotica* 54 (1985), 113–45. Roberta Kevelson's *Inlaws/Outlaws. A Semiotics of Systemic Interaction: "Robin Hood" and the "King's Law"* (Bloomington: Indiana University Press, 1977) also looks at Robin Hood from a semiotic standpoint, and Tom Hayes's *The Birth of Popular Culture. Ben Jonson, Maid Marian, and Robin Hood* (Pittsburgh: Duquesne University Press, 1992) brings a poststructuralist perspective to the changing Robin Hood legend of the early modern period. George Swan's "Robin Hood's 'Irish Knife': Irony in the Guy of Gisborne Ballad" [*University of Mississippi Studies in English* 11–12 (1993–95), 51–80] offers a rather intricate reading of one of the Percy Folio ballads of Robin Hood. Folklorists, once active participants in Robin Hood studies, have not often been heard on the subject in recent decades; for a few examples, see Tim Lundgren, "The Robin Hood Ballads and the English Outlaw Tradition," *Southern Folklore* 53 (1996), 225–47; Evelyn M. Perry, "The Battle to Possess Sherwood," *Journal of American Folklore* 109 (1996), 437–40; Joseph Falaky Nagy, "The Paradoxes of Robin Hood," *Folklore* 91 (1980), 198–210.

21. Knight, *Robin Hood*, 15.

22. Stephen Knight and Thomas Ohlgren, eds., *Robin Hood and Other Outlaw Tales*, TEAMS Middle English Texts Series (Kalamazoo, Mich.: Medieval Institute Publications, 1997).

23. James D. Stokes, "Robin Hood and the Churchwardens in Yeovil," *Medieval and Renaissance Drama in England* 3 (1986), 1–25; Sally-Beth MacLean, "King Games and Robin Hood: Play and Profit at Kingston-upon-Thames," *Research Opportunities in Renaissance Drama* 29 (1986–1987), 85–94; John Wasson, "The St. George and Robin Hood Plays in Devon," *Medieval English Theatre* 2 (1980), 66–69. Also of interest is a collection of articles on Robin Hood drama in general, *Playing Robin Hood: The Legend as Performance in Five Centuries*, ed. Lois Potter (Newark, Del.: University of Delaware Press, 1998).

24. Holt, *Robin Hood*, 36; cf. 111. For example, Dobson and Taylor have argued that the skill displayed in the surviving works suggest that "the early 'rymes and tales' were the work of professional minstrels" [Dobson and Taylor, "Medieval Origins of the Robin Hood Legend: A Reassessment," *Northern History* 7 (1972), 24]. Douglas Gray is rather unusual in arguing that the surviving texts are only a fragment of the original corpus [Gray, "The Robin Hood Poems," 3].

25. See R. M. Wilson, *Lost Literature of Medieval England*, 2nd ed. (London: Methuen, 1970).

26. Knight, *Robin Hood*, 29–31.

1

Robyn Hod in Scherewod Stod

For many ben of swyche manere
That talys and rymys wyl blethly here;
Yn gamys, & festys, & at the ale,
Love men to lestene trotevale,
That may falle ofte to vylanye
To dedly synne, or other folye.

[For many are of such sort that they will gladly hear tales and rimes; at games
and feasts and at the ale men love to listen to rubbish that may often lead
toward villany, to deadly sin, or other unwisdom.]

—Robert Mannyng, *Handlyng Synne* ll. 45–50

After two centuries of Robin Hood scholarship, the earliest certain reference to
the outlaw remains the passage first identified by Ritson in the B-version of
Piers Plowman [c. 1378], where Sloth, the drunken priest, confesses his profane
tastes in entertainment:

I can nouȝte perfitly my pater-noster, as the prest it syngeth,
But I can rymes of Robyn Hood, and Randolf erle of Chestre,
Ac neither of owre lorde ne of owre lady the leste that evere was made. [1]

[I know not perfectly my Paternoster, as the priest sings it, but I know rimes of
Robin Hood, and Ranulf, Earl of Chester; but neither of our lord nor our lady
the least that ever was made]

This casual allusion would seem to suggest that tales of Robin Hood were
already a familiar part of English culture in the latter half of the fourteenth
century, although there are no further references to the legend prior to 1400.

However, there is some possible evidence as early as the late thirteenth century. Historians have found eight instances of the surname "Robinhood" and others resembling it between 1261 and 1296. This evidence is highly suggestive: full names of this sort are rarely used as surnames, and in five of the eight cases, the name is applied to known or suspected criminals, or even outlaws, suggesting the possibility that it was a nickname for a malefactor. The names occur in Huntingdonshire, Suffolk, Essex, Berkshire, Hampshire, and Sussex, which might indicate that the legend was already widely diffused in England by that time. Regrettably, this evidence is not fully conclusive. In several cases the names take the form "Robehod"; even if we regard this as a variant for "Robinhood," it is by no means certain that the legendary outlaw lies behind the name. One early fourteenth-century instance of the name, Katherine Robinhood of London, belongs to the daughter of one Robert Hood; the earliest example, William Robehod in Berkshire, also appears as Hobbehod. Both should stand as warnings against too much confidence in our ability to interpret Middle English surnames.[2]

Actual Robin Hood texts first appear in the fifteenth century, initially as fragments of verse, then in a handful of complete tales. The earliest fragment is inscribed in an early fifteenth-century manuscript of miscellaneous Latin works, now at Lincoln Cathedral:

> Robyn hod in scherewod stod, hodud and hathud, hosut and schod; Ffour and thuynti arowus he bar in hit [*read:* his] hondus.[3]

> [Robin Hood in Sherwood stood, hooded and hatted, hosed and shod; four and twenty arrows he bore in his hands]

The verse appears to have been a stereotyped opening for a Robin Hood ballad. Versions of the phrase "Robin Hood in Sherwood stood" recur in diverse contexts in the fifteenth to seventeenth centuries, with "Barnsdale" and "greenwood" as variants for Sherwood. One early instance is concealed in a Wiltshire parliamentary return of 1432. At the end of each line of the return, the scribe, apparently looking to liven up a monotonous task, inserted an extra word; when read together, they reveal a few more clues as to the content of the Robin Hood legend:

Adam / Belle / Clyme / Ocluw / Willyam / Cloudesle / Robyn / hode / Inne / Grenewode / Stode / Godeman / was / hee / lytel / Joon / Muchette / Millersson / Scathelok / Reynoldyn.[4]

Robin is here associated with the legendary Cumbrian outlaws Adam Bell, Clim of the Clough, and William Cloudesley (discussed later in this chapter); Little John, Much the Miller's Son, and Scathlock all appear in the medieval Robin Hood texts (the identity of "Reynoldyn" is unclear).[5]

TALES OF ROBIN HOOD

From the mid-fifteenth century onward, actual Robin Hood tales begin to appear in the written record. The earliest datable example is not actually in English, nor was it even recorded in England: it is a story incorporated by the Scottish historian Walter Bower in his continuation of John Fordun's *Scotichronicon* [c. 1445]. Bower places the outlaw in the year 1265, in the context of Simon de Montfort's rebellion against Henry III. He relates the following story:

De quo eciam quedam commendabilia recitantur, sicut patuit in hoc, quod cum ipse quondam in Barnesdale iram regis et fremitum principis declinans missam ut solitus erat devotissime audieret—nec aliqua necessitate volebat interumpere officium—quadam die cum audiret missam, a quodam vicecomite et ministris regis eum sepius per prius infestantibus in illo secretissimo loco nemorali ubi misse interfuit exploratus, venientes ad eum qui hoc de suis perceperunt ut omni annisu fugeret suggesserunt. Quod ob reverenciam sacramenti quod tunc devotissime venerabatur omnino facere recusavit. Sed ceteris suis ob metum mortis trepidantibus, Robertus in tantum confisus in eum quem coluit inveritus cum paucissimis qui tunc ei forte affuerunt inimicos congressus eos de facile devicit, et de eorum spoliis ac redempcione ditatus ministros ecclesie et missas in majore veneracione semper et de post habere preelegit. Attendens quod vulgariter dictum est: "Hunc Deus exaudit qui missam sepius audit." [6]

[Concerning this man they do tell some commendable things, as in one instance when he, hiding in Barnsdale from the king's ire and rage, was devoutly hearing Mass as he was accustomed—nor would he interrupt this service for any need. One day when he was hearing Mass, he was spied out in that secret woodland place where he was at Mass by a certain sheriff and some officers of the king, who had often hounded him. Those of his men who had discovered this came to him and suggested that he make every effort to flee. This he entirely refused to do, out of reverence for the sacrament which was at that moment being devoutly venerated. But while the rest of his men were terrified for fear of death, Robert had so much faith in Him whom he worshiped that he fearlessly set out to meet whatever enemies might be there, taking those few men who happened to be with him; he easily defeated them, and, enriched with their spoils and ransom, he decided to hold the masses and ministers of the church forever in even greater respect. For he heeded what they say: "To him God gives ear who does often Mass hear."]

Bower gives his story a predictably clerical cast, yet its outline is consistent with other surviving Robin Hood tales. The basic premise of Robin endangering himself by insisting on hearing Mass has an analogue in the medieval ballad of *Robin Hood and the Monk*, and the references to Barnsdale and the sheriff agree with other early Robin Hood material.

For the most part, the rest of the early tales take the form of verse narratives, commonly labeled ballads. The term ballad is somewhat problematic because of its musical connotations. It is a convenient label, and valid in that the early

Robin Hood ballads are very similar in form to folk ballads of later centuries, but it must be remembered that there is in most cases no evidence whether the surviving early ballads were sung.

The *Gest of Robin Hood*

The most substantial early ballad is the piece described in its earliest versions as *A Little Gest of Robin Hood*. The *Gest* survives in about a half-dozen printed editions in various states of preservation: the earliest was probably printed some time around 1500, the latest about a century later.[7] The actual date of composition is uncertain and rendered more complex by the likelihood that the surviving text incorporates several layers of composition by which discrete stories were assembled into a longer narrative. William Clawson, writing early in this century, argued that the frequency and diversity of -e(- inflections in the *Gest* suggest that it was written before 1400, when these were still a current feature of the spoken language.[8] His dating is not impossible, but his evidence is not sufficiently strong to support a date of composition so much earlier than the surviving versions, and in general his conclusions reflect an intellectual milieu in which scholars were eager to assign their texts to the earliest possible dates. In fact, poetry of this period was notoriously conservative and continued to preserve -e(- inflections well into the fifteenth century—John Lydgate, for example, uses them extensively. Clawson's argument also presupposes metrical regularity, which is not always a feature of Middle English verse, especially at a more popular level. In the absence of any recent analysis of the language of the *Gest*, we can meaningfully read it as a text of the fifteenth century, but not as a work predating 1400.

The *Gest* is long and intricate, comprised of several interwoven narrative threads. It runs to 456 stanzas divided into eight fits. In the following plot summary, the titles in brackets are intended as labels for identifying the component narratives of the *Gest*.

Fit 1 ["Robin Hood and the Knight"]: Robin Hood and his men are in Barnsdale, and Robin resolves not to have dinner until some unusual guest has been found. Little John is detailed to Wentbridge with Much and Will Scarlok to watch the road; they bring back a knight of sorrowful cheer. The knight is given dinner and afterward is asked to pay. He pleads poverty, claiming that he has only ten shillings. The knight's coffer is examined and reveals the truth of his words. The knight explains that his son killed a knight and a squire in a tournament, and he has had to pledge his lands to the Abbot of St. Mary's in York as security for a £400 loan to save his son. Robin proposes to lend the knight the money to recover his lands if the knight can find proper surety. The knight says he has none to offer save God, but Robin scoffs at the idea; when the knight suggests the Virgin Mary, the outlaw willingly agrees. At the end of the fit, the knight is sent off with the money, new equipment and clothes, and Little John to be his servant.

Fit 2 ["Robin Hood and the Knight" continued]: In York, the Abbot of St. Mary's is gloating over the imminent acquisition of the knight's lands, in the company of a justice and other officials whom he has involved in the affair. The knight arrives and at first asks for leniency, but neither the abbot nor any of the others will grant it. At last the knight produces the money, to the abbot's profound disappointment. The knight returns home and gathers the money to repay Robin Hood. He sets out to meet Robin at the appointed time, but is delayed on the way as he stops to rescue a yeoman who has won a wrestling contest and is in danger of harm from his irate opponents.

Fit 3 ["Little John and the Sheriff"]: John, while in the knight's service, takes part in an archery contest. His skill so impresses the Sheriff of Nottingham that he takes John into his service—apparently unperturbed by John's rather unlikely alias of "Reynold Greenleaf." John sleeps in one morning while the Sheriff is out hunting. By midday he is famished: he breaks into the larder, thrashing the butler, and helps himself to a large meal. The Sheriff's cook attacks him, and proves a doughty opponent. The two eventually call a truce, and John convinces the cook to join the outlaws. They plunder the Sheriff's valuables and repair to the forest, where they join Robin and the band. John sets out through the forest and finds the Sheriff, whom he promises to lead to a particularly large deer. The Sheriff, never a quick study in his dealings with the outlaws, follows and is led straight to Robin Hood's lair. The outlaws serve him a feast using his own tableware, then strip him of his finery and compel him to spend the night on the ground like one of them. Robin offers to make the Sheriff a fine outlaw, but the Sheriff begs to be either released or killed. Robin frees him, after exacting a promise that he will do the outlaws no harm.

Fit 4 ["Robin Hood and the Knight" concluded]: Robin once again puts off dinner until a guest can be found—he is distressed that the knight has not paid and that the Blessed Virgin has failed to live up to her part of the bargain. Little John, Much, and Scarlok set out and encounter two monks accompanied by an escort of fifty-two men. They shoot one monk, the escort flees, and the remaining monk is brought to Robin. The outlaws feed him and ask what abbey he comes from. He proves to be the cellarer of St. Mary's Abbey, and Little John suggests that the Virgin has at last arranged repayment. The monk claims to be carrying only twenty marks, but when searched, he is found to bear over £800—Little John exults that the generous Virgin has repaid the knight's debt twice over. The knight finally arrives with the money, but Robin refuses it, saying he has already been paid, and hands the extra £400 to the knight to purchase new equipment suitable to his station.

Fit 5 ["Robin Hood and the Sheriff"]: The Sheriff announces an archery contest. Robin and his men take part, and Robin, naturally, wins; but he is identified and a fight ensues in which Little John is wounded. The outlaws are forced to take refuge in the castle of Sir Richard atte Lee, identified with the knight of fits 1, 2, and 4.

Fit 6 ["Robin Hood and the Sheriff" concluded]: The Sheriff lays siege to Sir Richard's castle, calling on the knight to yield his prisoners, but Sir Richard refuses, and the Sheriff withdraws. The Sheriff seeks assistance from the king (identified at the end of the fit as "Edwarde, our comly kynge"), who promises to come to

Nottingham and deal with the knight and Robin in person. The outlaws return to the forest, and soon after, the Sheriff captures Sir Richard while the knight is out hawking. Sir Richard's wife informs Robin of her husband's plight, and Robin leads a rescue by force, killing the Sheriff in the process. The knight joins the outlaws in the forest.

Fit 7 ["Robin Hood and the King"]: The king comes north and is further enraged to discover that Robin's poaching has depleted the deer stock of his parks. After half a year in Nottingham, he is still unable to find Robin Hood. On the advice of a forester, he disguises himself as an abbot, with five of his knights as monks to be his followers. They enter the forest and are captured by the outlaws. Robin asks the abbot for "charity": Edward cheerily gives him the £40 he is carrying. After feasting, the outlaws take part in a shooting contest, in which each unsuccessful shot is rewarded with a buffet. When Robin fails, he invites the abbot to strike him, and the hearty blow he receives convinces him that this abbot is worth a closer look. The king is recognized and pardons Sir Richard and the outlaws, telling them they must give up their forest life.

Fit 8 ["Robin Hood and the King" concluded]: The king dons the outlaws' Lincoln green, and they all process into Nottingham, competing at archery en route. Robin and his men join the court, but in time Robin's men abandon him, and he finds his wealth rapidly consumed. Robin yearns to return to the forest and asks the king for leave, under pretext of visiting a chapel he had built in Barnsdale. The king grants him a week for this purpose, but once he is back in the greenwood, Robin helps himself to the deer and gathers his men around him once again, never again to return to the king. At the end there is a brief account of Robin's death, in which he goes to his kinswoman the Prioress of "Kirkesly" (Kirklees) to be let blood and is killed by her and a Sir Roger of Doncaster.

The *Gest* is widely thought to have been written not as a single work but as a compilation crafted from several earlier tales. It includes at least four distinguishable narratives, here labeled "Robin Hood and the Knight" (Fits 1, 2, and 4), "Little John and the Sheriff" (Fit 3), "Robin Hood and the Sheriff" (Fits 5 and 6), and "Robin Hood and the King" (Fits 7 and 8). Most of its constituent stories can be shown to have medieval analogues of some sort, a matter of some importance when it comes to establishing the history of the legend. The motif of the impoverished knight in "Robin Hood and the Knight" has parallels in the romances of *Amadace*, *Isumbras*, and *Launfal* and the humorous tale of *Cleges*; the money-counting episodes closely resemble incidents in the romance of Eustace the Monk.[9] "Little John and the Sheriff" has close analogues in the tale of Fulk Fitz Warin and the *Gesta Herewardi*, as well as in the ballads *Robin Hood and the Potter* and *Robin Hood and the Butcher* (all discussed later in this chapter). "Robin Hood and the King" is a reflex of the common folk motif of the King Incognito, K1812 in Stith Thompson's classification. The story of Robin Hood's death occurs in an early ballad of its own, and its analogues are discussed below. Only the story of "Robin Hood and the Sheriff" can be said to be particularly unusual, although the motif of the archery contest is also found in

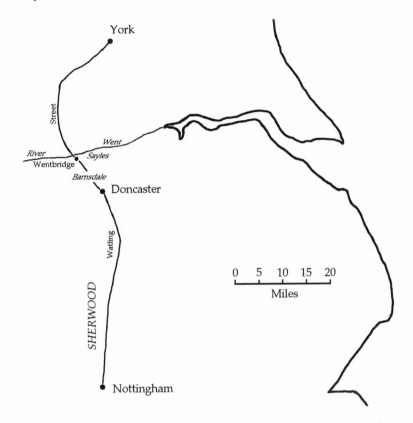

York

Street

Went

River   Sayles
Wentbridge

Barnsdale

Doncaster

Watling

0   5   10   15   20
Miles

SHERWOOD

Nottingham

The Geography of the Legend

"Little John and the Sheriff," *Robin Hood and Queen Katherine*, and the story of Adam Bell, Clim of the Clough, and William of Cloudesley. Significantly, this is the part of the *Gest* that connects its dominant story, "Robin Hood and the Knight," with its concluding climax in "Robin Hood and the King." It seems likely that some version of the other stories predated the *Gest*, while this one was created specifically for the compilation. This might help explain the fact that in this part of the *Gest* the previously anonymous knight is identified as Sir Richard atte Lee; the name may allude to someone known to the compiler, perhaps a patron.

The *Gest* shows some real signs of craftsmanship, particularly in "Robin Hood and the Knight," which has been especially praised for the balance of the narrative. The dialogue in many cases is quite vivid and evocative, as in stanzas 103–4, when the knight arrives at the abbey:

"Do gladly, syr abbot," sayd the knyght,
    "I am come to holde my day."

> The fyrst word the abbot spake,
> > "Hast thou brought my pay?"
>
> "Not one peny," sayd the knyght,
> > "By God that maked me;"
> "Thou art a shrewed dettour," sayd the abbot;
> > "Syr justyce, drynke to me."

The text is also pervaded by a dry sense of humor, as in the following scene after the cellarer of St. Mary's has been robbed of £800, nominally as payment for his food:

> The monke toke the hors with spore,
> > No lenger wolde he abyde;
> "Aske to drynke," than sayd Robyn,
> > "Or that ye forther ryde."
>
> "Nay, for God," than sayd the monke,
> > "Me reweth I cam so nere;
> For better chepe ['a better deal'] I myght have dyned
> > In Blythe or in Dankestere." [st. 258–59]

The compiler has apparently undertaken to create a substantial and semibiographic story of Robin Hood using the romance device of narrative interlacing. He begins with "Robin Hood and the Knight," a tale unusual in the Robin Hood canon for its well-balanced intricacy. He has interwoven this tale with "Little John and the Sheriff" through Little John's service with the knight. He has then linked both narratives to "Robin Hood and the Sheriff": he identifies the knight of "Robin Hood and the Knight" with Sir Richard atte Lee of "Robin Hood and the Sheriff," while the Sheriff's oath not to harm the outlaws in "Little John and the Sheriff" is violated by his plot against Robin in "Robin Hood and the Sheriff." Finally, he has connected "Robin Hood and the Sheriff" to "Robin Hood and the King" through the escalation of the conflict after the archery contest, by which the king is plausibly brought into the struggle.

The process of compilation has left a few seams in the narrative, suggesting that the compiler has not completely rewritten his material. The knight of "Robin Hood and the Knight" only acquires a name in "Robin Hood and the Sheriff." There are some curious allusions to a pilgrimage overseas by the knight [st. 56–57, 89, 97], apparently the vestige of some episode excised in the process of compilation. The compiler nonetheless deserves credit for the skill with which he has managed to turn discrete episodes into an integrated narrative with a strong sense of logical progression from beginning to end.

Robin Hood and the Monk

Although the *Gest* may be the oldest Robin Hood ballad according to date of composition, *Robin Hood and the Monk* is the earliest in its extant form. It is preserved in Cambridge University MS. Ff. 5. 48, a manuscript dating to the mid-fifteenth century, and containing a variety of devotional, comic, and didactic works. A single fifteenth-century manuscript leaf in the British library also contains some half-dozen stanzas of the same text. The ballad comprises some ninety stanzas, although some of the text has apparently been lost in transmission.[10]

In this ballad, Robin Hood decides to leave Sherwood and visit St. Mary's Church in Nottingham to hear Mass on Whitsuntide. He refuses to bring an escort of his followers, but says that Little John will accompany him to carry his bow. Little John tells Robin to carry his own bow, but accompanies him nonetheless. En route, Robin and John compete at archery; Robin loses and quarrels over payment of the bet. John forsakes Robin's service, and Robin proceeds alone to Nottingham. While in church, Robin is spotted by a "great-headed monk," who reports to the Sheriff. Guards are sent to capture the outlaw, whose sword fails him at the crucial moment. A section of the story is missing, but Robin is evidently captured, and the monk is sent to London with a page to inform the king. News of Robin's capture reaches Sherwood, and Little John and Much the Miller's Son set out to intercept the messengers. John kills the monk, while Much dispatches the page "ffor ferd lest he wold tell," and they themselves take the message to the king. He is delighted with the news and rewards the two handsomely. They return with royal letters, and the Sheriff feasts them. Once the Sheriff is asleep, John kills the jailer and frees Robin, and they return to Sherwood. John, still rankling at his treatment by Robin, prepares to leave. Robin contritely offers John the captaincy of the band, but John declines and decides to remain after all. The outlaws make merry with wine, ale, and venison, while the king bemoans the humiliating episode.

Robin Hood and the Monk is among the more distinctive tales in the early Robin Hood canon. Certain of its motifs can be found elsewhere. *Robin Hood's Death* and *Robin Hood and Guy of Gisburn* include the motifs of Robin Hood's escort and his quarrel with his followers; the latter also uses the device of a rescue through ruse; the general premise of Robin endangering himself by his insistence on hearing Mass appears in Bower's Robin Hood story; but the ballad lacks the close analogues found elsewhere in the tradition, and its violent spirit and extended exploration of the relationship between Robin and John set it apart from most of the other tales.[11]

Robin Hood and the Potter

The last ballad to survive in an early source is *Robin Hood and the Potter*. The piece is a bit over eighty stanzas long; a few stanzas are defective. It survives in Cambridge University MS. Ee. 4. 35, a manuscript comprised of short religious pieces, and probably written shortly after 1500.[12]

The story begins one summer's day when Robin sees a certain potter who has never paid him "pavage" (road tax) in years of using the road. Little John, who once fought with the Potter at Wentbridge, wagers that Robin will be unable to defeat him. Robin approaches the Potter and demands payment; the Potter chooses to fight, and Robin soon finds himself bested. He calls a truce and offers to buy all the Potter's wares. The Potter agrees, and Robin goes to Nottingham where he sells the pots at cut-rate prices. His last pots he sends as a gift to the Sheriff's wife, who invites him to take dinner in the Sheriff's hall. The mealtime conversation turns to archery, prompting a competition afterwards, during which the disguised guest reveals to the Sheriff that he has taken part in competitions with Robin Hood. The Sheriff expresses interest, and the guest offers to take him to find the outlaw. The next day he leads the Sheriff to the forest; Robin summons his men, and the Sheriff spends a miserable evening in the greenwood. The next day he is sent back to Nottingham, stripped of his possessions, and leading a white palfrey as a gift to his wife from Robin Hood.

The story of *Robin Hood and the Potter* closely resembles "Little John and the Sheriff" in the *Gest*, and the Percy manuscript ballad of *Robin Hood and the Butcher*. It has an analogue in the twelfth-century *Gesta Herewardi*, in which the Anglo-Saxon outlaw disguises himself as a potter; similar incidents also feature in the thirteenth-century romance of Eustace the Monk and the fifteenth-century Scottish legend of William Wallace. *Robin Hood and the Potter* also forms the basis of a fragmentary folk play printed in the sixteenth century. The combat in which Robin is bested by a doughty yeoman with whom he afterward becomes friends is one of the commonest motifs in the Robin Hood tradition.

The Percy Ballads

In addition to those ballads surviving in copies dating to 1500 or earlier, two of the Robin Hood ballads in the Percy folio manuscript, *Robin Hood and Guy of Gisburn* and *Robin Hood's Death*, correspond to tales known to have been circulating in the fifteenth century. The Percy manuscript was compiled in the mid-seventeenth century, but it contains versions of several demonstrably medieval texts, and whether or not these two ballads were ultimately copied from medieval sources, their form and content is consistent with that of the medieval ballads. The Percy manuscript is in imperfect condition: the lower half of the first twenty-nine leaves is torn away. As a result, all of the Robin Hood ballads, save *Robin Hood and Guy of Gisburn*, are in mutilated state, with only about half of each text surviving at best; however, it is possible to estimate the original length of the texts based on the space they occupied in the manuscript, and in most cases other versions of the stories survive to elucidate them.[13]

Robin Hood and Guy of Gisburn consists of fifty-eight stanzas; it is the only complete Robin Hood ballad in the manuscript, although certain obscurities in the story suggest corruption of the text in the process of transmission.[14] The opening of the story is unclear, but apparently Robin has a dream in which he foresees combat with some yeomen. He and Little John set out to find these antagonists, competing at archery on the way. They come upon a stranger in the woods and quarrel over who should approach him. Little John leaves, and finds that two of the outlaws have been slain by the Sheriff's forces, who are now pursuing Scarlet. John looses an arrow at the pursuers, but his bow breaks, and he is captured. Robin meanwhile learns that the stranger has come in search of him, but the outlaw conceals his identity. The two compete at archery. Robin wins, and the stranger reveals that he is Guy of Gisburn, an evildoing man. When Robin discloses his own identity, they fight, and Guy is killed. Robin dons Guy's clothes and sticks his head on his bow, disfiguring the face with a knife so that it cannot be recognized. He comes to the Sheriff representing himself as Guy and claiming to bear the head of Robin Hood, and he asks to be allowed to kill John as a reward. The request is granted, Robin cuts John's bonds, and John shoots the Sheriff dead as he flees.

Robin Hood and Guy of Gisburn is an unusual tale, comparable in its violent spirit as well as certain motifs with *Robin Hood and the Monk* and *Robin Hood's Death*. The story evidently enjoyed some currency in its day: it also appears in the fifteenth-century folk play known as *Robin Hood and the Sheriff*, and "Gy of Gysborne" is mentioned in association with "Robein under bewch" ["Robin under bough"] by the Scottish poet William Dunbar in the early sixteenth century.[15]

Robin Hood's Death (A) tells a more detailed version of the story of the outlaw's death as recounted in Fit 8 of the *Gest*; there is also a late seventeenth-century broadside ballad on the same subject. About twenty-seven stanzas survive; the original total was probably fifty or more.[16] The ballad opens very similarly to *Robin Hood and the Monk*. Robin declares his intention of going to be let blood by the Prioress of "Church Lees." His imperious treatment of his fellows puts their backs up. When Scarlet suggests he bring fifty men as an escort, Robin insinuates that he is cowardly, provoking him to threaten to quit the band. Robin will take only Little John, to carry his bow, but John tells him to carry it himself. Robin and John compete at archery en route (again a detail found in *Robin Hood and the Monk*). They come across an old woman kneeling at a stream cursing Robin Hood: the scene is fragmentary, but is probably an omen of Robin's death.[17] As in the version of Robin's death found in the *Gest*, the prioress bleeds Robin to death, although the outlaw fights and kills the Prioress's apparent confederate Red Roger before giving up the ghost.

Aside from its parallels with *Robin Hood and the Monk*, the story of Robin's death has a possible remote analogue in *The Hermit and the Outlaw*, a verse narrative preserved in a fifteenth-century manuscript but possibly composed in the late fourteenth century. In this story an outlaw dies by cutting open a vein and drinking his own blood in order to keep his penance of drinking no water for a day.[18]

Of the Robin Hood ballads in the Percy folio, only these two are demonstrably medieval, but the remaining six—*Robin Hood and the Beggar*, *Robin Hood and the Butcher*, *Robin Hood and Friar Tuck*, *Robin Hood and the Pinner of Wakefield*, *Little John and the Beggars*, and *Robin Hood and Queen Katherine*—are also best considered in the context of the premodern tradition, as is the story of "Robin Hood and the Bishop," mentioned in passing at the end of *Robin Hood and Queen Katherine*. These Percy ballads are by no means free of the influence of printing: *Robin Hood and Queen Katherine* alludes to the *Gest*, and *Robin Hood and the Pinner of Wakefield* existed in printed form as early as the mid-sixteenth century. Yet the inclusion of these ballads in the Percy manuscript suggests that the mid-seventeenth-century compiler thought them old-fashioned. None of them obviously postdate 1600—several are actually alluded to in Elizabethan sources—and on the whole the Robin Hood legend seems to have circulated mostly in oral forms until the end of the sixteenth century, suggesting that these ballads are likely to have been shaped for the most part by traditional modes of transmission. Indeed, almost all of them in length, language, and form more closely resemble the medieval examples than they do the printed ballads of the seventeenth century.

Robin Hood Rescuing Three Squires [Robin Hood and the Beggar (A)]. About eighteen stanzas survive in the Percy folio of an original total probably upward of thirty-five. The beginning of the ballad has been lost; in the eighteenth-century version of the story, Robin Hood meets a widow, who tells him that three squires, companions of his, are to be hanged for poaching. The Percy text opens with Robin exchanging clothes with a beggar and making plans with his men for a raid on Nottingham. There is another gap; in the broadside version Robin comes disguised to the gallows where the Sheriff is about to hang the three squires and volunteers to act as hangman. The manuscript resumes with Robin blowing his horn to summon his men, who help him rescue the prisoners. The conclusion is wanting, but at the end of the broadside, the Sheriff is hanged on his own gallows.[19] Percy labeled this ballad "Robin Hood and the Old Man, or rather the Beggar"; the seventeenth-century broadside ballad called *Robin Hood and the Beggar* has a similar plot, but the Percy ballad's closest narrative and verbal parallels are to be found in the eighteenth-century broadside called *Robin Hood Rescuing Three Squires*. The story is used in Anthony Munday's *Downfall of Robert Earl of Huntingdon* in the 1590s. The rescue motif is common in Robin Hood stories, and this one particularly resembles that in *Robin Hood and Guy of Gisburn*.

Robin Hood and the Butcher (A). About thirty-one stanzas of this ballad are preserved in the Percy folio, of an original total probably around sixty. The story resembles that of "Little John and the Sheriff" in the *Gest* and is almost exactly the same as *Robin Hood and the Potter*, even down to the role of the Sheriff's wife; another version of the story appears in a seventeenth-century broadside ballad.[20] Robin Hood meets with a butcher on the road and fights with him. There is a gap: presumably he finds himself overmatched, calls a truce, and buys the butcher's wares. When the text resumes, Robin is in Nottingham enjoying ale and wine in the company of some ladies, including the Sheriff's wife, who has apparently invited him to dinner later that day. Robin proceeds to market, and sells his wares at bargain prices. The text breaks again and resumes with Robin taking the Sheriff into the forest to see his "horned beasts," evidently having promised to sell the Sheriff his livestock for an irresistibly low price. Robin summons his men, robs the Sheriff, and strips him to his shirt, but spares his life for his wife's sake and sends him home to her.

Robin Hood and the Friar (A). About twenty-one stanzas survive; the original was probably forty or more. Robin sets out one day in May to encounter a certain "cutted friar" at Fountains Abbey. Robin finds the Friar at a river and insists on being carried across. At the other side, the Friar forces Robin at swordpoint to carry him back. Then Robin apparently forces the Friar to carry him over once again, the Friar dumps him in the middle and a fight ensues. Robin obtains permission to blow his horn, and his followers appear; the Friar blows his whistle, and fifty dogs come to his aid. Robin calls a halt to the combat, at which point the text is cut off. Presumably the ballad ended with Robin taking the Friar into his band.[21] This story is also preserved in a seventeenth-century broadside ballad and is alluded to in the Sloane life of Robin Hood, dating to c. 1600. The Friar is unnamed in the ballad, but the Percy scribe titles the piece *Robine Hood and Ffryer Tucke*; the same story appears in a folk play printed in the mid-sixteenth century, in which the Friar is so named. Tuck appears to have entered the tradition through the Robin Hood games and is discussed more fully in Chapter 2. This particular story, however, appears to predate its folk play version, which includes a vestigial allusion to the dogs. The Friar does not actually appear in any other early ballads, although he is mentioned in passing in *Robin Hood and Queen Katherine (A)*. However, he does appear as a member of Robin's band in the folk play *Robin Hood and the Sheriff* in the late fifteenth century.

Little John and the Beggars (A). Only eleven stanzas of this ballad survive. Little John trades clothes with a beggar. On the road, he meets three palmers, who set upon him. The end is defective, but in a seventeenth-century broadside version of the story, John's antagonists are soundly thrashed. The motif of impersonating a practitioner of a certain trade recalls *Robin Hood and the Potter* and *Robin Hood and the Butcher*.[22]

Robin Hood and the Pinner of Wakefield (A). Only six stanzas from the end of this ballad survive. In the seventeenth-century broadside version of this story, Robin, Scarlet, and Little John get into a fight with George a Green, the Pinner of Wakefield, and find themselves overmatched. All that remains in the Percy manuscript is Robin's invitation to the Pinner to join his band. This story was very familiar in the late sixteenth century: it is mentioned in the Sloane life and in Munday's *Downfall*, and it formed the basis of the late sixteenth-century play

George a Greene. A "Ballad of Wakefield and a Grene" appears in the Stationer's Register in 1557-58; since the story was printed so early, the orality of the Percy version is questionable. [23]

Robin Hood and Queen Katherine (A). Some thirty-eight stanzas of this ballad survive; it may originally have numbered upward of eighty.[24] Robin Hood plunders the king's receivers; there is a gap in the manuscript, but in other versions Robin sends the money as a present to Queen Katherine. As the text resumes, the queen is summoning the outlaws to shoot on her behalf in a contest with King Henry's archers on St. George's Day (April 23). There is another gap, in which it appears that the outlaws win and reveal their identities. Robin adds insult to injury by refusing to take service with the king, although he professes himself willing to serve the queen any time she calls for him. There are two seventeenth-century ballads that closely parallel the Percy version of this story, one of which echoes its wording as well. The ballad has an analogue in the story of Adam Bell, Clim of the Clough, and William of Cloudesley, which shares the motif of the archery contest and the patronage of the queen. This ballad is unusual in that it refers in passing to Friar Tuck and Maid Marian, who do not otherwise appear in Robin's band in the ballads. The queen gives Robin the alias of "Loxly," which could represent the earliest appearance of this name in connection with the outlaw. The ballad shows the direct influence of the *Gest*: the archery contest recalls Fits 3 and 5 of the *Gest*; one of the lords who takes the queen's part is Sir Richard Lee; and the text opens with the line "List you, lithe you, gentlemen," echoing the opening line of the *Gest*, "Lythe and listin gentilmen." The king and queen of this ballad are probably Henry VIII and Katherine of Aragon, since the former was the subject of a number of popular tales.[25] All of these factors suggest that the ballad was composed after 1500, but it may date to before 1600. It is certainly very long in comparison to surviving printed versions of the same story, and it may reasonably be taken as standing at a point of transition between the early and modern ballads.

"Robin Hood and the Bishop." This story survives only in a broadside version of the seventeenth century, but it is alluded to near the end of *Robin Hood and Queen Katherine* when the Bishop of Hereford, one of the spectators at the archery contest, learns that the victor is actually Robin Hood:

> "Is this Robin Hood?" says the bishopp againe;
>   "Once I knew him to soone;
> He made me say a masse against my will,
>   Att two a clocke in the afternoone.
>
> "He bound me fast unto a tree,
>   Soe did he my merry men;
> He borrowed ten pound against my will,
>   But he never paid me againe." [st. 31–32]

Although its place in the premodern tradition is questionable, this story is quite in keeping with the early ballads: the robbery of a churchman under color of a loan recalls the *Gest*, and the outlaw's interest in hearing a Mass is also found in *Robin Hood and the Monk* and Bower's story of Robin Hood.

The Sloane *Life of Robin Hood*

One last source of early Robin Hood stories is a quasi-biography of Robin Hood preserved in MS. Sloane 715, f. 157.[26] The text may predate the seventeenth century, as there is no mention of the earldom of Huntingdon, generally attributed to Robin after the success of Anthony Munday's Robin Hood plays in the late 1590s; the manuscript has been variously dated to the late sixteenth or early seventeenth century. This account of Robin Hood shows the influence of printed sources—it draws on Richard Grafton's *A Chronicle at Large* (1569), and the bulk consists of a prose rendering of the *Gest*—but there are also elements evidently culled from oral tradition. It includes two stories corresponding to seventeenth-century broadside ballads; these differ so much from the broadside versions that they are more likely to reflect oral than printed transmission. The first, similar to the broadside ballad *Robin Hood's Progress to Nottingham*, may be designated "Robin Hood and the Foresters (A)":

One of his first exployts was the goyng abode into a forrest, & bearing with him a bowe of exceeding great strength, he fell into company with certayne rangers or woodmen, who fell to quarrel with him, as making showe to use such a bowe as no man was able to shoote withall; wherto Robin replyed that he had two better then that at Lockesley, only he bare that with him nowe as a byrding bowe; at length the contention grewe so hote, that there was a wager layd about the kylling of a deere a great distance of, for performance wherof, Robin offred to lay his head to a certayne somme of money, of the advantage of which rash speach the others presently tooke; so the marke being found out, one of them, they were both to make his hart faynt & hand unsteady, as he was about to shoote, urged him with the losse of his head if he myst the marke; notwithstanding Robin kyld the deare, and gave every man his money agayne, save to him which at the poynt of shooting so upbrayded him with danger to loose his hed, for that <. . .>ey he sayd they would drinke togeyther; & herupon the other stomached the matter, & from quarelling they grewe to fighting with him, but Robin getting him somewhat off with shooting dispact them, & so fled away.[27]

The motif of the archery contest recalls several other early Robin Hood tales, both formal contests as in the *Gest* and informal competitions as in *Robin Hood and the Monk*, *Robin Hood and Guy of Gisburn*, and *Robin Hood's Death*. This tale is evidently intended as an origin story for the outlaw. It is not mentioned in any other early source, and it may have been just one among many origin stories in circulation. Another, recorded by Roger Dodsworth in the seventeenth century, places Robin at Bradfield and attributes his outlawry to having mortally wounded his stepfather at the plow.[28] The probable existence of multiple accounts of Robin's origin is supported by the indeterminate opening of the Sloane life itself, where the outlaw is said to have been born "at Lockesley in yorkeshyre, or after others in Notinghamshire."[29]

The Sloane life proceeds to allude to several other stories, including one corresponding to the broadside ballad *Robin Hood and Allen a Dale*, which may be designated "Robin Hood and the Lovers (A)":

Wheresoever he hard of any that were of unusual strength & hardynes, he would disgyse himselfe, & rather then fayle go lyke a begger to become acqueynted with them, & after he had tryed them with fyghting never give them over tyl he had used means to drawe them to lyve after his fashion; after such maner he procured the pynner of Wakefeyld to become one of his company, & a freyr called Muchel. . . . Scarlock he induced upon this occacion: one day meting him as he walked solitary, & lyke to a man forlorne because a mayd to whom he was affyanced was taken from by the violence of her frends & given to another that was auld & welthy; wherupon Robin understandyng when the maryage day should be, came to the church as a beggar, & having his company not far of, which came in so sone as they hard the sound of his horne, he toking the bryde perforce from him that was in hand to have maryed her, & caused the preist to wed her & Scarlocke togeyther.[30]

Again, this story has parallels in other Robin Hood tales, especially the story of *Robin Hood and the Beggar*, in which the outlaw disguises himself as a beggar to effect a rescue. The high-handed treatment of the clergy recalls several other stories, particularly that of "Robin Hood and the Bishop."

The Wider Tradition

This corpus of stories offers a fairly substantial basis on which to analyze the Robin Hood legend, yet it is still only a part of the early tradition as a whole. We do not know how many tales have been lost—the numerous allusions to the legend in the fifteenth and sixteenth centuries would seem to suggest that the tradition was quite extensive, and its formulaic and generative quality would certainly have allowed the corpus to expand prodigiously. In assessing the early Robin Hood legend, we must always remind ourselves that our knowledge of it is limited to those rare points at which the oral tradition left a surviving mark in the written record. Behind every recorded reference to the legend lie an unknown number of lost manifestations that cannot actually be recovered, but for which a space must always be allowed in our calculations.

One indication of the sheer scale of the tradition is its geographical distribution. Fifteenth-century references to the outlaw in England extend from Yorkshire to Norfolk to Devon. Not only was Robin a familiar figure across England, but he was also known in other parts of the British Isles. The earliest datable description of the great English hero appears in the riming chronicle of a Scottish author, Andrew of Wyntoun, written in about 1420. Wyntoun places the outlaw under the year 1283:

> Lytill Jhon and Robyne Hude
> Wayth-men ware commendyd gud:
> In Yngilewode and Bernysdale
> Thai oysyt all this tyme thare trawale.[31]

We have already seen the early reference in Bower's *Scotichronicon*, and there are records from Aberdeen mentioning a ship called "Robyne hude" or "ly Robert hude" in 1438.[32] Scottish interest in the legend is also reflected in Gavin Douglas's *Palice of Honour* (c. 1501), which has a list of legendary figures who appear in Venus's mirror, including "Robene Hude, and Gilbert with the quhite hand."[33] Robin was also known in Wales: each of the songs in a fifteenth-century collection in MS Peniarth 53 ends with the tag *Robin Hwd a'i kant*, "Robin Hood sang it."[34] By the late sixteenth century the legend appears to have been known in Ireland too, to judge by a reference in Richard Staniehurst's *History of Ireland*:

There standeth in Ostmantowne greeene an hillocke, named little John his shot. The occasion proceeded of this.

In the yeere one thousand one hundred foure score and nine, there ranged three robbers and outlaws in England, among which Robert Hood and little John were cheefeteines, of all theves doubtlesse the most courteous. Robert Hood being betraied at a nunrie in Scotland called Bricklies, the remnant of the crue was scattered and everie man forced to shift for himself. Whereupon little John was faine to flee the realme by sailing into Ireland, where he sojornied for a few daies at Dublin. The citizens being done to understand the wandering outcast to be an excellent archer, requested him hartilie to trie how far he could shoot at randon; who yeelding to their behest, stood on the bridge of Dublin, and shot at the mole hill, leving behind him a monument, rather by his posteritie to be woondered than possiblie by anie man living to be counterscored. But as the repaire of so notorious a champion to anie countrie would soone be published, so his abode could not be long concealed: and therefore to eschew the danger of lawes, he fled into Scotland, where he died at a towne or village called Moravie. Gerardus Mercator in his cosmographie affirmeth, that in the same town the bones of an huge and mightie man are kept, which was called little Iohn, among which bones, the huckelbone or hipbone was of such largeness, as witnesseth Hector Boetius, that he thrust his arme through the hole thereof. And the same bone being suited to the other parts of his bodie, did argue the man to have beene fourteene foot long, which was a pretie length for a little John. Whereby appeereth hath he was called little John ironicallie, like as we term him an honest man who we take for a knave in graine.[35]

This legend reminds us that a significant part of the Robin Hood tradition resided in geographical lore. A number of Robin Hood place-names appear in fifteenth- and sixteenth-century sources, and doubtless many more have been lost. The earliest example, from 1422, is a "stone of Robin Hood" located near Doncaster. In 1500 near Nottingham there is a "Robynhode Well." During the sixteenth century there was a "Robyn Hood Walke" in Richmond, perhaps associated with Henry VIII's penchant for Robin Hood festivities. In 1540 there was a Robin Hood's Stone near Whitby, possibly to be identified with the monolith standing in the field later known as Robin Hood's Close. Robin Hood's Bay in Yorkshire is recorded as early as 1544, perhaps related to the story told in the seventeenth-century ballad *The Noble Fisherman.* "Robin Hood buttes" occurs as a field name in Cumberland in 1598. Even more place-names are recorded after 1600.[36] From the sixteenth century there is additional evidence of geographic lore popularly associated with the legend. Kirklees Priory in Yorkshire is mentioned by Leland and Camden as the site of Robin Hood's burial. Grafton's *Chronicle* (1569) describes Robin Hood's graveslab at Kirklees, "wherin the names of Robert Hood, William of Goldesborough, and others were graven"; this stone was sketched in 1665 by the antiquary Nathaniel Johnston.[37] The Sloane life mentions Little John's gravesite as being noted as a source for good whetstones; the author may have had in mind the still-frequented site in Hathersage, Derbyshire, mentioned by Dodsworth in the seventeenth century.[38] John Ray in the mid-seventeenth century mentions Robin Hood's bow at Fountains Abbey in Yorkshire.[39]

Further evidence of the oral tradition behind written survivals is furnished by Robin Hood proverbs. One has already been mentioned: the phrase "Robin Hood in Sherwood stood" had an extensive life of its own, appearing even as a legal formula from the fifteenth to the seventeenth centuries. "Many speak of Robin Hood who never shot in his bow," meaning that many talk of subjects beyond their knowledge, is found in numerous texts in the same period. "Robin Hood's mile," a circuitous route, is recorded as early as 1559, and "Robin Hood's pennyworths," a commodity sold at a rate far below its value (as in *Robin Hood and the Potter* and *Robin Hood and the Butcher*), occurs from 1565. "To outshoot Robin Hood" appears in Sir Philip Sidney's *Apology* (1581). Alexander Hume's *Of the Orthographie of the Britan Tongue* (1620) records the saying "If Roben Hud wer nou leving, he wer not able to buu his aun bou," evidently meaning that the reputation of a hero far exceeds the reality.[40] The expression "Good even, good Robin Hood" seems to have referred to complaisance produced by fear, as used by Skelton in 1522–23 in "Why Come Ye Nat to Court?" in which Wolsey addresses the lords of Star Chamber:

> He sayth, "How saye ye, my lordes?
> Is nat my reason good?"
> Good evyn, good Robyn Hode![41]

Some modes of transmission were not even verbal. The existence of Robin Hood iconography is witnessed by one late sixteenth-century household inventory, which includes a painted cloth depicting Robin Hood, probably used as a wall hanging.[42] Of course, Robin Hood as a visual figure was most fully developed in the Robin Hood games. The games are an enormous subject and for practical reasons require a chapter of their own; but for contemporaries, dramatic forms of the legend were fully integrated with other manifestations, and any contextualist reading of the legend must take into account the games as well.

These diverse and prolific manifestations should warn us against identifying the Robin Hood legend too closely with the Robin Hood stories. Robin Hood studies have generally focused on the stories as the primary component of the tradition, although a few scholars have suggested that the games during their heyday may have been the principal form of transmission. The latter may indeed be nearer the mark; as we shall see, there are reasons for believing that Robin Hood's vital core was not truly narrative in character and that the timelessness of proverbs, place-names, iconography, and ritual better represents the heart of his mystery.

STRUCTURES OF THE LEGEND

Nonetheless, even if the Robin Hood stories cannot assume pride of place as the most important manifestation of the legend, they are the form in which its content is most fully articulated, and therefore offer the best point of access from which to begin an analysis. Scholarship on the Robin Hood legend has traditionally accorded little attention to its fictive dimension. Most of the study of the legend, whether on the part of folklorists or of historians, has been dominated by antiquarian aims, gravitating especially toward the age-old question of the "real" Robin Hood. Even those who show an interest in the later development of the legend have tended to read the ballads as if they were sources to be strip-mined for historical nuggets.

While questions of historical context are undoubtedly among the most interesting aspects of the Robin Hood tradition, the texts must be understood first as fictions before they can be interpreted historically. There are significant historical elements in these tales, but as fictive creations they embody self-contained worlds that relate firstly to themselves and to their literary context, and only secondarily to the external world of the historian.

A literary text may be legitimately approached in any number of ways. If our goal is to understand the Robin Hood legend as a whole, the obvious starting point is to look for the distinctive and recurrent features that give the tradition its characteristic shape and impart some measure of unity and consistency in its various manifestations.

At an immediately obvious level, the legends are consistent in their frequent reliance on a limited stock of narrative motifs. The single most common of these is the "sportful combat" between two good-natured antagonists who become friends at the end of the fight. This motif, among the most enduring in the legend across the centuries, is already well attested in the early tales: it appears in *Robin Hood and the Potter*, *Robin Hood and the Butcher*, *Robin Hood and the Pinner of Wakefield*, *Robin Hood and the Friar*, and "Little John and the Sheriff" in the *Gest*. This motif is commonly combined with a theme of disguising, in which one of the outlaws pretends to be the practitioner of a

certain trade or calling, and a theme of entrapment in which an outlaw captures
an enemy. Such is the case in *Robin Hood and the Potter*, *Robin Hood and the
Butcher*, and "Little John and the Sheriff." In other cases disguising is linked to
a "rescue by ruse," as in *Robin Hood and the Monk*, *Robin Hood and the
Beggar*, and *Robin Hood and Guy of Gisburn*; a variant on the same theme
occurs in "Robin Hood and the Lovers." Also common is the archery contest:
this topos appears in formalized versions in "Robin Hood and the Sheriff" and
Robin Hood and Queen Katherine, and in more informal versions in *Robin
Hood and Guy of Gisburn*, *Robin Hood's Death*, and "Robin Hood and the
Foresters." Finally, there is a particularly interesting recurrent motif of a quarrel
among the outlaws, appearing in *Robin Hood and the Monk*, *Robin Hood and
Guy of Gisburn*, and *Robin Hood's Death*.

This list of motifs is by no means authoritative or exhaustive: it includes only
the most common, particularly those that were most significant to the legend's
development in the long term. These motifs are among the building blocks from
which the stories are constructed: they are used in various combinations in some
tales, while they are wholly absent in others. Underlying them, however, are
structural foundations common to all the tales that may be considered integral to
the legend as a whole. Of these, the most important is a fundamental polarity
between the forest and outlawry on the one hand and the outside world and law
on the other.

At the heart of the Robin Hood tradition, and in structural terms perhaps more
important than Robin himself, is the greenwood, identified variously with
Barnsdale or Sherwood. The geography of the Robin Hood legends is
characteristically specific, detailed, and prominent, and the forest was probably
part of the legend from the start. The forest is mentioned in the stereotyped verse
"Robin Hood in Sherwood stood"; and in all the surviving stories, the forest
setting occupies a central structural position—one can scarcely envision them
without it. In the world of Robin Hood, the forest is the spatially organizing
principle, the stationary, gravitational center around which the tradition
revolves. The standard Robin Hood ballad opens with an evocation of the forest,
from the simple lines of stanza 3 of the *Gest*,

> Robyn stode in Bernesdale,
>   And lenyd hym to a tre

to the more elaborate setting in the opening stanzas of *Robin Hood and the
Monk*:

> In somer when the shawes be sheyne,
>   And leves be large and long,
> Hit is full mery in feyre foreste
>   To here the foulys song.

To se the dere draw to the dale
 And leve the hilles hee
And shadow hem in the leves grene,
 Under the grene wode tre.

Hit befel on Whitson[tide],
 Erly in a May mornyng
The sun up feyre can shyne,
 And the briddis mery can syng.

Similar opening lines appear in *Robin Hood and Guy of Gisburn*, *Robin Hood and the Potter*, and *Robin Hood and the Butcher*. Such openings are stereotypical, not only for Robin Hood balladry, but for much Middle English verse. Even a historical poem like *The Siege of Calais* may use the topos:

In Juyll whan the sonne shone shene
Bowes burgoned, and leves grene
Gan change thair coloures.[43]

Even as the words of the ballads echo verbal formulae common in late Middle English literature, so the whole forest topos of the Robin Hood tradition reflects a characteristic literary theme of the Age of Romance. The forest is a common fixture of romance literature, figuring as a place of mystery, of liberation, of danger, and of chaos. As Robert Hanning has expressed it, "The forest . . . is a *locus classicus* of romanticism; within the forest, the rules and forms of normal society are suspended or defied."[44] From Gawain to Rosalind, literary figures of this genre typically find in the greenwood a realm of possibilities wherein they may escape, experience, grow, and re-create. The Robin Hood legends share in this literary tradition, since his forest too is a place whose physical impenetrability prevents exterior social structures from imposing themselves, and allows the exploration of alternative possibilities.

Yet the Robin Hood tradition evokes the forest topos with a difference. The literary forest, as a space outside the human world, normally occupies the periphery. Romance stories typically begin and end in the human world, even when most of the action takes place in the forest. In the Arthurian tradition, the center of the world is the human institution of Camelot, embodying order and civilization, while at the perimeter is the forest as the locus of danger, mystery, and chaos. Characters leave Camelot in search of adventure and return to it to enjoy the fruits of their efforts.

In the Robin Hood legend, the protagonists begin in the forest, experience some adventure through contact with the outside world, and return to the forest and their idyllic state at the end. Sherwood is Robin Hood's Camelot: he and his men venture from the forest into the outside world in search of adventure just as Arthur's knights venture from the human world into the forest for the same purpose. The geography of Robin Hood's world is thus inside out relative to romance convention, with the forest at the center and the human world relegated to the periphery.

As Robin Hood's greenwood is a familiar medieval topos presented from a radically different perspective, so Robin himself as an outlaw hero is the scion of a venerable literary tradition who turns that tradition on its head.

The earliest surviving English outlaw legend is that of Hereward the Wake, a historical Anglo-Saxon nobleman who was one of the leaders of a rebellion against William the Conqueror in 1069–70. The early twelfth-century *Gesta Herewardi* tells a complex story in which Hereward is exiled in the late years of the Anglo-Saxon kingdom, returns after the Conquest, and gathers a band of followers whom he leads in a struggle against the Normans, initially from Ely, and later from forested lairs.[45] His story includes some material strongly reminiscent of Robin Hood. While on Ely, Hereward decides to spy out the enemy: he persuades a potter to lend him his pots, and enters the Norman camp under the pretence of selling them (cf. *Robin Hood and the Potter*). Once inside, he claims to have encountered Hereward; he is later taken in by some cooks, who eventually get in a fight with him (cf. Fit 3 of the *Gest*).[46] Like Robin Hood, Hereward captures a monk (Turold, Abbot of Peterborough, in this case; cf. Fit 4 of the *Gest*)[47] and is eventually reconciled with the king (cf. Fit 7 of the *Gest*), although unlike Robin Hood he does not return to the outlaw's life.[48]

Another historical outlaw who became the object of legend was Fulk Fitz Warin, a nobleman who lived during the reign of King John. According to the thirteenth-century Anglo-Norman *Fouke li Fitz Warin*, Fulk was disinherited by John, and took to a life of exile and outlawry.[49] The story recounts a wide range of adventures, including one obvious analogue with Robin Hood: on one occasion Fulk exchanges clothes with a charcoal burner, meets the king on a hunt, and offers to show him a great stag; John follows and is led into the arms of Fulk's followers; he is released only after promising to make good Fulk's losses [pp. 49–50; cf. Fit 3 of the *Gest*]. Like Hereward, Fulk is ultimately reconciled with the king [p. 57].

The last of the historical outlaws of English legend was Eustace the Monk, a twelfth-century figure whose deeds formed the basis of the thirteenth-century Anglo-French *Romans de Wistasse li Moine*. In the *Romans*, Eustace leaves the monastic life to take up the inheritance of his father, a nobleman of the Boulonnais region, but is disinherited by his feudal overlord, the Count of Boulogne. Eustace takes to an outlaw's life and harrasses the count with an endless series of ruses, including one in which he disguises himself as a potter [ll. 1072 ff.]. On another occasion, he captures a merchant, who admits to carrying forty pounds, and escapes not only unplundered but with the gift of a horse. Later, he captures the Abbot of Jumièges, who claims to be carrying only four marks; when searched, he is found to have thirty, of which Eustace returns four and keeps the rest [ll. 930 ff. and 1746 ff.; cf. Fits 1 and 4 of the *Gest*]. At the end Eustace manages to win the favor of the King of France and dies in his service in a sea battle against the English [ll. 2225 ff.].[50]

In addition to these historical figures there are some outlaw heroes for whom there is no known historical basis. One of these is Gamelyn, the hero of a fourteenth-century verse narrative incorporated into several manuscripts of *The Canterbury Tales*. Gamelyn, the youngest son of a gentleman, is dispossessed of his inheritance by his eldest brother after his father's death. He takes to the forest and becomes king of the outlaws, while his brother becomes sheriff. The sheriff has Gamelyn declared an outlaw, and when Gamelyn appears in court to clear his name, he is cast in prison, but Gamelyn's second (and virtuous) brother Ote stands surety for him for the pending trial, and he is released. On the appointed day, Ote is about to suffer execution, but Gamelyn shows up with his outlaw followers, takes over the court, holds a trial of his own, and has the sheriff hanged. In the end, he receives a pardon from the king.[51] The tale shares a number of features with the Robin Hood legend. In addition to the prominent roles of the sheriff and the outlaw band, Gamelyn takes part in a wrestling match [ll. 169 ff.], and he thrashes a party of churlish abbots and priors [ll. 435 ff.]. Like Robin Hood, Gamelyn is a gentle robber: "No man for him ferde the wors But abbotes and priours, monk and chanoun" [ll. 780–81].

Finally, there is the Cumbrian trio of Adam Bell, Clim of the Clough, and William of Cloudesley, whose story is preserved in a printed ballad of the sixteenth century, although their legend is attested in the Wiltshire parliamentary return of 1432. In the ballad, the three men are outlawed for poaching and take to the forest. William goes to visit his wife and children in Carlisle, where he is captured and imprisoned. His companions rescue him by force of arms, and all three ultimately win a pardon from the king through the queen's intercession. They demonstrate their skill at archery in a contest before the king and are taken into his service.[52]

These legends are part of a wider tradition of outlaw stories, particularly prominent in the Scandinavian and Irish traditions and in areas influenced by them; these stories include several Icelandic sagas and the legend of William Wallace. The genre is akin to the ancient tradition of exile literature of which the *Odyssey* is the most famous example. Outlawry in these stories resembles the forest of the Romances in that it is a space where the ordering structures of the human world do not operate, allowing for possibilities that cannot be explored within the more structured space of society.

Robin Hood resembles other literary outlaws in the basic fact of his outlawry and in the freedom that his outlawry bestows, and he even has some adventures in common with them, but he is unlike them in a few crucial respects. All the other outlaws have social connections to root them in the human world, but Robin Hood has neither title, pedigree, nor relatives (aside from the Prioress of Kirklees, with whom his relationship is tangential). Robin's operative social connections are within his outlaw band.

Closely related is the difference in the biographic profile of the legends. The stories of the other outlaws include many unconnected incidents, yet these are fitted into a biographic framework: origin, outlawry, adventures, readmission into society, and death. Even the fictional outlaws are biographized. Gamelyn has a father and family, and his outlawry has a beginning and an end; so too the outlawry of Adam Bell, William of Cloudesley, and Clim of the Clough has a beginning and an end. In all of these stories there is an implicit goal of restoration to society, realized at the end of the story. In the case of Robin Hood, the entire narrative scheme is episodic, a collection of adventures without any kind of linear progression from one state to another. Even in the *Gest*, which consciously attempts to consolidate the legend, this episodic nature predominates: Robin's readmission into society in Fit 8 is reduced to the status of another episode, since he returns to his outlaw state at the end. The story of his outlawry as described in "Robin Hood and the Foresters" and the tale of his death in the *Gest* and *Robin Hood's Death* are biographic, but relatively marginal to his legend as a whole; the former in particular seems to have lacked authority as an origin story.

As the geography of the Robin Hood ballads displaces the forest from a marginal to a central position, so too these alterations of the normal pattern of outlaw literature similarly transform Robin's outlaw status. In other legends, outlawry marginalizes the characters with respect to the world of the story. Even if most of the events of the narrative take place while the characters are outlaws, the legends invariably involve a separation from lawful society at the beginning, which casts the outlaw or exilic state as aberrant, while the connections between the outlaw and society make his outlaw state unstable: in the end the protagonists choose to return to an in-law state as their position of equilibrium. Robin Hood begins and ends as an outlaw, and only makes temporary journeys into the world of lawful society. With Robin Hood, outlawry is the normal state: it is relocated from the margin into the center, turning the social as well as the geographical world inside out.

In most narratives of the romance and outlaw traditions, outlawry and the forest are associated with chaos, but in the Robin Hood legend, they serve as the organizing center around which the narrative revolves, and as such they require an order of their own. This order is embodied in the concept of yeomanry. Although Robin and his followers lie outside the social structure, the ballads frequently make use of the ethos of yeomanry within the forest context. Robin is called a "yeoman" or "good yeoman" [e.g. *Gest* st. 1, 26, 129; *Robin Hood and the Potter* st. 3, 4; *Robin Hood and the Monk* st. 12]; so too are his followers [e.g. *Gest* st. 3, 212; *Robin Hood and the Potter* st. 9, 20; *Robin Hood and the Monk* st. 8, 12, 38, 41]. The ballads' emphasis on a yeoman hero and yeomanly values is a distinctive feature of this tradition that sets it apart from other surviving literature of the Middle Ages.

The term yeoman is problematic, as it belongs to a subtle, complex, and sometimes contradictory system of social classification. It could apply to the upper stratum of free landholding commoners; this sense appears in the fifteenth century, and predominates in the sixteenth, but it is rare before 1400. J. C. Holt has associated Robin Hood's yeoman status with the "yeoman in service": in the hierarchy of service, whether personal, household, or military, a yeoman ranked just below a gentleman and just above a groom. This appears to be the commonest meaning of the word in Middle English texts. Holt notes in particular Robin's courtesy and his lack of a family, which he sees as suggestive of the service milieu.[53]

Yet the word yeoman had other meanings too. In the fifteenth century, it was also applied in certain guilds to craftsmen who had finished their apprenticeship but had not yet become freemen of the guild.[54] In a more general sense it could be used loosely to designate the upper stratum of freeborn commoners in general, a meaning already well established in the late fourteenth century, when the miller in Chaucer's *Reeve's Tale* is described as insisting on a wife of a certain breeding "to saven his estaat of yomanrye" [l. 3949].

Of the possible associations of the word, the most general is clearly the best match. None of the characters who are described as yeomen in the ballads correspond to any of the technical senses of the word—the closest example is where Robin gives Little John into the knight's service, promising that "In a yeman's stede he may the stande, / If thou greate nede have" [*Gest* st. 81]. The yeomanry of Robin Hood's world are neither landholders, servants, nor guildsmen, but the upper crust of free commoners, self-confident and proud of their status. Robin's yeomanly status associates him with the values, culture, and prestige attributed by the audience to the yeoman. From the point of view of the legend, the myth of the yeoman is more important than the reality. Nor should we imagine that Robin's yeomanry associates him only with those who would legally be classed as yeomen. Just as everyone of gentle birth partook in the myth of chivalry and in the image of the knight, so any commoner might identify with the idea of yeomanry as represented in Robin Hood. The cult of yeomanry in the Robin Hood ballads reflects the system of values and aspirations of commoners generally.

Robin's yeoman status is a key organizing principle in the legend, for it defines the entire point of view and ethical outlook of the stories. The concept of yeomanry fulfills much the same function in Robin Hood's world as chivalry does in the world of the romances, serving as the yardstick by which all acts are measured. The knight in the *Gest* demonstrates his moral worth by saving a yeoman in adversity: "He sayde that yoman shulde have no harme, / For love of Robyn Hode" [*Gest* st. 139]. Robin enjoins his followers to harm no "gode yeman" [*Gest* st. 14], and his views are echoed by the Potter:

"Het is ffol leytell cortesey," seyde the potter,
    "As y haffe harde weyse men saye,
Yeffe a pore yeman com drywyng on the wey,
    To let hem of hes gorney." [*Robin Hood and the Potter* st. 22]

Robin heartily concurs:

"Be mey trowet, thow seys soyt," seyde Roben,
    "Thow seys god yeme[n]rey;
And thow dreyffe fforthe yevery day,
    Thow schalt never be let ffor me." [st. 23]

The closing words of *Robin Hood and the Potter* sound a keynote for the entire
tradition:

God haffe mersey on Roben Hodys solle,
    And saffe all god yemanrey!

The concept of yeomanry as manifested in the Robin Hood legend knits
together a number of mutually reinforcing strands in the world of the outlaws.
As yeomen, the outlaws represent the ideal of the free commoner; the principle
of freedom strongly informs the perspective of the ballads. The importance of
freedom to the medieval commons was demonstrated by the rebels of 1381, who
placed the abolition of villeinage among their foremost demands, even though it
appears that in practical terms villeinage was no longer an enormously
burdensome status. In the ballads, the freedom of the yeoman manifests itself in
a highly developed sense of personal self-worth, particularly evident in the
"sportful combat" motif. When Robin Hood waylays the Potter and demands
pavage, the commodity at stake is obviously not money. By demanding this
feudal toll, Robin is symbolically questioning the Potter's status as a free man, a
challenge to which the Potter can only respond by proving himself in combat.
The interaction yields an interesting perspective on social status: the yeoman's
position is determined not by external legal parameters, but by an internal sense
of personal worth and self-reliance, as manifested in his willingness and ability
to assert his status by violence if necessary. This ideal of personal freedom and
self-reliance is of course well suited to the forest world of the outlaws.

Although Robin's challenge to the Potter sets up an ostensibly adversarial
relationship, it is also ultimately the means by which they become friends: at the
end of the fight Robin offers his opponent a "fellowship." This concept of
fellowship is also integral to the yeoman world of the outlaws. [55] Its importance
to the myth of yeomanry in late medieval England is corroborated strikingly in
independent sources: the *Medulla Grammaticæ*, a fifteenth-century Latin-
English vocabulary, gives "yeoman" as the translation of *colega* ["companion"],
and in several of the lists of "terms of association" from the fifteenth century,
the technical term for a grouping of yeoman is said to be "a fellowship of
yeomanry." [56] The spirit of camaraderie pervades the Robin Hood ballads; as in
Robin's interaction with the Potter, it is by no means a straightforward
amicality, but a relationship in which loyalty and competition are inextricably
linked. Many of the stories hinge on this kind of fellowship. It is crucial to
Robin Hood and the Monk, and equally present in the stories based on the
"sportful combat" motif. It is evident in Robin's friendship with Little John, a

relationship so prominent both in the stories and in external references to the legend that it is probably one of the oldest features of the legend. Given the interrelationship between friendship and competition in the ballads, it is not surprising that the stories also stress what we would call sportsmanship: characters are expected to take their knocks with good grace, and when they fail to do so, as Robin does at the opening of *Robin Hood and the Monk*, we are obviously meant to perceive this lack of sportsmanship as blameworthy. The same is presumably implicit when Robin tells his followers not to harm knights or squires who are willing to be "a good fellow": if they will be good sports and play along with the game by handing over the cash demanded of them, they will receive no harm.

The importance of fellowship in the Robin Hood tradition is highlighted by the prominent role of Robin's outlaw band. Where most medieval heroes are distinguished for their prowess, Robin's personal abilities are more limited. He is a skilled archer, but this skill rarely influences the outcome of the stories: his success is more often owing to the assistance of his band. As the status of the hero is limited, that of his followers is correspondingly enhanced. In most outlaw legends, the rank and file of the outlaw band are faceless supernumeraries, but in Robin's band, they have names: Scarlet, Much the Miller's Son, and especially Little John. Scarlet and Much play relatively passive roles in the stories, yet they are constantly present: their names are mentioned consistently even in the earliest references to the legend. Little John yields little in the way of importance to Robin himself: he is invariably present and active, and he is the *de facto* hero of several of the stories. The prominence accorded to Robin's followers and diminished focus on Robin himself emphasize the community while downplaying the hierarchy.

Nonetheless, it might seem that the band employs the terms and structures of hierarchy. The outlaws make use of many forms borrowed from the feudal world, with Robin Hood standing in the role of lord or king: he entertains guests, he demands tolls from travelers, and, like King Arthur in *Gawain and the Green Knight*, he delays his dinner until some remarkable event occurs.[57] Little John is said to be Robin Hood's man [*Gest* st. 177], and Robin's followers address him as their master [*Gest* st. 449] and are dressed in livery [*Gest* st. 230]. When the king comes to Sherwood, Robin gives him livery as well [*Gest* st. 420 ff.]. New members of the band are offered terms corresponding exactly to those of feudal service, as in those offered by Little John to the cook in the *Gest*:

> "Two times in the yere thy clothinge
> > Chaunged shulde be;
>
> And every yere of Robyn Hode
> > Twenty merke to thy fe." [*Gest* st. 170-71][58]

There is even an explicit comparison between the feudal structure of external society and the structure of Robin Hood's band, in that Robin's men prove more loyal than the king's [*Gest* 391].

A closer examination reveals significant structural differences between this outlaw society and the society of the outside world. Robin is the leader of the band, yet he holds no actual title, in contrast with other fictional or semifictional outlaw figures who are styled kings. [59] His followers are far from servile: they often refuse to follow his orders and do not take well to Robin's occasionally overbearing manner. Robin's status seems rather to be that of *primus inter pares*. His relationship with Little John is particularly telling. John appears to be the lieutenant of the band, yet it is impossible to be sure whether this status is in any way formal, or whether it merely reflects his particular friendship with Robin. In *Robin Hood and the Monk*, Robin even offers John the leadership of the band, testimony to the informality of the arrangement. The feudal elements in Robin Hood's band do not make it a feudal society: rather, they are a vocabulary drawn from feudalism that colors but does not define the structure of the outlaw's world. Indeed, as P. R. Coss has pointed out, there is a strong current of irony in the outlaws' use of feudal forms: when Little John kneels before the knight and bids him welcome [*Gest* st. 24-25], or when Robin Hood draws attention to the impropriety of a yeoman paying for a knight [st. 37], the real transaction is highway robbery. [60]

The social egalitarianism of the ballads is facilitated not only by the outlaws' common status as yeomen, but by the absence of hierarchizing distinctions of age and gender. The term "yeoman" is thought to derive from "young man," and this is precisely what Robin Hood and his followers would seem to be—their physical vigor and unmarried state in particular contribute to this impression. At the same time, the outlaws' status as young men, like their status as yeomen, has associations with freedom. A child was subject to its elders, while a householder and husband, standing in a position of authority over others, was by the same token burdened with exterior responsibilities. Conceptually at least, the unmarried young man was free from the restrictions imposed by both states. The status of outlaws as young men also relates to the nearly complete absence of female characters or sexual themes. The world of Robin Hood is overwhelmingly masculine in both content and perspective. Maid Marian was not a part of the premodern Robin Hood ballads, and sexual elements enter the legend only tangentially, as in Robin's interactions with Queen Katherine or the Sheriff's wife—never do they penetrate the fastness of the greenwood.

The myth of yeomanry is reflected symbolically in the outlaws' choice of weapons. One of the most consistent elements in the legend is Robin's prowess as an archer, and the practice of archery figures prominently in many of the early ballads. Robin's association with bowmanship is evident in the Lincoln Register fragment mentioned early in this chapter, and might even be attested as early as 1385 in Chaucer's *Troilus and Criseyde*:

For swich manere folk, I gesse,
Defamen Love, as nothing of hym knowe;
Thei speken, but thei benten nevere his bowe! [2.860-62]

These lines appear to echo a proverb well-attested in the fifteenth century and later, "Many speak of Robin Hood who never bent his bow." The earliest certain examples of the proverb date to shortly after Chaucer's death. Hugh Legat, a monk of St. Albans, in a sermon of about 1410, reproves clerics who preach on matters beyond their level of education, observing that "mani, manime seith, spekith of Robyn Hood that schotte never in his bowe" ["Many people say that many a man speaks of Robin Hood who never shot with his bow"].[61] In about 1419–20, the *Reply of Friar Daw* chastises the antimendicant satirist "Jack Upland" for preaching patience when he possesses none of his own:

On old Englis it is seid, unkissid is unknowun;
And many men speken of Robyn Hood & shotte nevere in his bowe.[62]

Fifteenth-century readers were certainly interpreting Chaucer's lines as a version of this proverb: the Huntington manuscript of *Troilus and Criseyde*, dating to about 1435, adds the gloss "of Robyn hode," while Harleian 2392, written in the mid-fifteenth century, emends the text itself to "speken of robynhod."[63]

Archery is not a common theme in Middle English literature: its prominence in the Robin Hood tradition is one of the defining and distinctive characteristics of the legend, and possibly one of its oldest features. Longbow archery was first cultivated in England by Edward I, who had seen in the prowess of Welsh archers a military resource to be exploited. The longbow is not inherently a superior weapon. In the hands of a weaker archer, it is less useful than a smaller bow with a lighter draw, while the crossbow is easier to use and can be significantly more powerful. However, the longbow is significantly cheaper and faster than a crossbow, and in the hands of a properly trained archer it can penetrate steel plate. From the late thirteenth century onward the crown fostered archery in England as a means of creating a relatively cheap and powerful military force, requiring regular archery practice of freemen and forbidding other forms of recreation.[64] The laws against other games may not have been zealously observed, yet official efforts did yield fruit, as evidenced by the success of English archers during the Hundred Years' War.

The longbow as represented in the Robin Hood tradition was an icon of considerable social significance to the medieval audience, and is to be directly associated with the myth of the yeoman. Although J. C. Holt has pointed out that archery was not exclusively the province of commoners, the longbow as a symbol was very much associated with the stalwart commoner, and its prominent place in the legend is obviously related to its idealization of the yeoman.[65] The longbow is emblematic of the one respect in which society

accorded commoners a position of prestige and importance. The myth of the
English bowman is reflected in such fifteenth-century sources as John Lydgate's
Debate of the Horse, Goose, and Sheep:

> Bi bowe & arwis sith the werr began,
> Have Ynglysshmen, as it is red in story,
> On her enmyes had many gret victory.[66]

The success of English military archery on the battlefield made it increasingly
possible for commoners to mythologize their own role in society: the longbow
represented empowerment, even if this empowerment was as yet more symbolic
than substantive. Armed with the longbow, the English commoner could
imagine himself capable of redressing the evils in his society and even
prevailing where his social superiors could not, just as he had brought victory
for the king at Crécy, Poitiers, and Agincourt.

The yeoman myth is also reflected in the sword and buckler, as used by
Robin in *Robin Hood and the Potter* [st. 15] and by the Friar in *Robin Hood and
the Friar* [st. 6]. Although the sword itself was considered a mark of gentle
birth, the sword and buckler were more likely to be associated with commoners
or ruffians: Chaucer's Miller (who is both) is armed with this combination; so
too is his Knight's Yeoman. While the sword is a dangerous weapon, the
combination of sword and buckler would not necessarily convey an image of
violence or murderousness. They were in fact the weapons used in the medieval
precursor of fencing, and, like fencing in later centuries, sword-and-buckler play
was a popular sport and form of public entertainment.[67] Robin's choice of
weapons emphasizes both his status as a commoner and his capacity to use
violence for playful as well as lethal ends.

Robin's yeoman ethos defines his relationships to the various elements in
society, relationships that are vital motivating agents in the stories. At the
opening of the *Gest*, Little John asks Robin to articulate a policy for the band:

> "Tell us wheder that we shal go
>   And what life that we shall lede;
>
> "Where we shall take, where we shall leve,
>   Where we shall abide behynde,
> Where we shall robbe, where we shal reve,
>   Where we shal bete and bynde." [st. 11–12]

Robin's response is a blueprint for the actions of the outlaws, not only in the
Gest, but in all the early texts:

> "Thereof no force," than sayde Robyn;
>   "We shall do well inowe;

"But loke ye do no husbonde harme
    That tylleth with his ploughe.

"No more ye shall no gode yeman
    That walketh by grene wode shawe;
Ne no knyght ne no squyer
    That wol be a gode felawe.

"These bisshoppes and these archebisshoppes,
    Ye shall them bete and bynde;
The hye sherif of Notyingham,
    Hym holde ye in your mynde." [st. 13–15]

Robin's attitude to commoners is unequivocal: they should suffer no harm. This is certainly in keeping with our received view of Robin Hood, although J. C. Holt's early article on Robin Hood suggested that the reality of Robin's conduct is otherwise, observing that Robin's only victim in the medieval ballads, aside from officials and monastics, is the Potter from whom he attempts to exact a toll in *Robin Hood and the Potter*.[68] Such a misreading of the "sportful combat" topos illustrates the danger of ignoring the literary parameters of the texts.

Holt has also called into question the traditional view that Robin Hood "robbed from the rich and gave to the poor." He points out that Robin never robs a secular landlord. Furthermore, he sees in the Robin of the legends "no positive intention to help the poor." Strictly speaking, he denies that Robin robs the rich *for the purpose of giving to the poor*, an element of the legend that he sees as postmedieval in origin.[69] Although Robin's one major act of charity in the surviving stories is to a knight, the absence of charity to the poor is not reliable evidence that it did not figure in the tradition as a whole. We have already seen that the surviving corpus probably constitutes only a fragment of the original, and even in later eras, when charity to the poor was demonstrably an element of the legend, it was still not a prominent part of the narratives themselves. There is a reference in Martin Parker's *True Tale of Robin Hood* (1632), but few in other commercial ballads of the early modern period, when Robin's benificence is well attested. This aspect of the legend is more likely to have circulated at the subliterary level, as common knowledge about the outlaw, rather than as part of actual stories. In the *Gest*, there is an explicit reference in st. 210, where Robin says that if his highwaymen bring him a "pore man," "Of my good he shall have some." By the early sixteenth century, such charity was clearly an integral part of the story, as witnessed by the Scottish historian John Major (1521):

Circa haec tempora ut auguror, Robertus Hudus Anglus et parvus Joannes, latrones famatissimi, in nemoribus latuerunt, solum opulentorum hominum bona diripientes. Nullum nisi eis invadentem vel resistentem pro suarum rerum tuitione ceciderunt. ... Foeminam nullam opprimi permisit, nec pauperum bona surripuit, verum eos ex abbatum

bonis ablatis opipare pavit. Viri rapinam improbo, sed latronum omnium humanissimus
et princeps erat.[70]

[Around this time, as I gather, the Englishman Robert Hood and Little John, the famous
robbers, hid in the forests, stealing the goods only of the rich. They never killed anyone
unless he attacked or resisted them in defence of his things. . . . He permitted no woman
to be harmed, nor did he take the goods of the poor, but richly supported them with the
goods taken from abbots. The man's robbery I condemn, yet he was the most humane
and the prince of thieves.]

Major's description is very much in keeping with the epitaph of the *Gest*:

> Cryst have mercy on his soule,
>   That dyed on the rode!
> For he was a good outlawe
>   And dyde pore men moch god. [st. 456]

Robin's benificence, like his outlawry, is taken for granted. Whether Robin
stole *for the purpose of* giving to the poor is a subtle distinction that cannot be
made on the basis of the surviving texts: even today, it circulates primarily at the
subliterary, even subverbal level. The prominence given by Major and the *Gest*
to Robin's charity suggests that this was as important a feature of the legend
then as now: even if it was not a prominent element in the stories, it stands as
background to them.

Robin's relationship to the aristocracy is less straightforward. His policy
statement in the *Gest* does not reveal a fundamental antipathy, since he instructs
his men that they should not, as a rule, harm a knight or a squire. However, he
qualifies this, stating that it applies to those "that wol be a gode felawe." At the
opening of the *Gest* Robin is deliberately looking for a rich guest from whom to
extract money:

> Than bespake hym gode Robyn:
>   "To dyne have I noo lust,
> Til that I have som bolde baron,
>   Or some unketh gest.
>
> "Till that I have som bolde baron,
>   That may pay for the best,
> Or som knyght, or some squyer
>   That dwelleth here bi west." [*Gest* st. 6–7]
>
> "Be he erle, or ani baron,
>   Abbot or ani knyght,
> Bringhe hym to lodge to me;
>   His dyner shall be dight." [*Gest* st. 19]

Robin's willingness to despoil the aristocracy is demonstrated in the events immediately following, when Robin forestalls the knight from leaving after dinner before paying the bill:

"But pay or ye wende," sayde Robyn;
    "Me thynketh it is gode ryght;
It was never the maner, by dere worthi god
    A yoman to pay for a knyhht."

"I have nought in my coffers," saide the knyght
    That I may profer for shame."
"Lytell Johnn, go loke," sayde Robyn,
    "Ne let nat for no blame."

"Tel me truth," than saide Robyn,
    "So God have parte of the."
"I have no more than ten shelynges," said the knight,
    "So God have parte of me." [*Gest* st. 37–39]

The outlaws are evidently quite prepared to rob the knight (presuming he is actually as rich as one would presume from his social rank), but they will not commit violence against him if he will acquiesce in their game. While Robin is not hostile to the aristocracy as such, he is willing to fill his own coffers at their expense. This suggests a commoner's-eye view of *noblesse oblige*, in which the aristocrat's duty to be generous may be enforced by the commoner if necessary.

There is also something decidedly insolent about Robin's expectation that knights and squires must be "a gode felawe." Partly it seems to refer to a willingness to play along with the outlaws' game by handing over the money they demand. At the same time, the normal meaning of the expression in Middle English is "a boon companion." As P. R. Coss has observed, the outlaws are inclined to violate the distance that is supposed to separate the commoner from the aristocrat.[71] Underneath Robin's ironic courtesy to his social superiors lies a confirmed disregard for the official hierarchy: gentlemen can escape violence at the outlaws' hands only by casting aside any claims to deference.

One of the reasons for the success of the Robin Hood legend is that the villains of the stories were widely acceptable scapegoats. Robin's statement of policy in the *Gest* reflects anticlerical trends of the period in specifically instructing his men to beat and bind bishops and archbishops, and the ballads extend this hostility to monastics as well. Throughout the ballads, monks are among Robin's most consistent adversaries. The portrait of the Abbot of St. Mary's is vivid, and far from flattering:

"Do gladly, syr abbot," sayd the knyght,
    "I am come to holde my day."
The fyrst word the abbot spake,
    "Hast thou brought my pay?". . .

"Now, good syr abbot, be my frende,
        For the curteyse,
And holde my londes in thy honde
        Tyll I have made the gre . . ."

The abbot sware a full grete othe,
        "By God that dyed on a tree,
Get the londe where thou may,
        For thou getest none of me." [*Gest* st. 103 ff.]

Robin's greatest nemesis is the Sheriff, again a figure often vilified in public sentiment. As the principal royal official in his shire, the sheriff wielded considerable power, and could attract commensurate hostility. Even after 1300, when the actual power of sheriffs was waning, their unpleasant reputation persisted: they appear in a negative light in such works as *The Tale of Gamelyn* and *Piers Plowman*.[72] The Sheriff is utterly a cipher in the Robin Hood ballads. Not only does he fall for Robin's tricks every time, but he is repeatedly killed (as happens in the *Gest* and in *Guy of Gisburn*, and, perhaps, *Robin Hood and the Beggar*).

While Robin Hood is perpetually at odds with the Sheriff, he appears to be deeply loyal to the king:

Robyn behelde our comly kynge,
        Wystly in the face,
So dyde Syr Rycharde at the Le,
        And kneled downe in that place.

And so dyde all the wylde outlawes,
        Whan they se them knele:
"My lorde the kynge of Englonde,
        Now I knowe you well." [*Gest* st. 410–11. Cf. *Gest* st. 386–87]

Yet the relationship between the outlaw and the king is not really so simple. The world of Robin Hood is not always kind to the monarch. Robin's loyalty is symbolic at best: in practice, as a confirmed outlaw, he is a rebel against royal authority. Robin's very existence as *de facto* lord of Sherwood denies the king's authority, indeed in a geographical location specifically marked as the king's own. His poaching of deer likewise impinges on royal prerogatives, and his antipathy to the Sheriff sets him at odds with the enforcement of royal policy.[73] In the *Gest*, Robin takes some relish in playing "pluck-buffet" with the king:

And many a buffet our kynge wan,
        Of Robyn Hode that day:
And nothynge spared good Robyn
        Our kynge in his pay. [st. 425]

In *Robin Hood and the Monk* the monarch is the butt of humor as much as the Sheriff:

> Then bespake our cumly kyng,
>> In an angur hye:
> "Little John hase begyled the schereff,
>> In faith so hase he me. . . ."
>
> "He is trew to his maister," seid our kyng,
>> "I sey, by swete Seynt John,
> He lovys better Robyn Hode
>> Than he dose us ychon." [*Robin Hood and the Monk* st. 84, 88]

Particularly significant is the reconciliation between Robin and the king in the *Gest*. Robin makes his peace with the king and joins his court: here we recognize the modern ending of the tale. But for the *Gest*, the story continues. Robin pines for his old life and returns for a visit to the forest:

> Whan he came to the grene wode,
>> In a mery mornynge,
> There he herde the notes small
>> Of byrdes mery syngynge.
>
> "It is ferre gone," sayd Robyn,
>> "That I was last here;
> Me lyste a lytell for to shote
>> At the donne dere."
>
> Robyn slewe a full grete harte;
>> His horne than gan he blow,
> That all the outlawes of that forest
>> That horne coud they knowe,
>
> And gadred them togyder,
>> In a lytell throwe.
> Seven score of wyght yonge men
>> Came redy on a rowe,
>
> And fayre dyde of theyr hodes,
>> And set them on theyr kne:
> "Welcome," they sayd, "our mayster,
>> Under this grene wode tre."
>
> Robyn dwelled in grene wode
>> Twenty yere and two;
> For all drede of Edwarde our kynge,
>> Agayne wolde he not goo. [*Gest* st. 445–50]

Indeed, Robin had already boldly warned the king of this possible outcome before he left Sherwood:

But me lyke well your servyse,
  I wyll come agayne full soone,
And shote at the donne dere,
    As I am wonte to done. [*Gest* st. 417]

In an age when the monarchy carried considerable weight in the popular imagination—even the peasant rebels of 1381 expressed their loyalty to Richard II—Robin Hood's lack of real respect for the king seems all the more subversive.

CONTEXTS OF TRANSMISSION

While the internal structures of the tradition are the essential first stage in understanding the Robin Hood tradition, meaning is produced at the point of interaction between text and context, and it is to the world of premodern England that we must now turn to understand the structures by which the legend interacted with the culture that transmitted it. Any attempt to interpret the language of the ballads will naturally involve some assumptions about whose language it is. This brings us to the most vexed question of modern Robin Hood scholarship.

The traditional view of the outlaw holds that he was a popular hero whose stories reflect the discontent of the peasantry of late medieval England. M. J. C. Hodgart expressed the classical interpretation in calling the ballads "yeoman minstrelsy,"[74] while Maurice Keen associated them with "the attitude of the oppressed classes" and "the peasant's outlook."[75] In an article in *Past and Present* in 1960, J. C. Holt rejected this view, arguing that the Robin Hood ballads were "originally the literature, not of a discontented peasantry, but of the gentry."[76] Holt's *Robin Hood* (1982) offered a more nuanced version of his original position, arguing that it is among the "retainers and dependents" of "the crown, the aristocracy, and the landed gentry ... gathered together in circumstances which allowed for entertainment, that the original audience of the tales of Robin Hood must first be sought."[77] In this way he maintains a privileged context for the genesis of the ballads, while allowing the principal audience to be yeomen, in the sense used in the hierarchy of service.

Holt's high-profile book has proved very influential. Popular literature on the legend invariably quotes him as gospel. R. B. Dobson and J. Taylor stated in the 1976 introduction to their *Rymes of Robyn Hood* that "'yeoman minstrelsy' remains the most appropriate description for the *Gest*, *Robin Hood and the Monk*, and *Robin Hood and the Potter*, all works which reflect a deliberate appeal to the patronage of the yeoman rather than of the landed nobleman," but they concede in their Foreword to the 1989 edition that "the case for a positive 'household influence' on the greenwood legend looks much stronger than it did when this anthology originally appeared."[78] Others, like Rodney Hilton, have adhered emphatically to the old view, identifying the ballads as the "obvious fantasy of a discontented rural population" and connecting them with the discontent that exploded into violence in 1381: "The sentiments [of the Robin Hood ballads] . . . are as near as we shall get, in imaginative literature, to those favoured by the peasantry at the time of the rising."[79]

Were we to rely entirely on the testimony of contemporary commentators, we would have to conclude that the audience of the Robin Hood legends were those of debased tastes. We have already seen the passage in *Piers Plowman* in which the drunken priest Sloth reveals that

> I can rymes of Robyn Hood, and Randolf erle of Chestre . . .
> I am occupied eche day, haliday and other,
> With ydel tales atte ale, And otherwhile in cherches;
> I haue levere here an harlotrie, Or a somer game of souteres,
> Or lesynges to laughe at . . .
> Than al that evere Marke made, Mathew, John, & Lucas.[80]

> [. . . I would rather hear some bawdry, or a summer-game of cobblers, or lies to laugh at . . . than everything that Mark made, Matthew, John or Luke.]

Scholars have generally looked to the pairing of Robin with Ranulf Earl of Chester to provide some clue as to the nature of the ballads in Langland's day. As Ranulf de Blundeville, an early thirteenth-century Earl of Chester, was the subject of now-lost romances, one might at first conclude that an aristocratic audience is implied.[81] However, the logic of the alliterative verse calls for a different approach. Verse in this tradition is characterized by half-lines closely bound within themselves but connected with each other only by alliteration and loose association of ideas, which makes it possible to read the first half of this line independently of the second: it is to "rimes," not Ranulf, that we should first look for meaning.

In fact, the phrase "rymes of Robyn Hood" is echoed by a family of expressions current in the fifteenth to seventeenth centuries. A "tale of Robin Hood" during this period meant a false, foolish, or idle story; in the words of a proverb current in the sixteenth and seventeenth centuries, "Tales of Robin Hood are good enough for fools."[82] Sir Thomas Chaloner, writing in the early sixteenth century, echoes the very words of Sloth:

If one that is sandblynde woulde take an asse, for a moyle, or an other praise a rime of Robyn hode, for as excellent a makyng, as Troilus of Chaucer, yet shoulde they not straightwaies be counted madde therefore?[83]

Sloth's allusion to "rymes of Robyn Hood" suggests that by 1377 Robin Hood may already have become a byword for the literature of the profane, coarse, or foolish. Fifteenth-century allusions to the legend corroborate this view. In about 1405–10, the author of the devotional tract *Dives and Pauper* rebukes those who "han lever ['would rather'] gon to the taverne than to holy chirche, lever to heryn a tale or a song of Robyn Hood or of som rybaudye than to heryn messe or matynys or onything of Goddis servise or ony word of God."[84] In a sermon from an early fifteenth-century manuscript, the author complains that "Mony men wol leve ['believe'] fablesse rathyr than the gospell; remaunce of Robyn Hode lever than Powles pystylles"[85]; another fifteenth-century homilist lamented that

Many of these ley pepyll dispise presthode, ne they take none hede to the worde of God. They 3eve no credens to the Scripture of almy3ti God. They take more hede to these wanton proficijs, as Thomas of Arsildowne and Robyn Hoode, and soche sympyll maters, but thei 3efe not so fast credens to the prophettis of God.[86]

The moral debasement attributed by these authors to aficionados of the Robin Hood tales need not imply low social status, but such sources as are explicit on the point of social context associate these tales with the commonality. The Scottish historian Bower in the mid-fifteenth century described the outlaw as

ille famosissimus sicarius Robertus Hode, cum Litiljohn et eorum complicibus, de quibus stolidum vulgus hianter in comediis et in tragediis prurienter festum faciunt, et super ceteris romanciis mimos et bardanos cantitare delectantur.[87]

[that most famous thief Robert Hood with Little John and their accomplices, concerning whom the foolish commonality eagerly make entertainments in comedies and tragedies, and love for minstrels and poets to recite about, above all other romances.]

A similar audience is suggested in the fifteenth-century comic poem *How the Plowman Learned His Paternoster*, in which two plowmen

Eche had two busshelles of whete that was gode,
They songe goynge home-warde a gest of Robyn Hode. [88]

Turning from external testimony to that of the texts themselves, we find further evidence of a popular audience. One distinctive feature of the early Robin Hood ballads that has received little attention is the meter in which they are composed.[89] They are invariably in the classic ballad meter, consisting of four-line stanzas riming *abcb*, alternating between 4 and 3 feet in each line. This meter has doubtless escaped notice because it is the most common meter in the corpus of traditional English balladry. However, it is extremely unusual in medieval poetry. The quatrain itself is surprisingly rare in Middle English: it occurs mostly in fifteenth-century carols, with some instances among the lyric poems of the same period. [90] In the corpus of Middle English narrative verse, it is virtually nonexistent: among edited texts, there are scarcely more than a dozen.[91] Given the quatrain's rarity in contemporary narrative verse, its ubiquity in the Robin Hood ballads calls for explanation.

The most obvious conclusion to be drawn is that the Robin Hood ballads represent a genre not otherwise well documented in surviving Middle English texts. This militates against an aristocratic context for the ballads, since it is popular rather than aristocratic genres that have left the fewest traces in the written record. Since the meter also corresponds to that of later popular ballads, and in Middle English is most commonly found in popular forms (particularly those that are apparently sung), a popular context for the Robin Hood ballads seems all the more likely.[92]

The ballads' apparently low rate of survival in medieval versions also argues against an aristocratic context. To judge by contemporary references, the Robin Hood legend would seem to have been as popular with its audience as were tales of King Arthur. Yet countless Arthurian texts survive from late medieval England, while the surviving Robin Hood material is minimal. Had these tales been favored in privileged circles, we would expect more of them to have found their way into writing. All in all, there appears to be ample reason to take seriously the ballad of *Robin Hood and the Potter* when it addresses the audience as "yeomen" [st. 2].

Nonetheless, Holt rightly identifies a number of elements in the *Gest* suggestive of the privileged milieu of the aristocratic household. He accounts for this aristocratic strain in the legend of the yeoman outlaw by postulating an audience of commoners in service to aristocratic masters, but this explanation is needlessly tortuous. Aristocratic elements in the ballads could easily be explained by the general process of downward cultural diffusion, as suggested by P. R. Coss.[93] Nor need one reject as mere politeness the opening stanza of the *Gest*, which addresses itself to "gentilmen that be of frebore blode." The very survival of Robin Hood ballads from the fifteenth and sixteenth centuries proves that Bower's *stolidum vulgus* were not the sole audience. In this period literacy was virtually the exclusive property of the elite. Plowmen may have delighted in gests of Robin Hood, but all the literate plowmen in England would not have constituted a sufficient market to justify even a single printing of the *Gest*, let alone a half-dozen before 1600. The *Gest* in particular shows aristocratic influences, but the manuscripts of *Robin Hood and the Monk* and *Robin Hood and the Potter* also bespeak a privileged audience, whatever their content.

There is no necessary contradiction between the existence of a privileged audience and the popular audience generally indicated by exterior sources. As Peter Burke explains in his analysis of the structure of popular culture in the early modern period, there was no absolute division between the culture of the aristocracy and that of the commoners. There was a "high" culture that belonged to the elite and was transmitted in forms inaccessible to the lower classes, such as courtly performances and the written text. Popular culture, by contrast, was accessible to the entire population to a greater or lesser extent: certain aspects were restricted to specific subgroups, but in general both commoner and aristocrat participated in the same popular culture, albeit in different roles and often with different attitudes.[94] The evidence connecting these legends with a popular audience does not mean that they were the exclusive province of commoners: rather, it indicates that they were full participants in its transmission. Because of sheer numbers, full participation meant that the content of the legend was largely shaped by their perspective, although the influence of aristocratic culture was disproportional to the aristocracy's limited numbers.

The arguments offered so far do not necessarily obviate Holt's view of the legend. Holt himself acknowledges the existence of a popular audience in the fifteenth century. His claim regarding Robin Hood ultimately focuses not on the legend's history, but its prehistory: he does not deny that the ballads were popular fare, but challenges the idea that they originated in a plebeian context. As the origins of the ballads predate our external evidence, the question of their original social context can only be answered by analysis of the texts themselves.

Holt undertakes to identify elements in the ballads that point to a specific social milieu, and in particular he tries to discern which stories are of the greatest antiquity and to find in them characteristics that shed light on the earliest stages of the legend. He sees a distinction in the *Gest* between "Robin Hood and the Knight" on the one hand and "Robin Hood and the Sheriff" and "Robin Hood and the King" on the other. He notes that first is associated with the obscure setting of Barnsdale and that it lacks obvious literary parallels, while the latter two are associated with Nottingham and have readily identifiable analogues. He concludes that "Robin Hood and the Knight" represents the historical kernel of the legend, and that since this part of the *Gest* is most aristocratic in its content, the legend emanates from an aristocratic milieu. [95]

Closer examination of the evidence casts doubt on these conclusions. To begin with, Holt's pattern is contradicted by *Robin Hood and the Potter*, which he characterizes as a plebeian text but which associates the outlaw with the Barnsdale area. The analogues for *Robin Hood and the Monk* are no closer than those for "Robin Hood and the Knight," yet the one is connected with Nottingham, the other with Barnsdale. In the "plebeian" Fit 8 of the *Gest*, Robin Hood apparently returns, not to Sherwood, but to Barnsdale. Indeed, Robin Hood continued to be associated with both localities at least until the seventeenth century: at any time in this period, a Barnsdale story could be shifted to Sherwood, and vice versa. The analogue test is unreliable, depending as it does on the scholar's knowledge of the possible sources and judgment of degrees of narrative similarity. Holt identifies *Robin Hood's Death* as lacking analogues, yet it bears a suggestive resemblance to *The Hermit and the Outlaw*;[96] as we have seen, "Robin Hood and the Knight" shares several of its principal motifs with other medieval tales. Even a genuinely unique tale could reflect literary invention rather than historical antiquity. The absence of recognizable historical characters or events also bodes ill for the search for a historical kernel in the legend. The knight, the abbot, the sheriff, the king, are all nameless, the adventures fictive in character rather than historical—indeed, the knight only acquires a name in the part of the story which would be more recent by Holt's criteria.

There is an inherent danger in using details from the texts to identify the original social milieu. Holt sees no reason "for thinking that the surviving written versions are atypical of the legend as a whole,"[97] but the very fact of their preservation in written form makes them atypical. If the Robin Hood corpus was substantial, as contemporary references seem to suggest, then the surviving tales constitute only a small fragment of the whole; and the fact of their preservation in writing skews them toward aristocratic interests. Holt acknowledges the possibility that a plebeian oral tradition may have existed, but dismisses the idea as "guesswork," for which there is "no evidence."[98] However, if such a tradition did exist, it would naturally have left little obvious evidence of itself: we know very little about popular literature in the time when the legend was forming. Such evidence as survives does support its existence, and even if this evidence is taken as inconclusive, our interpretation must allow for the possibility of an undocumented popular tradition, in which case any tendency toward aristocratic interests in the surviving tales has little value as evidence.

Perhaps the greatest problem with Holt's approach is that it requires us to believe that the details of the *Gest* can be used as evidence of the content of the original Robin Hood story, which he himself believes to predate the mid-thirteenth century. The assumption is simply untenable. As suggested earlier in' this chapter, the current state of our knowledge will not support a date for the *Gest* prior to the fifteenth century. This allows a lengthy period of oral transmission, which may have preserved broad structural features of the legend, but is unlikely to have left the details intact.

Under these circumstances, we must presume that the details of "Robin Hood and the Knight" reflect the literary choices of an author or authors some time around 1400 or later, rather than the original content of the legend in the earlier part of the fourteenth century or before. This seems even more probable given what has already been said (by Holt among others) regarding the literary skill apparent in the text. If the author places Robin in Barnsdale, it is not because he was instinctively following the older strand of the tradition, but because he was more interested in northern than in southern settings. If his tale is one that would particularly appeal to a privileged audience, this is not because he had a unique handle on the roots of the tradition, but because an author of his skill would probably be looking for the patronage of a privileged audience.

Ultimately, our best guide to the original audience of the ballads will be the same structural features that distinguish them from other medieval literature, as these are the elements most consistent in all Robin Hood tales, and least subject to authorial innovation. Of these, several would seem to have distinct implications as to the nature of the original audience.

The structural centrality of the plebeian perspective and the idea of yeomanry is the most immediately obvious. While it was not unknown for aristocrats to idyllicize the life of their social inferiors, the Robin Hood legend is organized from the point of view of its plebeian protagonists.[99] Yeomanry is not just an alternative to the pressures of courtly existence: it is a fully functional system of values embodied permanently in the social arrangements of the outlaws. It is also unlikely that the gentry would deliberately choose a hero for themselves who is of ungentle birth. Aristocratic literature of the Middle Ages is singularly devoid of dynamic plebeian heroes. There are humorous tales featuring plebeian protagonists, and there are some genuine heroes who are of temporarily low status—examples include Perceval, Havelok, and Gamelyn—but this low status is typically a stage between their aristocratic origins and the recuperation of their aristocratic rights. As we shall see, Robin's eventual incorporation into official culture entailed the rewriting of his story to fit this very pattern.

The interest in bowmanship, so closely allied to the theme of yeomanry, would also point toward a more popular origin. The longbow may not have been the exclusive province of the commoner, yet even if an aristocrat might employ a bow in the hunt, this did not make the bow a significant part of aristocratic culture. For the commons, on the other hand, the bow was a symbol of self-worth and empowerment, as well as an integral part of their material world.

Bowmanship and the concept of yeomanry may not have been fully developed at the time of the legend's inception, and it is difficult to be sure what form they took in the early stages of its development. At the more abstract level, the narrative shape of the legends is equally difficult to reconcile with Holt's theory of an aristocratic milieu. The tales are constructed on a cyclical and episodic pattern typical of popular culture and very unlike the linear imperatives of aristocratic literature, with its emphasis on heredity, assertion of social status, and progeny. The unaristocratic nature of the legend is vividly demonstrated by the difficulty that the *Gest* poet has faced in making his ballad suit the expectations of aristocratic taste. He has been at great pains to construct a lengthy story with a sense of progression, narrative intricacy, and historicity: his inability to create such a tale without leaving obvious structural seams suggests that the material available to him simply did not fit this pattern.

The evidence strongly suggests that the Robin Hood tradition as known in the later Middle Ages had been transmitted and shaped primarily by the *stolidum vulgus* since its earliest stages. Within this general context, there may still be some basis for Holt's distinction between a plebeian and an aristocratic strand in the surviving texts. On the one hand there is *Robin Hood and the Potter*, "Robin Hood and the Sheriff," and "Robin Hood and the King," which tend to reflect the popular background of the legend, although they must have appealed to a privileged audience as well. On the other there is "Robin Hood and the Knight," displaying the marks of the legend's popular origins, but also showing aristocratic cultural influence. There may also be a latent geographical distinction beneath this obvious social one. "Robin Hood and the Knight" is not only set in Barnsdale: its entire axis of attention looks northward, to York and the abbey of St. Mary's. The Sherwood tradition looks southward, to Nottingham. The two strands might represent trends in the legend as it evolved in two adjoining counties: Nottinghamshire, looking toward the culture and society of southern England, and Yorkshire, the cultural and political heart of the north. This would also explain why Scottish authors consistently place Robin in Barnsdale, since the Scots would most likely have received their information via northern England. The contrasts between "Robin Hood and the Knight" and the other tales might reflect two geographical tendencies in the legend: a northern strain, transmitted in a society characterized by scattered settlement patterns and a correspondingly greater cultural influence of the aristocratic household, and a southern one, transmitted in more densely populated areas where there was greater opportunity for the development of plebeian culture independent of aristocratic influences.

The ultimate origins of the Robin Hood legend are likely to remain a perpetual mystery. There is a limit to how much can be known about the origins of folk tales that were not recorded until after a century or two of oral transmission, in a period when vernacular popular culture was rarely given any attention in written sources. Yet based on the information presented here, we can at least construct a plausible scenario for the early evolution of the legend.

The figure of Robin Hood was widely known by the latter half of the fourteenth century, and perhaps even a century before. We can only guess at the original content of the legend, but its basic shape during the centuries prior to the first recorded Robin Hood tale was probably determined by the same structural features that define the surviving early stories: Robin and his followers, dwelling as outlaws in the forest, have a series of adventures through contact with the human world, each one ending with the outlaws returning to their forest life. The intense interest in archery may date to the late thirteenth or fourteenth century, when the crown initiated its policy of fostering bowmanship among the English commons. The concept of yeomanry may be a fourteenth-century addition, reflecting a new self-conscious pride among the commons, but it seems likely that the tales must always have had some ordering ethos underlying them, whether or not there was a concept such as yeomanry to encapsulate them.

If there was a historical Robin Hood, it is doubtful that we will ever be able to identify him, since the recorded legends are shaped by narrative rather than historiographic forces. There is little in the ballads on which to base an identification beyond Robin's name, the fact of his outlawry, and perhaps his presence in Barnsdale. Indeed, one of the most crucial shaping principles in the legend is its very ahistoricity. The strength and uniqueness of Robin Hood as a legendary figure did not lie in the stories told about him: after all, these stories could have been told about any number of other characters, and many of them actually were. Robin's peculiar advantage was that he was perpetually an outlaw: his world lacks a sense of time, since every adventure ends where it began, allowing the legend to be limitlessly generative. The permanence of Robin's outlaw state is embodied in his very name, with its connotations of thievery and mystery—and the peculiar aptness of the name for an outlaw robber should at once make us question its historical plausibility. The legend's atemporality facilitated its adoption into non-narrative modes and was in turn reinforced by them. Robin's appearance in place-names and proverbs confirmed his timelessness, and, as we shall see in the following chapter, the legend found one of its most successful modes of expression when interpreted by its own audience in dramatic and ritual form.

NOTES

1. *The Vision of William Concerning Piers the Plowman in Three Parallel Texts*, ed. W. W. Skeat (London: Oxford University Press, 1886), 5.4002.

2. J. C. Holt, *Robin Hood*, 2nd ed. (London: Thames and Hudson, 1989), 187–89; John Bellamy, *Robin Hood: An Historical Enquiry* (London: Croom Helm, 1985), 135–36.

3. George E. Morris, "A Ryme of Robyn Hode," *MLR* 43 (1948), 507–8.

4. Holt, *Robin Hood*, 69. A variant also occurs in st. 3 of the *Gest*. See Joseph Ritson, *Robin Hood: A Collection of All the Ancient Poems, Songs and Ballads Now Extant*. (London: T. Egerton, 1795), 1.lxxix-lxxx for other examples.

5. A character named "Reynold" is mentioned as being one of Robin's band in the fifteenth-century *Gest of Robin Hood* [st. 243], and "Reynold Grenelefe" is used as a pseudonym by Little John in the same text.

6. Walter Bower, *Scotichronicon* (Aberdeen: Aberdeen University Press, 1987), 5.354.

7. These are Richard Pynson's *Gest*, ?1500 [*STC* 13688]; Wynkyn de Worde's edition, ?1506 [*STC* 13689]; an edition printed at York by H. Goes, ?1506–9 [*STC* 13689.3]; the Lettersnijder edition, attributed to the press of Jan van Doesborch at Antwerp, ?1510–15 [*STC* 13689.5]; J. Notary's edition, ?c1515 [*STC* 13690]; William Copland's *Mery Geste of Robyn Hoode*, ?1560 [*STC* 13691]; a second edition of the same, perhaps published by Copland, ?1565 [*STC* 13691.3]; and a reprint of Copland by "Edward White," ?c. 1590 [*STC* 13692]. For modern editions of the text see R. B. Dobson and J. Taylor, *Rymes of Robin Hood*, 2nd ed. (Gloucester: Alan Sutton, 1989), 71–112; F. J. Child, *The English and Scottish Popular Ballads* (Boston: Houghton, Mifflin, and Co., 1882–98; rpt. New York: Cooper Square, 1962), #117.

8. William Hall Clawson, *The Gest of Robin Hood*, University of Toronto Studies, Philological Series (Toronto: University of Toronto, 1909), 3–6; Douglas Gray, "The Robin Hood Poems," *Poetica: An International Journal of Linguistic and Literary Studies* (Tokyo) 18 (1984), 23n.58.

9. *Amadace* in John Robson, *Three Early English Metrical Romances*, Camden Society 18 (London: Camden Society, 1842), 27–56; *Isumbras* in J. O. Halliwell, *The Thornton Romances*, Camden Society 30 (London: Camden Society, 1844), 88–120; *Launfal* in Walter Hoyt French and Charles Brockway Hale, *Middle English Metrical Romances* (New York: Prentice-Hall, 1930), 345–80; *Cleges* in G. H. McKnight, *Middle English Humorous Tales in Verse* (Boston: D. C. Heath, 1913), 38–59.

10. Dobson and Taylor, *Rymes*, 113–22; Child #119.

11. J. C. Holt has argued that it is akin to the tale of Adam Bell, in which the outlaw William Cloudesley goes to Carlisle to visit his wife, is captured, and must be rescued by his fellow outlaws [Holt, *Robin Hood*, 73], but the resemblance is marginal: Robin is rescued by ruse, William by force, and the basic scenario of an outlaw going into town and being captured is too general to constitute a significant analogue.

12. Dobson and Taylor, *Rymes*, 123–32; Child #121.

13. On the manuscript, see D. C. Fowler, *A Literary History of the Popular Ballad* (Durham, N.C.: Duke University Press, 1968), 132 ff.

14. John W. Hales and Frederick J. Furnivall, eds., *Bishop Percy's Folio Manuscript* (London: Trübner, 1868), 2.227; Dobson and Taylor, *Rymes*, 140–45; Child #118.

15. Dunbar, "Of Sir Thomas Nonry," ll. 25–28, in *The Poems of William Dunbar*, ed. W. Mackay Mackenzie (London: Faber and Faber, 1932), 64.

16. Hales and Furnivall, *Bishop Percy's Folio Manuscript*, 1.50–58; Dobson and Taylor, *Rymes*, 133–39; Child #120.

17. The scene is reminiscent of one preceding the death of the Irish hero Cú Chulainn, in which the hero finds a fairy woman kneeling at a river and lamenting as she tries to wash a blood-stained garment [Eleanor Hall, *The Cuchullin Saga in Irish Literature* (London: David Nutt, 1898), 247–48].

18. Max Kaluza, "Kleinere publikationen aus me. handschriften," *Englische Studien* 14 (1890), 171–77.

19. Hales and Furnivall, *Bishop Percy's Folio Manuscript*, 1.13–18; Child #140.

20. Hales and Furnivall, *Bishop Percy's Folio Manuscript*, 1.19–25; Dobson and Taylor, *Rymes*, 150–57; Child #122.

21. Hales and Furnivall, *Bishop Percy's Folio Manuscript*, 1.26–31; Dobson and Taylor, *Rymes*, 158–64; Child #123.

22. Hales and Furnivall, *Bishop Percy's Folio Manuscript*, 1.47–49; Child #142.

23. Hales and Furnivall, *Bishop Percy's Folio Manuscript*, 1.32–36; Child #124; Dobson and Taylor, *Rymes*, 146–49. The status of this Percy ballad may be compared to that of the Percy version of *Adam Bell* [Hales and Furnivall, *Bishop Percy's Folio Manuscript*, 3.76 ff.], which also corresponds to a ballad printed in the sixteenth century. The Percy *Adam Bell* is quite close to its printed counterpart.

24. Hales and Furnivall, *Bishop Percy's Folio Manuscript*, 1.37–46; Child #145A.

25. Cf. Roger Thompson, *Samuel Pepys' Penny Merriments* (New York: Columbia University Press, 1977), 24–32.

26. Edited in William J. Thoms, *Early English Prose Romances*, 2nd ed., Vol. 2, *Virgilius, Robin Hood, George a Green, Tom a Lincolne* (London: Nattali and Bond, 1858), 124 ff. The manuscript contains miscellaneous material in various hands, including medical and cooking recipes, a moral poem, and a description of the astrolabe [John Matthew Gutch, *A Lyttel Geste of Robin Hood* (London: Longman, Brown, Green and Longmans, 1847), 1.379].

27. *Ibid.*, 547–48.

28. Holt, *Robin Hood*, 44.

29. Thoms, *Prose Romances*, 547.

30. Thoms, *Prose Romances*, 548.

31. Andrew of Wyntoun, *The Orygynale Cronykil of Scotland*, ed. David Laing (Edinburgh: Edmonston and Douglas, 1872), 2.263 (VII.x.3523–26).

32. Anna Jean Mill, *Mediaeval Plays in Scotland* (Edinburgh and London: W. Blackwood and Sons, 1927), 23.

33. Gavin Douglas, *Palice of Honour* 1.65, in *The Poetical Works of Gavin Douglas Bishop of Dunkeld*, ed. John Small (Edinburgh: W. Paterson, 1874). Gilbert appears as a member of Robin's band in st. 401 of the *Gest*.

34. Holt, *Robin Hood*, 204.

35. Richard Staniehurst, *A History of Ireland*, in Raphael Holinshed, *The First-Laste Volume of the Chronicles of England, Scotlande, and Irelande* (London: H. Bynneman for J. Harrison, 1577), 6.28 [ch. iii].

36. On Robin Hood place-names see Dobson and Taylor, *Rymes*, 293–311.

37. Published in Richard Gough, *Sepulchral Monuments of Great Britain* (London: for the author, 1786).

38. Thoms, *Prose Romances*, 555; Holt, *Robin Hood*, 44.

39. John Ray, *Select Remains of the Learned John Ray*, ed. William Derham (London: George Scott, 1760), 161.

40. Alexander Hume, *Of the Orthographie and Congruitie of the Britan Tongue*, EETS o.s. 5 (London: Trübner and Co., 1865), 11.

41. Skelton, "Why Come Ye Nat to Court?" ll. 195–97, in John Skelton, *The Complete English Poems*, ed. John Scattergood (Harmondsworth: Penguin, 1983), 283. A similar expression may be found in Gascoigne's "Yea, Robin Hood" in 1559. On Robin Hood proverbs see Dobson and Taylor, *Rymes*, 288–92; Bartlett Jere Whiting, *Proverbs, Sentences, and Proverbial Phrases; From English Writings Mainly Before 1500* (Cambridge, Mass.: Harvard University Press, 1968), R155–56.

42. F. G. Emmison, *Elizabethan Life: Home, Work, and Land*, Essex Record Office Publications 69 (Chelmsford: Essex County Council, 1976), 22.

43. R. H. Robbins, *Historical Poems of the Fourteenth and Fifteenth Centuries* (Oxford: Clarendon Press, 1959), 78. Cf. also Carleton Brown and Rossel Hope Robbins, *The Index of Middle English Verse* (New York: Columbia University Press, 1943), #1456; Carleton Brown, *Religious Lyrics of the Fifteenth Century* (Oxford: Clarendon Press, 1939), 286.

44. Robert Hanning, *The Vision of History in Early Britain from Gildas to Geoffrey of Monmouth* (New York: Columbia University Press, 1966), 158.

45. *De Gestis Herwardi Saxonis*, ed. S. H. Miller (Peterborough: George C. Caster, 1895); Michael Swanton, *Three Lives of the Last Englishmen* (New York and London: Garland, 1984).

46. *De Gestis Herwardi*, 52 ff.

47. *Ibid.*, 62.

48. *Ibid.*, 67 ff.

49. *Fouke Le Fitz Waryn*, ed. E. J. Hathaway, P. T. Ricketts, C. A. Robson, and A. D. Wilshere, Anglo-Norman Texts Society 26–28 (Oxford: Blackwell, 1975).

50. *Le Romans de Wistasse li Moine*, ed. D. J. Conlon, University of North Carolina Studies in Romance Languages and Literature 126 (Chapel Hill: University of North Carolina Press, 1972).

51. *Gamelyn*, in *The Complete Works of Geoffrey Chaucer*, ed. W. W. Skeat (Oxford: Clarendon Press, 1894), 4.645–67.

52. Dobson and Taylor, *Rymes*, 258–73; Child #116.

53. Holt, *Robin Hood*, 123–28; Dobson and Taylor, *Rymes*, 35–36.

54. Richard Tardif, "The 'Mistery' of Robin Hood: A New Social Context for the Texts," in *Words and Worlds. Studies in the Social Role of Verbal Culture*, ed. Stephen Knight and S. N. Mukherjee, Sydney Studies in Society and Culture 1 (Sydney: Sydney Association for Studies in Society and Culture, 1983), 130–45.

55. The expression recurs frequently in the ballads, eg. *Gest* st. 14, *Robin Hood and the Potter* st. 24, 27.

56. *Medulla Grammaticae* in Stonyhurst College MS. A.1.10, fol. 15v; John Hodgkin, *Proper Terms*, Supplement to the Transactions of the Philological Society 1907–10 (?London: n. p., n.d.), 158.

57. *Gawain and the Green Knight*, ed. J. R. R. Tolkien and E. V. Gordon (Oxford: Clarendon Press, 1967), ll. 85 ff.

58. Cf. *Robin Hood and the Pinner of Wakefield (A)* st. 4; this element was probably also in *Robin Hood and the Friar*, as suggested by the broadside and folk-play versions.

59. *Gamelyn* ll. 660, 695; cf. Maurice Keen, *The Outlaws of Medieval Legend* (Toronto: University of Toronto Press, 1961), 200.

60. P. R. Coss, "Aspects of Cultural Diffusion in Medieval England: The Early Romances, Local Society, and Robin Hood," *Past and Present* 108 (1985), 75. Douglas Gray has similarly pointed out the irony latent in Robin's devotion to the Virgin Mary [Gray, "The Robin Hood Poems," 27–28].

61. D. M. Grisdale, ed., *Three Middle English Sermons from the Worcester Chapter Manuscript F. 10.* (Leeds: printed by T. Wilson of Kendal for members of the School of English Language in the University of Leeds, 1939), 8.

62. *Jack Upland* ll. 232–33, in *Jack Upland, Friar Daw's Reply and Upland's Rejoinder*, ed. P. L. Heyworth, Oxford English Monographs (Oxford: Oxford University Press, 1968). For other examples of the fifteenth to seventeenth centuries, see Dobson and Taylor, *Rymes*, 289–90.

63. Robert Kilburn Root, ed., *The Book of Troilus and Criseyde by Geoffrey Chaucer* (Princeton: Princeton University Press, 1926), p. 449; Dobson and Taylor, *Rymes*, 2.

64. Robert Hardy, *Longbow, A Social and Military History* (Portsmouth: Mary Rose Trust, 1986), 45 ff.

65. Holt, *Robin Hood*, 142–45.

66. Lydgate, *Debate of the Horse, Goose and Sheep* ll. 215–17, in *The Minor Poems of John Lydgate*, ed. H. N. McCracken, EETS o.s. 192 (London: Oxford University Press, 1934), 548.

67. Holt, *Robin Hood*, 145–46.

68. J. C. Holt, "The Origins and Audience of the Ballads of Robin Hood," *Past and Present* 18 (1960), 92.

69. Holt, *Robin Hood*, 38–39.

70. John Major, *Historia Majoris Britanniae*, ed. R. Freebairn (Edinburgh: R. Freebairn, 1740), IV.ii.56.

71. Coss, "Aspects of Cultural Diffusion," 75.

72. *The Vision of William Concerning Piers the Plowman* (A-Version), 2.128 ff.; cf. also John Bellamy, *Crime and Public Order in the Later Middle Ages* (London: Routledge and Kegan Paul, 1973), 13–14.

73. The poaching is mentioned in the *Gest* st. 366, 377, 417.

74. M. J. C. Hodgart, *The Ballads* (London and New York: Hutchinson's University Library, 1950), 133.

75. Maurice Keen, "Robin Hood, a Peasant Hero," *History Today* 8 (1958), 689.

76. Holt, "Origins and Audience," 90.

77. Holt, *Robin Hood*, 110.

78. Dobson and Taylor, *Rymes*, 10, xviii.

79. Rodney H. Hilton, *Class Conflict and the Crisis of Feudalism*, 2nd. rev. ed. (London and New York: Verso, 1990), 151, 152.

80. *The Vision of William Concerning Piers the Plowman*, 5.400 ff.

81. On Ranulf see R. M. Wilson, *Lost Literature of Medieval England*, 2nd ed. (London: Methuen, 1970), 117–18.

82. On the proverb, see Dobson and Taylor, *Rymes*, 291.

83. Sir Thomas Chaloner, *The Praise of Folie*, ed. Clarence H. Miller, EETS 257 (London: Oxford University Press, 1965), 53 (l. 9).

84. *Dives and Pauper*, ed. Priscilla Heath Barnum, EETS 275 (Oxford: Oxford University Press, 1976), 1.189 [Precept 1, ch. 51].

85. Alan J. Fletcher, "'The Unity of the State Exists in the Agreement of Its Minds': A Fifteenth-Century Sermon on the Three Estates," *Leeds Studies in English* n.s. 22 (1991), 126n.60.

86. Fletcher, "'The Unity of the State,'" 119 (ll. 57–61).

87. Bower, *Scotichronicon*, 5.354.

88. Thomas Wright, and J. O. Halliwell-Phillips, *Reliquiae Antiquae* (London: J. R. Smith, 1845), 1.45.

89. The principal exception is Fowler, but he is concerned with the literary rather than the social implications of the ballad form.

90. For the carols, see R. L. Greene, *Early English Carols* (Oxford: Clarendon Press, 1977).

91. Examples of narrative verse in quatrains, all dating to the fifteenth century, are: *The Battle of Otterburn* [Child #161]; *The Boy and the Mantle* [Melissa M. Furrow, ed., *Ten Fifteenth-Century Comic Poems*, Garland Medieval Texts 13 (New York and London: Garland, 1985), 301 ff.]; *The Adulterous Falmouth Squire* [*Zwei Mittelenglische Geschichten*, ed. Anne L. Leonard (Zürich: Druck des Art. Institut, 1891)]; *The Knight of Courtesy and the Fair Lady of Faguel* [ed. Elizabeth McCausland, Smith College Studies in Modern Languages 4:1 (Northampton, Mass.: Smith College; Paris: Librarie E. Champion, 1922)]; *Robyn and Gandelyn* [Child #115]; *The Blood of Hayles* [Carl Horstmann, *Altenglische Legenden* (Heilbronn: Henniger, 1881), 275 ff.]; *S. Editha sive*

Chronicon Vilodunense [ed. Carl Horstmann (Heilbronn: Henniger, 1883)]. Of these, only the first is in the same meter as the Robin Hood ballads. There are more examples, including *Adam Bell, Clim of the Clough and William of Cloudesley*, from the sixteenth century.

92. The similarity to the carol, a musical form, and the fact that the later Robin Hood ballads are normally sung may suggest that even if the surviving early ballads were not sung, they may have been composed in the style of others that were.

93. Coss, "Aspects of Cultural Diffusion," 73.

94. Peter Burke, *Popular Culture in Early Modern Europe* (New York: Harper, 1978), 24–28.

95. Holt, *Robin Hood*, 111.

96. *Ibid.*, 74.

97. *Ibid.*, 111.

98. *Ibid.*, 111; see also Holt, "Origins and Audience," 102.

99. Cf. Bruce A. Rosenberg, "Medieval Popular Literature: Folkloric Sources," in Thomas J. Heffernan, ed. *The Popular Literature of Medieval England*, Tennessee Studies in Literature 28 (Knoxville: University of Tennessee Press, 1985), 61–84.

2

Robin Hoodes Daye

Celle temps lan MCCCLVII entour le Pentecost le dit prince Dengleterre . . .
amenaunt soun adversarie de Frauns et soun fitz Philippe . . . les deliverra al
roy soun piere; en quel viage chivachaunt parmy la terre Dengleterre, le roy
Dengleterre avauntdit fist plusours seignours et autres gentz du pays les
encountrere par diverses voies; entre queux une iour pred de une foreste furent
enbuschez bien a v^c homes en cotes et mantels de verte; et quaunt le dit roy de
Frauns passa par le dite forest si moustrerent les ditz homes avaunt le roy de
Frauns et sa company come robbers ou gentz de male part od arkes et setes et
od espeys et talvasses; et de celle vieu le roy de Frauns se mervailla
graundement, demaundant quel maner de gentz qe ceux si furent; et le prince
respondist qils furent gentz Dengleterre foresters vivaunt par sauvagine en lour
dedute, et ceo fuist lour custome checun iour destre issint arrayes.

[At this time, in the year 1357 around Whitsun, the Prince of Wales . . . taking
the King of France and the Dauphin Philippe . . . delivered them to his father
the King of England. During this journey, as they rode through England, King
Edward arranged for numerous noblemen and other Englishmen to meet them
along the way. On one such occasion, one day near a forest, there were as many
as five hundred men hiding, clad in tunics and mantles of green, and as the
King of France passed by this forest, the men leapt out before him and his
company as robbers or malefactors with bows and arrows and swords and
shields. The King of France was astonished at the sight, and asked what sort of
men these were; the Prince of Wales replied that they were forest-dwelling
Englishmen who lived in the wild by choice, and that it was their custom to be
thus arrayed every day.]

—*The Anonimalle Chronicle*

Among the storytelling traditions of medieval England, the Robin Hood legend was distinguished by its extensiveness and popularity. Yet its most unique feature may have been the manner of its transmission. Very early in the recorded history of the legend, Robin Hood stepped out of the ballads to appear in the flesh in popular dramatic performances. In many parts of England by the end of the Middle Ages, Robin Hood the dramatic character may have been as familiar as Robin Hood the ballad hero. These portrayals of Robin Hood, known generally to scholars as Robin Hood games, encompassed a range of diverse phenomena, from scripted enactments of Robin's adventures to a kind of masquerading in which individuals would take the parts of Robin Hood and his men and act as hosts for a village fete.

In the case of the Robin Hood ballads, the surviving evidence includes a substantial corpus of texts but limited information on their performance context. With the Robin Hood games, the situation is reversed. Most of the surviving information relates to the context of performance: parish records detailing expenditures on costumes and accoutrements, household accounts recording donations to performers of folk plays, court documents relating to instances when the games got out of hand. There are a few scripts for actual plays, but for the most part the games were ephemeral observances and festivities whose content must be inferred from intermittent contextual evidence. Furthermore, the games did not constitute independent fictive worlds as did the ballads, but were public transactions in which the boundary between text and context was often fluctuating and always permeable. For these reasons, the sequence of this chapter is the reverse of the previous: it will first survey the contextual evidence and then turn to the task of reconstructing the actual content of the games.

CHRONOLOGY AND GEOGRAPHY

The earliest reference to a Robin Hood game occurs only half a century after the allusion to the outlaw hero in *Piers Plowman* and falls toward the beginning of the period from which the legend is well attested. It appears in the Exeter Receivers' Rolls for 1426–27, where we find the following entry:

Dato lusoribus ludentibus lusum Robyn Hood, xx d.

[Given to players playing a play "Robin Hood" (or "a Robin Hood play"), 20d.]

This laconic mention offers little insight on Robin's transition from balladic hero to dramatic character. One might expect that the plays had been around for some time prior to the first surviving reference; yet Exeter could conceivably have been the point of origin of the games. In the late fifteenth and the sixteenth centuries, when records of Robin Hood games become plentiful, Devonshire is one of their best-documented locations.

Nearly half a century passes before Robin Hood plays resurface in the written record, this time in a rueful letter from Sir John Paston of Norfolk to his younger brother John, written in 1473:

I have ben and ame troblyd with myn overe large and curteys delyng wyth my servantys and now wyth ther onkyndness. . . . W. Woode, whyche promysed you and Dawbenoy . . . at Castre that iff ye wolde take hym in to be ageyn wyth me that than he wold never goo from me; and ther-uppon I have kepyd hym thys iij yere to pleye Seynt Jorge and Robynhod and the shryff off Notyngham, and now when I wolde have a good horse he is goon into Bernysdale, and I wyth-owt a kepere.

Here, scripted plays are probably implied, to judge by the mention of the Sheriff of Nottingham. The allusion to St. George probably refers to other folk plays featuring England's patron saint. Apparently Sir John felt that Woode had devoted too much of his energy to amateur theatrics and not enough to his household duties. As we shall see, the only surviving medieval text of a Robin Hood play may have originated in the Paston household at about the time of this letter.

Evidence for Robin Hood games abounds for the rest of the fifteenth and sixteenth centuries. It is widely distributed across the map, but most plentiful in four distinct regions: the West, the Severn Valley area, the Thames Valley area, and Lowland Scotland.

The west of England, which yields the earliest reference to the Robin Hood games, also furnishes some of the fullest documentation for them. In Somerset, several of the references cluster around the cathedral town of Wells. Croscombe churchwardens' accounts document a "revel" or "sport" of Robin Hood for most years between 1476 and 1526, presided over by a parishioner who took the role of the outlaw; after 1526 he disappears, his place possibly taken by the "St. George ale" that figures in subsequent years. "Robin Hood's reckons," money generated by these Robin Hood games, were a significant source of funds for the parish. Records from Wells itself in 1498 mention a "Robynhode" who had collected money on behalf of the church and community.[1] In Glastonbury the parish of St. Johns had payments and income from Robin Hood games in 1500–1. Tintinhull held a "Robine Hood's All" in 1512–13, while the nearby town of Yeovil yields extensive references to Robin Hood games between 1516 and 1587. Dorset also furnishes instances of Robin Hood games, with Robin Hood collections in Poole in 1508–9, 1509–10 and 1510–11, references in Bridport to a "Robynhode Ale" in 1555 and to "Robyn hodes mony" in 1557–58, and church ales at Whitsun featuring Robin Hood and Little John in the parish of Netherbury in the years around 1567. Wiltshire yields at least one instance, with money paid to performers of a Robin Hood play in the house of Sir John Thynne at Longleat in 1562. In the great western port of Bristol, St. Nicholas Church paid for costuming Robin Hood and Little John in 1525-26.

Devonshire had a particularly well-documented tradition of Robin Hood games. These seem to have been especially popular in Exeter, the locus of the first example in 1426–27. The parish of St. Johns Bow received five shillings in 1487–88 from a "game [*lusione*] called Robin Hood." In 1508–9 the same parish had an "arrow of Saint Edmund the martyr" repaired "for Robin Hood"; the object was probably a prize for archery, such as mentioned in the *Gest*. Robin Hood games were restricted to specific days by an act of the town council in 1509–10; although this act regulated Robin Hood games, they were not prohibited altogether, and Robin Hood and Little John appear in the records of St. Johns as late as 1553–54, with collections from the sale of ale.

To the southeast of Exeter, in Woodbury, there are records in 1540–41, 1573–74, 1574–75, and 1576–77 of games featuring Robin Hood and Little John. There also appear two green coats in the records from 1581–82, probably costumes for the outlaws. Still further east, Farway chose a Robin Hood in 1567; in Honiton in 1571–72 a pound of gunpowder was purchased on the occasion of a visit from a Robin Hood from Colyton, and there was income from Robin Hood games in 1576–77.

Robin Hood games are well attested in the Dartmoor region. In Ashburton in 1526–27 money was paid to buy a new coat for Robin Hood, and in 1541–42 more was spent for coats for "Robert Hood" and his followers. In the churchwardens' accounts for Chagford in 1537, 35s. were paid "for dowing the office of the Howde Coat." This apparently refers to a Robin Hood game, as money was regularly handed in to the churchwardens between 1555 and 1564 by "Robin Hood's Company" or "howdesmen," and in 1562 another 35s. were paid to John Newcomb—listed in 1564 as one of the "howdesmen"—"for dowing the office of the Howde." In Chudleigh for the year 1561 there is an unusually substantial "Count of Robyn Hodde & Litle Iohn":

Recettes

	In primis received of theyr gathering in the parishe	xx s.
	Item received of the parishe	xl s.
	Item received of William Showbrocke	vj s. viij d.
	Item received for our alle solde	iij li.
	Sum totall vj li. vj s viij d	

Expences

	In primis paid for the clothe of vij cottes	xl s.
	Item paid for the Hoode cott cloth	xj s. iij d.
	Item paid for the vyces cott	ii s.
	Item paid for sylke & bottonse for the same cottes	vj s. iiij d.
	Item paid for sylke & whyplasse for the Hoodes cott	iij s.
	Item paid for making of ix cottes	x s.
	Item paid for the cuckes wages & the brewsters	iiij s.
	Item paid for a pere of showes for the vyce	xvj d.
	Item paid for wrytting this acount	ij d.
	Sum totall iij li. xviij s. j d.	

And so remaynethe declare xliiij s. vij d. finis. . .
Received of Robyn Hoode Richard Pynson xliiij s. vij d.

There were Robin Hood games on the north coast of Devon too. In Barnstaple in 1558–59 a payment was made to Robin Hood "for his pastime." Nearby Braunton made various expenditures between 1560 and 1562 for Robin Hood and his company.

Even further west, in Cornwall, Robin Hood games are documented late into the sixteenth century. Stratton records them between 1535–36 and 1538, and received money from the sale of "Robyn Hode is howse" in 1543. St. Breock had income from its Robin Hood in 1573–74, and gave money to a Robin Hood from St. Columb Minor in 1590–91 and to one from Mawgan in 1591–92. St. Ives had a Robin Hood game in 1584 and paid money to a Robin Hood from St. Columb Minor in 1588. St. Columb Major loaned out its Robin Hood costume in 1588 and collected "Robin hoodes monyes" in 1594.

The documentation for Robin Hood games in the Severn Valley area is less full than in the west, but is extensive enough for us to identify a tradition of such games in this region. The accounts of William More, Prior of Worcester in the reign of Henry VIII, yield a number of references in the area around Worcester. In 1519 a Robin Hood game from Worcester went on tour downriver to the northern end of Gloucestershire, as More gave money to "Robyn whod & hys men for getheryng to tewkesbury bruge ['bridge']." In 1529 "certen yong men" of the parish of St. Helen's in Worcester "pleyd Robyn Whod," in reward for which they received 12d. In 1530 players at Worcester or Battenhall collected money from the Prior in the "box of Robin Hood." In 1531 the Prior's tenants at the manor of Cleeve Prior played "Robin Whot, Mayde Marion, & other" at Crowle. Battenhall in 1535 had a visit from "Robyn Whod & litle Iohn of Ombursley."

Further upriver in Shropshire, Robin Hood plays were supported by civic authorities in all three market towns. Shrewsbury officials paid money in 1553 for clothing for a Robin Hood play and provided wine for the players. Officials in Ludlow reimbursed money given to Robin Hood in 1566–67; and in 1588 at Bridgnorth 2s. 6d. were disbursed by order of the bailiff "upon them which plaied Robin Hood." To the east of the Severn, residents of Staffordshire testified in 1498 that it was customary for inhabitants of Wolverhampton, Wednesbury, and Walsall to attend the fair at Willenhall on Trinity Sunday "with the capitains called the Abot of Marham or Robyn Hode to the intent to gether money with ther disportes to the profight of the churches."

Aside from the west, the richest evidence for Robin Hood games comes from the Thames Valley area. In Oxfordshire Robin Hood games are attested at Thame in 1474, 1496, and 1501 and at Henley-on-Thames in 1499, 1505, and 1520. Berkshire also yields several examples. In Reading, the parish of St. Lawrence received "gaderyngs" of "Robyn Hod" from 1498–99 to 1511. Finchamstead sent a Robin Hood game to Reading in 1505, and the parish of St.

Helens Abingdon in 1566 paid 18d. for setting up "Robin Hoode's bower." In Buckinghamshire, Amersham had a Robin Hood game in 1530. Further downriver, at Kingston-upon-Thames in Surrey, there are substantial references to Robin Hood games in the churchwardens' account books for most years between 1506 and 1539; the game toured to Croydon in 1515. The Kingston accounts of 1536–37 are particularly substantial:

The Charges for Robyn Hodde.
Item for II yerdes and a quarter of brode cloth for the fryer, 6s.
Item for IIII yerdes of cotton for the fooles cote, 2s.
Item for half a pice of fustian of gene for the morres dauncers cotes, 7s. 5d.
Item for II elles of Wustedde for maide marrion's Kyrtell, 6s. 8d.
Item for XIII C of Lyverey, 4s. 4d.
Item for VI payre of Dubble sollyd shows, 4s. 6d.
Item for VI payre of single sollid showis, 3s.
Item for XXIIII greate lyvereys, 4d.
Item for makyng of maide marrions kyrtell, 14d.
Item for makyng of the mores dauncers and the freyers cotes, 4s. 1d.

There are also instances of Robin Hood games in and around London. One possible reference may be found in the continuation of Robert Fabyan's *Chronicle*, where, under the year 1502, we read:

Also thys yere, about Mydsomer, was taken a felowe whych hadde renewed many of Robin Hodes pagentes, which named him selfe Greneleef.

This allusion could refer to professional or semi-professional drama. One of the criticisms offered against Bishop Stephen Gardiner in William Turner's *The Rescuynge of the Romishe Fox* (1545) is that he "forbad the players of london . . . to play any mo playes of Christe, but of Robin Hode and litle Johan, and of the Parlament of Byrdes and suche other trifles."[2] There is also evidence of parish Robin Hood plays: the church of Holy Trinity the Less, near the Tower of London, had fifteen "Robyne Hoodes Cottes" in its possession in 1552. The only actual description of a Robin Hood game in London, recorded by the diarist Henry Machyn in 1559, appears to reflect the declining days of the custom in the city: it suggests a rather formalized presentation combining a parade with civic tableaux, looking toward the Robin Hood pageants of the seventeenth century:

The xxiiij day of June ther was a May-game . . . with a gyant, and drumes and gunes . . . and then sant Gorge and the dragon, the mores dansse, and after Robyn Hode and lytyll John, and M[aid Marian] and frere Tuke, and thay had spechys rond a-bowt London.

In addition to these three major traditions of English Robin Hood games, there are other scattered references, which may or may not represent fully developed traditions of Robin Hood games in their respective regions. The southeast yields a small cluster of references. In 1528 the Lord Warden of the Cinque Ports forbade Robin Hood games in the coastal towns of Kent and Sussex under his jurisdiction. The ban was either transient or ineffective, since a Robin Hood game from Hythe performed in New Romney in 1532. The account books for the young Robert Sidney in 1574 include 3s. paid to a group who "played Robin Hood," probably some local country folk who presented a play at Penshurst for the Sidney children.

The Paston letters and the play of *Robin Hood and the Sheriff* prove that Robin Hood games were known in Norfolk in the late fifteenth century. A century later Thomas Nashe seems to describe Robin Hood and Little John taking part in a procession in Yarmouth, but the reference is probably not intended literally, suggesting that we should be warned by the title of the piece—*The Praise of Red Herring*. The Marprelate tract *Hay any work for cooper?* (1589) mentions Robin Hood games in Halstead in Essex, but again such a source cannot be taken at face value. Yet the games were certainly known in Hertfordshire, where Hexton was reported in the early seventeenth century as having recently abandoned its custom of Robin Hood games.

Recent research has also drawn attention to evidence of Robin Hood games in the East Midlands and North. In Leicester, an ecclesiastical visitation of the religious foundation at Newark College in 1525 found that Robin Hood games had been played there, although one cleric asserted that they were "for the benefit of the churches." In 1526 the parish of St. Leonards was complaining that 40s. from a Robin Hood play had not been rendered. In 1534 William Billar, the registrar of the Archdeaconry Court of Leicester, submitted an expense account for his service to Robin Hood. In Melton Mowbray (Leicestershire), just twenty miles from Nottingham, "Robin Hood's Money" was collected in 1555, 1556, and 1567. In Lancashire, there was a game in 1579 at Burnley, and a seventeenth-century tradition held that "the play of Robin Hood" was acted in Manchester during the reign of Mary (1553–58). In Yorkshire, a Robin Hood play was performed in the churchyard and church at Brandsby in 1615, with local recusants in the roles of Robin and the Sheriff.

In the first chapter, we already saw indications that this quintessential English hero also had some appeal for the Scots. Robin Hood games seem to have been at least as popular north of the Tweed as south of it. For a number of years, Robin Hood played an important ceremonial role in the life of Edinburgh, where he presented candidates for admission to the liberties of the city and was deputed to collect the "burgess money" paid for this privilege. References to this ceremony are to be found between 1492 and 1500; occasionally a Little John is also mentioned. References to Robin Hood games in Edinburgh recur throughout much of the sixteenth century. By 1518 he and Little John were said to have supplanted the traditional figure known as the Abbot of Narent, and in the same year one Francis Bothwell obtained a letter from the Earl of Arran to excuse him from "the office of Litiljohn, to the quhilk he was chosin for this yeir." There were also games in 1544, 1547, 1549, and 1550. In 1555 Robin Hood games were banned by the Scottish parliament, but the Edinburgh games did not disappear. Efforts by city authorities to suppress a revival of the games in 1561 provoked a riot, but the games seem to have taken place peacefully in 1572. Even as late as 1579 it was still deemed necessary to warn the residents of Edinburgh against accompanying "any sic as ar of mynde to renew the playes of Robene Hude."

Robin Hood games lasted even longer in smaller Lothian towns and villages. The Presbytery in Dalkeith felt it was necessary to warn against them in 1582. The town authorities in Haddington resolved to abolish them in 1588, but they were still taking place in 1589. Lasswade had games in 1583, Dirleton in 1585, Cranston in 1590.

Several other towns along Scotland's North Sea coast observed similar customs. The Lord Treasurer's accounts for 1503 refer to a donation to Robin Hood of Perth, and in 1545 burgess money in Perth was being paid to "robyn hwyd." In Dundee in 1521, Robin Hood was in charge of building archery butts. St. Andrews also had games: they were banned there in 1575, and a commission was sent by the General Assembly of the Kirk in the same year to inquire why the games had not been suppressed. The minister protested that they were the work of "certane servandis and young childering," and that he had consistently preached against the games and sought their suppression by the town magistrates.

As Edinburgh's Robin Hood replaced the Abbot of Narent, so in Aberdeen he and Little John supplanted the Abbot and Prior of Bonaccord. In 1508 the alderman, baillies, and council of Aberdeen decreed that all able-bodied citizens were to be ready with outfits of green and yellow, as well as bows and arrows, to attend upon Robin Hood and Little John whenever they should be required, particularly on Sundays in May and on St. Nicholas Day. Apparently there was some disagreement in the community over this practice, since warnings had to be issued in 1517 to certain "inobedientis & ȝoung" who refused to take part in the processions. Robin Hood games persisted in Aberdeen after the ban, although without official support, as evidenced by an action against one Henry Marshall for "making of robin huid & litill Iohnne" in 1565. Residents of the nearby parish of Arbuthnot were still holding games in 1570.

In the southern Lowlands, Dumfries had its own Robin Hood to admit candidates to the liberties of the city, a practice attested between 1534 and 1536. Robin Hood plays apparently continued to enjoy favor in Dumfries some time after they had been banned by Parliament, as witnessed by a case in 1570 when the council fined one disobedient citizen who had refused to "accept on hym the office of robert huyd & littill Iohn." Records from Ayr between 1538 and 1554 mention a Robin Hood who admitted candidates into the liberties of the city. In Peebles, Robin Hood was receiving "burgess silver" in 1555.

While most references appear in civic or parochial contexts, Robin Hood games also found their way into aristocratic circles. Aristocratic patronage of

Robin Hood games has already been seen at Longleat in Wiltshire and Penshurst in Kent. Such patronage might reach to the highest levels of society. Machyn, in recording the Robin Hood game in London in 1559, goes on to report that the next day the presentation went to Greenwich to play for the queen and council. Elizabeth's father Henry VIII appears to have been especially fond of such pastimes, which he organized for his court on at least two occasions. The first was in 1510:

His Grace, the earles of Essex, Wiltshire, and other noble men, to the number of 12, came sodainly in a morning into the Quene's chambre, all appareled in short cotes of Kentish Kendal, with hodes on their heddes, and hosen of the same, every one of them his bowe and arrowes, and a sworde and a bucklar, like outlawes, or Robyn Hodes men, whereof the Quene, the Ladies, and al other, there were abashed as well for the strange sight, as also for their sodain comyng; and after certain daunces and pastimes made, they departed.

A similar celebration took place in May 1515:

The king and the Queen, accompanied with many lords and ladies, rode to the high ground of Shooters Hill to take the open air; and as they passed by the way, they espied a company of tall yeomen, clothed all in green with green hoods and bows and arrows, to the number of two hundred. Then one of them, which called himself Robyn hood, came to the King, desiring him to see his men shoot, and the King was content. Then he whistled, and all the two hundred archers shot and loosed at once, and then he whistled again, and they likewise shot again; their arrows whistled by craft of the head, so that the noise was strange and great, and much pleased the King and Queen and all the company. All these archers were of the King's guard and had thus apparelled themselves to make solace to the King. Then Robyn hood desired the King and the Queen to come into the green wood, and to see how the outlaws live. The King demanded of the Queen and her ladies, if they durst adventure to go into the wood with so many outlaws. Then the Queen said, that if it pleased him, she was content. Then the horns blew till they came to the wood under Shooters Hill, and there was an arbour made of boughs, with a hall and a great chamber and an inner chamber very well made and covered with flowers and sweet herbs, which the King much praised. Then said Robyn hood, Sir, outlaws' breakfast is venison, and therefore you must be content with such fare as we use. Then the King and Queen sat down, and were served with venison and wine by Robyn hood and his men, to their great contentation.

Henry VIII's Robin Hood games hover at the margin of the folk tradition, being heavily reinterpreted by aristocratic interests and resources. Probably closer to the popular games is the patronage of several Scottish monarchs. In 1503 James IV gave money to Robin Hood of Perth; in 1531 the Treasurer disbursed money on behalf of James V for gray, yellow, and white taffeta for "the Kingis Robene Hudis baner," and in 1544, 1547, 1549, and 1550, during the regency of Mary, the crown gave money to Robin Hood. The games in

Dirleton in 1585 were enjoyed by James VI and several of the leading figures in the country.

After 1600 the records are largely silent on the subject of Robin Hood games, but silence is always a suspect form of evidence. Such few references as have turned up suggest that the practice proved surprisingly tenacious in a period when political, cultural, and socioeconomic pressures were conspiring to eliminate it. In Scotland, there was a Robin Hood game in Linton in 1610, over half a century after the official ban was first imposed. In Stratford-on-Avon in 1622 there were May games featuring morris dancing and a Robin Hood play, perhaps related to the Severn Valley tradition of Robin Hood games. The play of Robin Hood and the Sheriff in Brandsby, Yorkshire, in 1615 has already been mentioned.

Somerset yields two late examples of the games. In the summer of 1607, when St. Cuthberts in Wells needed to raise money for a new bell and repairs to the tower, the parish held a protracted ale spanning the Sundays in May and June. The entertainments on May 31 featured a large gathering in the marketplace with dancing; military displays with an ensign, a drum, and musketry; and a Robin Hood game. Two weeks earlier the parish of Westonzoyland also had a Robin Hood game—one of the best-documented examples of the phenomenon, thanks to a local Puritan's complaint against the parish priest:

Item Mr Wolfall the sundaye after Ascention daye last, at morninge prayer, presentlye after the second lesson, put of his Surplusse and willed his parishioners to departe, and followe Robin Hoode, accordinge to their auncient Custome, to the Alle, and to breakfast with him, and gave them libertye soe to doe the most parte of an howre, and then came to the Churche, and begann the service at the tenn Comandementes.[3]

Robin Hood games seem to have been especially tenacious in Oxfordshire. Woodstock in 1627–28 received profits at Whitsontide from "Robin whood & lille John." As late as 1652, when the Commonwealth was striving to reform the country according to Puritan ideals of godliness, a Swedish visitor to the village of Enstone witnessed games *quos sua lingua Rabben hüt vocabant*, "which in their language they called 'Robin Hood.'"

There are no known later examples, save perhaps for a few marginal appearances in traditional celebrations, none of which can be shown to have originated before 1700. The Abbots Bromley horn dance in Staffordshire includes a Robin Hood–like figure, but although the dance can be traced as far back as the seventeenth century, this particular character could have been introduced later in its history.[4] Certain nineteenth-century mummers' plays incorporated Robin Hood figures and stories, but this material derived from printed Robin Hood balladry.[5]

Robin Hood Games
before 1500

o indicates an
   uncertain reference

50 miles

Edinburgh

Severn Wednesbury

Caister o

Thame

Thames

Reading Henley

Croscombe
Wells
Glastonbury

Exeter

Robin Hood Games
1500–1525

○ indicates an
uncertain reference

Aberdeen

Dundee
Perth

Edinburgh

50 miles

Severn

Leicester

Worcester

Tewkesbury

Thame
Henley   London
Reading   Croydon
Finchamstead   Kingston

Thames

Croscombe
Glastonbury
Tintinhull
Yeovil

Poole

Exeter

Robin Hood Games

1526–1550

○ indicates an
uncertain reference

Perth

Edinburgh

Ayr

Dumfries

50 miles

Severn

Leicester

Worcester
Cleeve

Amersham

London

Bristol *Thames*

Kingston Faversham

Sandwich

Hythe

Croscombe

New
Romney

Stratton

Yeovil

Chagford

Woodbury

Ashburton

Robin Hood Games
1551–1575

o   indicates an
    uncertain reference

50 miles

Aberdeen
Arbuthnot
St. Andrews
Edinburgh
Peebles
Ayr
Dumfries
Manchester
Severn
Shrewsbury
Ludlow
Melton
Thames Abingdon
London
Longleat
Penshurst
Braunton
Barnstaple
Yeovil
Honiton
Farway
Netherbury
Exeter
Colyton
Bridport
Chagford
Woodbury
St. Breock
Chudleigh

Robin Hood Games
1576–1600

○ indicates an
uncertain reference

Dirleton
Edinburgh
Lasswade   Haddington
Cranston   Dalkeith

50 miles

Burnley

Severn   Yarmouth

Bridgnorth

Hexton   Halstead

Thames

Glastonbury

Yeovil
Honiton
Chagford
St.Columb St.Breock
Mi.   St.Columb
        Ma.
Woodbury
St.Ives
Mawgan

Robin Hood Games
after 1600

Linton

50 miles

Brandsby

Severn

Stratford

Enstone
Woodstock

Thames

Wells

Westonzoyland

CHARACTER OF THE GAMES

Several general parameters may be deduced from this survey of the Robin Hood games. One of the most important is that the tradition was not a monolithic entity, but a diverse range of practices that spanned upwards of two centuries and appeared in settings as diverse as the court at Greenwich, the towns of the Scottish coast, and the remotest villages of Cornwall. At the same time, the evidence argues its own incompleteness in representing this extensive and diverse phenomenon. In areas where references are abundant enough to suggest a living tradition, they are too widely and thinly scattered, both geograpically and temporally, to constitute full evidence of an ongoing custom. Even where instances are the sole occurrences for the locality in question, they may represent a more extensive tradition now lost to the record: since a Robin Hood game could involve a significant investment of capital for costumes and accessories, it would be economically advantageous to perform the game more than once. In some cases the language of the attestation implies an established local tradition of Robin Hood games. The games at Willenhall in 1498 are said to have been "of olde tymes used and accustumed," and at Westonzoyland in 1607 Robert Wolfall urged his parishioners to join Robin Hood "accordinge to their auncient Custome."

At the same time, the fact that the Robin Hood game is by far the best documented form of folk drama of the period strongly suggests that the tradition must have been quite extensive. This is borne out by sixteenth- and early seventeenth-century allusions to the Robin Hood games, which imply that they were a very familiar feature of English life. The games are frequently mentioned by nostalgists or reformers who wish either to praise or condemn the traditional practices of the English people. They would hardly have received such attention had their distribution been as limited as our references. As with the Robin Hood ballads, an intelligent reading of the tradition must allow for a significant body of lost information.

Such fragmentary sources adumbrate rather than illuminate the geographic and temporal diversity of the tradition, allowing us to see only the very broadest patterns. There is an evident contrast between the games in Scotland, where civic contexts for the games are especially common, and those in England, where parochial settings predominate. Also striking is the abundance of evidence from southern England and from Scotland compared with its extreme rarity in northern England, which might be taken to reflect the cultural division between northern and southern strands of the Robin Hood tradition mentioned at the end of the previous chapter. Yet the limitations of the evidence make any such conclusions conjectural at best. The parish account books which furnish most of our references to the English games survive unevenly, and they are much more plentiful for southern England than for the north. Until quite recently, it was believed that Robin Hood games were wholly unknown in northern England: the scattering of references discovered in the past two decades should warn us against overinterpreting the gaps in the record.[6]

The evidence likewise offers little information on the evolution of the games over time. The original point of contact between the stories and the games may be forever lost. One might suppose that the games began with scripted plays, since these are the form of the Robin Hood game closest to the ballads, sharing with them the element of narrative—in fact, all of the surviving plays have corresponding ballads with the same plot. On the other hand, there are instances in which narrative traditions became matter for unscripted playacting without the intervention of scripted plays. In courtly circles in the later Middle Ages there was a vogue for role-playing the court of King Arthur, a practice apparently independent of any actual dramatic enactments.[7] The incident from the *Anonimalle Chronicle* cited at the opening of this chapter would appear to be playacting of this sort and could even be the earliest example of a Robin Hood game.

As regards the later evolution of the games, not enough information survives to reconstruct much of the genetic relationships by which they were developed and disseminated. Some cases appear to represent living transmission of folk practices. This may be seen in such instances as the games of Somerset, Devon, and Cornwall, where attestations appear in geographically close locales over a compact period of time. Here one might even see a pattern of transmission, from such urban centers as Wells and Exeter into the smaller villages and remoter parts of the west, dying off first in the towns while enduring longer in the hinterland. In other cases, parallel traditions of games appear to evolve more or less independently. Such would seem to be the case of the games in Scotland, which are so strikingly different and geographically discontiguous from the English games as to constitute a separate tradition. Similarly, later instances of the games in England may represent deliberate revivals of a practice known only as a traditional and patriotic entertainment of a previous generation. This is particularly likely in such cases as Wells in 1607: there the last previous attestation of Robin Hood games was over a century before, and one witness testified regarding the festivities that he had "heard by his father and Grandmother that the same had ben an auncyent Custome, with certayne Pageantes, Maye games, and shewes."[8]

In the end, we can only understand the games as a generalized whole, acknowledging the variations of time and place, but declining the futile task of analyzing them. If the evidence is fragmentary relative to the tradition it represents and frustratingly thin in detailed examples of what actually took place in any one Robin Hood game, it is nonetheless substantial enough to reveal distinct patterns from which we may reconstruct the general contours of the Robin Hood games. The sources reveal a range of common features that may manifest themselves in whole or in part in any given instance; these features share certain themes with one another to constitute an organically if not logically integrated continuum.

One of the most consistent and fundamental patterns in the games is the context in which they took place. The Robin Hood games generally occurred in specific settings and at certain times of the year. The formalized contexts are immediately evident in the dates of performance, which are closely tied to the annual cycle of the festive calendar and agrarian life. Where a specific day is named, it is generally after Easter (March 22–April 25) and before the end of June. In England, the most common date is Whitsun, seven weeks after Easter (May 10–June 13). This is the date specified in the cases of Kingston-on-Thames in 1506, 1515–16, 1520–21, and 1528–29; Thame in 1474–75, 1496–97, and 1501–2; Reading in 1506; and Braunton in 1561–62. The Worcester games in 1529 also took place during the week leading up to Whitsun.

Other common dates are the holidays close to Whitsun. In Yeovil in 1572–73 Robin Hood seems to have been responsible for overseeing the bell ringing on Ascension Day, ten days before Whitsun. The Westonzoyland games occurred on the Sunday after Ascension. The fair at Willenhall that Robin Hood was accustomed to attend at the end of the fifteenth century was held on Trinity Sunday, one week after Whitsun; this was also the date of the Robin Hood game in Wells in 1607. The games at Worcester in 1519 and 1530 took place the week following Trinity Sunday.

Most other examples also fall in May or June. The Lord Treasurer of Scotland made payments to Edinburgh's Robin Hood on May 14, 1547. King Henry VIII's Robin Hood game in 1515 took place in May. In Aberdeen in 1517 burgesses were to be prepared to attend Robin Hood on all Sundays in May. The Edinburgh games in 1561 and 1572 occurred in May. Games took place in and around Worcester the week of May 30–June 5 in 1535. The Robin Hood game at Enstone in 1652 took place on June 21. In 1503 James IV of Scotland dispensed money to Perth's Robin Hood on June 26. Robin Hood and Little John in Dumfries in 1532 were chosen at Easter, which suggests that their work was to take place in the same general period. Unusually late are the games at Crowle the week of July 23–29 in 1531; the earliest date is April 26, in Edinburgh in 1544. The only significantly deviant date occurs in Aberdeen in 1508, where the Robin Hood parade took place on St. Nicholas Day, December 6; here the date reflected a transferral of the games from their summer setting to the feast day of the town's patron saint.

Although Robin Hood games were often associated with particular days, they were not necessarily limited to a single occasion. The Exeter City Council act of 1509–10 felt it was necessary to halt the proliferation of the games by restricting them to the church holy day. Robin's gathering at Kingston in 1506 lasted two weeks, from Whitsunday to Fair Day, and a similar span may have been involved whenever Robin was involved in collecting grain and malt for the festival.[9] Touring Robin Hood games necessarily involved multiple days of activity. Some of the Scottish references imply that Robin's activities lasted for a month or more.[10]

Aside from actual feast days, Robin Hood games might occur on Sundays in general, as these were days of leisure for both performers and audience. The burgesses of Aberdeen were expected to attend Robin on all Sundays in May. The playing of Robin Hood games on Sundays is also attested by Scottish reformers during the latter half of the sixteenth century, who characterized the games as profanations of the Sabbath.[11]

In most documented instances, the Robin Hood games appear to have taken place not as an independent activity, but within the context of an established social event organized by the civic or parochial community. In England, the occasion may be termed a church holy day, as in Reading in 1503–4 where money was paid for bread and ale for Robin Hood and his company on the "church holy day"; Exeter in 1509–10 banned Robin Hood games from all times "but oonle the Churche holyday." In other instances, it is called a church ale or parish ale. The Robin Hood in Yeovil in 1577–78 rendered money made "by kepinge the Churche ale"; the Robin Hood game in Wells in 1607 was part of a church ale; and the Westonzoyland game in 1607 took place in the context of a "parishe Alle."

Other kinds of ales also figure. The Thame accounts in 1501–2 list receipts "of the may ale of the gderyng [sic] of Robyn Hodde at Whitsontyed." The Bridport game was called a "Robynhode Ale." Alternatively, the context of the games may be described as a May game or a May play. The disruptions at Burnley in 1579 were "aboute Robyn hoode and the May games." Machyn describes the Robin Hood game in London in 1559 as being part of a "May-Game"; this instance illustrates that the term referred generally to the time of year, not to the specific month, since the display took place on June 24–25. The Kingston records for 1519–20 list receipts "of the Maye game and Robyn Hode." The Robin Hood plays printed by Copland in the sixteenth century are said to be "verye proper to be played in Maye Games." The Reading games in 1501–2 are called a "May play."

In some cases, the Robin Hood games coincided with local fairs; all known examples again fall in May or June. In 1498 the inhabitants of Wolverhampton, Wednesbury, and Walsall were said to have been accustomed to visit Willenhall fair on Trinity Sunday with Robin Hood. In Reading in 1501–2 the games took place on "the fayre day" (May 1). In Kingston in 1506 Robin Hood's gathering is said to have run from "Whitsunday unto Fair Day" (the Wednesday two weeks later).

Most English instances of the games come from small towns. This is likely to reflect more on the nature of the evidence than on the existence of Robin Hood games in cities or rural settings, both of which are certainly attested. Even in urban contexts, the English games are usually associated with parochial rather than civic structures, although again there are exceptions. In Scotland this connection between the games and the parish church is unattested. Public sponsorship of the games is through civic authorities or the crown, and although the games take place during the same season, there is no evidence of a close connection with church holy days.

There is also evidence of Robin Hood games transpiring outside official jurisdictions. The Robin Hood game organized by Roger Marshall of Wednesbury in 1498 does not appear to have been officially sanctioned. The City Council in Exeter in 1509–10 forbade any "riot kept in any parysh by the yong man of the same parish called Robyn hode but oonle the Churche holyday." The games in Edinburgh in 1561 were organized by the servants of craftsmen in defiance of the civic authorities; those in Aberdeen in 1565 and 1570 were also unauthorized. The games in St. Andrews that prompted an inquiry in 1575 were the work of "certane servandis and young childering," and those in Haddington in 1588 and 1589 were blamed on "the insolence of the ȝouth." Unauthorized games also feature in Dalkeith in 1582, Lasswade in 1583, Cranston in 1590, and Linton in 1610. Such unofficial games are identifiable only when they come into conflict with the authorities of church and state, which is why they are particularly well documented in Scotland after the games were officially banned. Yet unofficial games were not necessarily lawless by nature. Many of the instances of the games known through rewards paid to players rather than through records of civic or parochial involvement could also represent Robin Hood games organized independently of official communal structures. Again, all datable examples of unofficial games fall in May and June.

From this diversity of dates and names of occasions, we can abstract two principal contexts for the Robin Hood games. The first, which we may term the communal May festival, is a public festivity organized by either parochial or civic authorities, taking place after Easter and before July, typically in May or June. In England the occasion is often in observance of a holy day or the feast day of the parish church; in market towns it may coincide with the town fair. In Scottish towns the festival is more secularized and urbanized, being associated with civic structures and dissociated from the church calendar.

The second setting, which may be designated the subcommunal May game, is organized by individuals acting outside of official communal structures. It is akin to the first in that it takes place during the same part of the ritual year; it differs in the degree of official communal involvement and control. There were probably marginal examples in which Robin Hood games were organized by a social subgroup in conjunction with the communal festivity but without communal oversight. Subcommunal games are attested in both England and Scotland, but are generally harder to detect because of their unofficial character.

The Robin Hood games in general are principally recognizable in the records by the personnel involved. Chief of these is Robin himself; he is often accompanied by Little John.[12] In many instances, there is also a band of followers, sometimes called "Robin Hood's men," or "Hoodsmen," as in Chagford.[13] The records even offer some hints as to their numbers: nine coats were purchased for the games in Chudleigh in 1561, presumably including those for Robin himself, Little John, and the "Vice"; a total of fifteen "Robin Hood cottes" were in the inventory of the London church of Holy Trinity the Less in 1551; Kingston in 1519–20 provided fourteen coats, apparently all for the supernumerary characters, and rented twenty hats "for Robin Hode" in 1522–23. Apart from Little John, other outlaw characters from the ballads, such as Will Scarlett and Much the Miller's Son, are not specifically mentioned. Perhaps they were not sufficiently defined as visual characters to be recognizable by their appearance—which would suggest that already by this time Little John had acquired his own distinctive physical characteristic (a feature attested by Staniehurst in 1577).

The Sheriff of Nottingham is also mentioned in several cases.[14] His presence may indicate scripted plays enacting Robin Hood's adventures, although it is possible that he sometimes interacted more informally with the audience. Testimony from Yeovil in 1607 describes a mock sheriff apparently involved in gathering money from the parishioners:

One Thomas Jarvis being in the street . . . & seing the company cominge toward him . . . he went into a house thinkinge to escape them, but on John Traske & John Peek went in after him . . . & brought him forth to the company, whear on Thomas Ffantstone, which they called the Shrive amonges them, commanded som to bear him away; the said Thomas Jarvis offendinge the said shrive, he begane to drawe his sword, & not withstandinge they very much molested the said Thomas Jarvis of his peace.[15]

While some ballad characters did not make it into the Robin Hood games, other new ones were added. One of these was Friar Tuck, a character apparently representing one version of the mock clerics who feature in popular rituals of the period in various guises, including the Boy Bishop, and the Abbot of Unreason, Marham, or Bonaccord.[16] The earliest reference to Tuck's name occurs in 1417, when Henry V issued a commission to arrest one assuming the name "Frere Tuck" and other evildoers of his retinue who had committed various "murders, homicides, robberies, depredations, felonies, insurrections, trespasses, oppressions, extortions, offenses, and misprisions" in Surrey and Sussex.[17] The next year he issued another commission to inquire into reports regarding one "Frere Tuk" and his followers, who had entered parks, warrens, and chases in Surrey and Sussex, "hunting and carrying off deer, hares, rabbits, pheasants, and partridges, burning houses and lodges for keeping the parks, and threatening the keepers."[18] In 1429 a pardon was granted to this wrongdoer, in which he was identified as a chaplain named Robert Stafford of Lyndefeld, Sussex.[19]

Stafford may have adopted the preexisting name of a mock cleric figure, or his alias may have later been applied to the character. An intimate interaction was at work in this period between ritual and folk drama on the one hand and lawlessness and protest on the other. This close relationship could extend to the point of sharing of names: several leaders of popular riots in the early seventeenth century adopted the name "skimmington," the term for an English form of the ritual charivari.[20] Tuck's name referred to the tucking up of the skirts of a clerical habit; it was of course particularly appropriate for a friar who pursued a life more active than contemplative.

By 1475, Friar Tuck was a figure in Robin Hood folk plays, as witnessed in the play of *Robin Hood and the Sheriff*, where he is the only named character besides Robin and the Sheriff. He also appears in the play and ballad versions of *Robin Hood and the Friar*, both probably dating to the sixteenth century, and in commercial plays from the 1590s onward; not until Sir Walter Scott's *Ivanhoe* (1819) does he become an integral part of the band in a nondramatic context.[21]

However, he may have had something of a life of his own outside of the Robin Hood stories. Oxford Bodleian MS. Ashmole 61 includes a verse narrative known as *The King and the Hermit* which may shed some light on this character. The manuscript dates to around 1500 and contains a variety of short pieces, including devotional texts, romances, and works of moral instruction.[22] *The King and the Hermit* is incomplete: it runs to a bit over 520 lines in twelve-line rhymed stanzas. The story is set in "god Edwerd deys" and begins with a royal hunt in Sherwood Forest. The king becomes separated from his men and comes upon a hermitage. The hermit, who is referred to anonymously throughout as a "hermit" or "friar," reluctantly grants the stranger lodging. The king asks for food, slyly observing that if he led the hermit's life, he would surely go hunting while the foresters were asleep. The friar is suspicious, but after much cajoling he relents, observing that his guest "semys a felow," and brings forth venison. The king convinces the friar to visit him in turn, identifying himself as Jack Fletcher, a yeoman at the court. The friar shows off his bedchamber, adorned with broad arrows and a bow so mighty that the king can scarcely draw the string. The next morning the king rejoins his hunting party. At this point the narrative breaks off, but on the basis of analogues in the "King Incognito" motif, we may surmise that the friar returns the visit and receives some reward from his guest, now revealed as the king.

There is no mention of the friar's name, but by the time of the manuscript, Friar Tuck was an established figure in the Robin Hood tradition, at least in dramatic contexts, so that a tale about a poaching friar in Sherwood would strongly suggest Tuck. It is more difficult to speak with certainty about intent of the poem's author, due to the uncertain date of composition. The setting in "god Edwerd deys" implies that an Edward was not on the throne at the time of composition, which would put the date between 1377 and 1461, or after 1483. Given that Robin Hood was popularly associated with Sherwood by the early fifteenth century, the otherwise unnecessary and unparalleled reference to Sherwood could well be a deliberate allusion to the Robin Hood tradition.[23] Even if we feel our evidence is insufficient to prove the intent of the author, this tale would certainly have been interpreted as a Robin Hood tale for most of its history; it was to be revived in precisely this way by Scott in *Ivanhoe*.

In the early sixteenth century, we begin to have evidence for the inclusion in May festivals of a friar character, sometimes under the name "Friar Tuck"; he is often associated with the morris dance, and particularly with the lady who features in the dance. A friar was a regular part of the Robin Hood games in Kingston-on-Thames from 1508 onward, apparently doubling as a part of Robin Hood's entourage and as a morris dancer.[24] This dancing friar was apparently not the source of Robin Hood's friar, as the 1475 play predates references to morris dancing in England. On the whole, it makes most sense to suppose that Tuck was a mock cleric who occasionally appeared in conjunction with Robin Hood, as did the Abbot of Marham at Willenhall in 1498, and thereby came to be incorporated into his story; this same figure was adopted by the morris dance as an appealingly burlesque character to dance with Maid Marian.

Tuck may also have engaged in other activities appropriate to a mock cleric, as suggested in Skelton's *Magnificence*:

> Another bade shave halfe my berde,
> And boyes to the pylery gan me plucke,
> And wolde have made me freer Tucke,
> To preche oute of the pylery hole.[25]

The possibility that Tuck may have preached mock sermons is supported by an allusion in Michael Drayton's *Poly-Olbion* (1612) to "*Tuck* the merry Frier, which many a Sermon made,/ In praise of *Robin Hood*, his Out-lawes, and their Trade."[26]

Maid Marian also entered the Robin Hood legend through the May festival. In sixteenth-century sources she takes various forms, not always named and not always paired with Robin Hood, but recognizable as the only female figure in the games. She too was in origin probably a ritual figure, appearing in two versions: one was played by a woman and was akin to the ritual May Queen; the other was played by a man and related to the tradition of ritual cross-dressing. Thomas Nashe in the late sixteenth century describes such a portrayal:

Martin himself is the Maid Marian, trimly dressed up in a cast gown and a kercher of Dame Lawson's, his face handsomely muffled with a diaper-napkin to cover his beard, and a great nosegay in his hands. [27]

Like the Friar, Marian was incorporated into the morris dance. She does not seem to have been incorporated into the legend outside of dramatic contexts. A character in Barclay's *Eclogues* (c. 1513–14) asks to hear "some merry fit of Maid Marion or else of Robin Hood,"[28] but the allusion is probably just one of association, as in one of the *Merie Tales of the Mad Men of Gotam* (c. 1565):

Theare was two men of Gotam, and the one was goyng to the market to Nottyngham to buye sheepe and the other dyd come from the Market, and bothe met together uppon Nottingham bridge. . . Marye sayd the other, I wyll brynge them ouer thys bridge. By Robyn hoode sayd he that cam from Nottingham, but thou shalte not. By Mayd Maryon sayde he that went to the market, but I wyll.[29]

Marian appears in none of the early ballads, although an unnamed lady does show up briefly at the end of the play of *Robin Hood and the Friar*, where she is offered as a "reward" for the Friar—an obvious device for making the transition to the dance, which she performs with the Friar. Marian appears in the accounts for Kingston-on-Thames from 1509 onward, as a morris dancer and probably as part of the Robin Hood game as well. She is included in the Robin Hood games performed by the tenants of Cleeve Prior at Crowle in 1531. Maid Marian is attested only in the Thames and Severn Valley Robin Hood games.

Given that Robin and his outlaw band in the ballads are all young unmarried men, one might expect their roles to have been fulfilled by their counterparts in the community, especially since informal social groupings of young men were a common feature of European popular culture in this period.[30] In some cases this is supported by the sources. In the Paston letters we see an irresponsible servant playing the role; in the parish of St. Helens in Worcester in 1519 it is specified that it was "certen yong men" who "pleyd Robyn Whod." In *Londons Artillery* (1616) Richard Niccols lamented:

How is it that our London hath laid downe
This worthy practise . . .
. . . when her *Robin Hood*
Had wont each yeare, when May did clad the wood,
With lustie greene to lead his yong men out,
Whose brave demeanour, oft when they did shoot,
Invited royall Princes from their courts,
Into the wilde woods to behold their sports?[31]

Subcommunal Robin Hood games seem particularly likely to have been the purvey of young men, a possibility supported by some evidence. In Exeter in 1509–10 it is the young men of the city who have to be restrained from their enthusiasm for unauthorized Robin Hood games. In Edinburgh in 1561 the games are organized by craftsmen's servants; in St. Andrews in 1575 it is "certane servandis and young childering"; in Haddington in 1589 the games are blamed on "the insolence of the ȝouth." Some communal May festivities apparently delegated responsibility for the Robin Hood games to the young men of the community, as in Amersham in 1530 where the churchwardens received money from the "lades" for the Robin Hood game, and Chagford in 1554–55, where the games were in the hands of "the yongemen off the parysche."

In other cases, the roles of Robin Hood and his followers were taken by persons of standing in the community. The men who impersonated Robin Hood in Croscombe were in several instances churchwardens or former churchwardens.[32] In Yeovil too Robin Hood was frequently a past or future churchwarden, and the offices were held simultaneously in one instance.[33] The Yeovil Robin Hoods include a smith, a shoemaker, a yeoman, and an innkeeper; some of them were or had been married; one of them was also a constable.[34] In

Leicester in 1534 Robin Hood's attendants included the registrar of the Archdeaconry Court. Wells's Robin Hood in 1607 was a yeoman, his assistant (perhaps Little John) a tailor.

In the towns of Scotland, where the Robin Hood games were closely integrated into the civic life of the community, Robin's followers were men of substance, in some cases required by civic edict to attend on the outlaw. In both England and Scotland there are instances in which the leading roles in the Robin Hood games were treated as community offices. There are indications that Robin Hood was elected in Chagford and Farway, and in Edinburgh in 1518. At Dumfries in 1532 Robin Hood and Little John were chosen at Easter, doubtless giving them time to organize the upcoming festivities. The choosing of Robin Hood at Reading in 1501–2 seems to have been something of a festival in itself, since minstrels were hired for the occasion.[35] In many cases Robin Hood was paid, and in Ayr 1549 one man's labors for a year in the office were considered to have earned him admission to the liberties of the town.[36] In Reading in 1515–16 Robin Hood was paid 12d. for his efforts; Little John received 10d., Friar Tuck 8d., and another 8d. were given to "Roben Hodes men." In Chagford in 1537 and 1562 the "office of the Howde coat" involved the substantial recompense of 35s., probably implying reimbursement for expenses incurred. The position could be subject to communal oversight: in 1567 Farway chose Walter Bucknoll as its Robin Hood, but afterward removed him from office. In some Scottish towns service as Robin Hood or Little John was considered a civic responsibility, with fines imposed on those who declined to serve.[37] With this responsibility came some authority, as in Aberdeen in 1518 Robin and Little John are authorized to require people to attend upon them in their parades. This degree of status, authority, and responsibility is hardly surprising for an individual who might be called on to handle significant sums of money and in some cases pay immediate expenses out of pocket.[38]

The records suggest a certain measure of consistency in the visual interpretation of the legend. The attire of the outlaws appears to have been stereotyped: in the play of *Robin Hood and the Friar*, there is nothing in the dialogue itself to identify Robin, implying that the visual cues were sufficient, and in Chagford and Chudleigh, the role of Robin Hood seems to have been characterized by the costume, since the office was known as the "Howde coat." The attire was predictably dominated by green and could be quite elaborate. In Aberdeen in 1508, it is specified that those attending Robin Hood are to be decked out in green and yellow, with bows and arrows. The Chudleigh accounts mention silk adornment for the coats. Yeovil in 1568 bought a ribbon lace for Little John's horn, and in 1572 a green silk ribbon was purchased for the Sheriff, as well as arrows for Robin Hood. The Leicester accounts for 1534 suggest that Robin's followers were attired in Kendal (a green woolen cloth) and might be equipped with swords and bucklers. Kingston's Robin Hood costumes were especially costly, doubtless reflecting the town's wealth and prestige: the records mention not only Kendal coats but satin, gloves, hats, and ostrich feathers. The description of Henry VIII's Maygames offer the fullest details: the men are attired in hoods, hose, and short coats of Kentish Kendal and armed with bows and arrows as well as swords and bucklers.

There were also ambient decorations associated with the games. Woodbury in 1574–75 purchased thirty yards of canvas and paid "for maken of Roberte Hoodes Howse." In 1543 Stratton had "Robyn Hode is howse"; Bridport in 1555 had a "bowth" for the Robin Hood ale; Abingdon in 1566 had a "Robin Hoodes bowere." Henry VIII's Robin Hood game in 1515 also involved a bower, serving as a kind of rustic palace for the outlaw and his guests. Its plebeian counterparts may have fulfilled similar ritualized functions, but given Robin's involvement with the sale of ale, they are just as likely to have functioned as beer tents for the public at large. The festive spirit of the games was further enhanced by spectacles of sight and sound. Banners are mentioned in Kingston in 1506 and Edinburgh in 1531; drums and guns appear in association with the games in some instances,[39] and purchases of gunpowder at Honiton and Ayr suggest firework displays.

Although the records of the Robin Hood game deal mostly with money and materials, there is also evidence of the actual activities involved. Perhaps the most straightforward manifestation of the game was the scripted folk play, enacting the sort of adventure found in the ballads. We are singularly fortunate in the survival of no less than three scripts of such plays, which constitute unique examples of texts of English folk plays of the period. The oldest is a cryptic playlet known as *Robin Hood and the Sheriff*, preserved on a single manuscript leaf (Trinity College Cambridge MS. R. 2. 64). On the dorse are some account entries, and there is reason to believe that the leaf originally came from the Paston collection.[40] The entries date to 1475–76, and the play seems to be of roughly the same period, making *Robin Hood and the Sheriff* one of the oldest Robin Hood texts extant. The text is quite brief:

> Syr sheryffe for thy sake Robyn hode wull y take
> I wyll the gyffe golde and fee This be hest thu holde me
> Robyn hode ffayre and fre undre this lynde shote we
> with the shote y wyll Alle thy lustes to fullfyll
> Have at the pryke And y cleve the styke
> late us caste the stone I graunte well be seynt Iohn
> late us caste the exaltre have a foote before the
> syr knyght ye have a falle And I the Robyn qwyte shall
> owte on the I blowe myn horne hit ware better be unborne
> lat us fyght at ottraunce he that fleth god gyfe hym myschaunce
> Now I have the maystry here off I smyte this sory swyre
> This knyghtys clothis wille I were And in my hode his hede woll bere
> welle mete felowe myn what herst Thu of gode Robyn
> Robyn hode and his menye with the sheryffe takyn be
> sette on foote with gode wyll And the sheryffe wull we kyll
> Be holde wele ffrere tuke howe he dothe his bowe plucke

Ʒeld yow syrs to the sheryffe Or elles shall yor bowes clyffe
now we be bownden alle in same ffrere <T>uke this is no game
Co<m>e thu forth thu fals outlawe Thu shall <be> hangyde and y drawe
Now <oute> allas what shall we doo we <m>oste to the prysone goo
Op<en> the yatis faste Anon An <le>te theis thevys ynne gon. [41]

Reconstruction of the play is difficult, as there is no indication of speakers or actions. The first half clearly corresponds to the story of *Robin Hood and Guy of Gisburn*: a knight is engaged by the Sheriff to kill Robin Hood; the knight and outlaw compete at archery, stone-putting, axle-tossing, and wrestling. They then fight to the death, and Robin takes his defeated enemy's clothes and head. There is a break in the action at this point, and the plot becomes more obscure: there is a fight between the Sheriff's forces and Robin Hood's band in which the latter are defeated, which could correspond to the similar battle in *Robin Hood and Guy of Gisburn*. The play appears to be incomplete, the remainder presumably dealing with Robin's rescuing of the band by means of his disguise, as in the ballad. [42] The story calls to mind Sir Richard Morison's reference in the reign of Henry VIII to "playes of Robin hoode, mayde Marian, freer Tuck" in which "these good bloodes go about to take from the shiref of Notyngham one that for offendyng the lawes shulde have suffered execution." [43]

The other two plays are found in Robert Copland's edition of the *Gest*, first printed around 1560, and in Edward White's reissue, perhaps dating to about 1590. They appear together under the heading "Here beginnethe the Playe of Robyn Hoode, verye proper to be played in Maye Games." [44] The first, known as *Robin Hood and the Friar*, is a verse playlet of some 120 lines, telling the familiar story of Robin Hood's encounter with Friar Tuck. The play opens with some dialogue between Robin and Little John regarding a certain "stoute frere" who has been giving Robin trouble. The outlaws exit in search of the interloper, and the Friar enters, armed with a quarterstaff, and boasts to the audience of his skill with the quarterstaff, bow, and sword and buckler. He explains that he has come to seek Robin Hood in Barnsdale to test his mettle, vowing to serve Robin if the outlaw proves the better man,

> But if that I be better man than he,
> By my truth my knave shall he be,
> And lead these dogges all three.

Robin appears and orders the Friar to bear him across the nearby river. The Friar does so, but dumps Robin in the middle of the water. Robin challenges him to fight, to which the Friar responds with a will:

> Then have a stroke for Fryer Tucke!

The fight begins, and Robin apparently finds himself overmatched, for he seeks permission to blow his horn to summon his dog. Tuck allows him to do so, and of course it is Robin's men who appear. Tuck similarly asks leave to blow his whistle, and summons two followers of his own (presumably Robin's followers are the same in number). A battle ensues, but in the end Robin calls a halt to the strife and proposes to take Tuck into his service, offering him "golde and fee," and presenting him with "a lady free." The Friar responds with lecherous delight, and his final words suggest that the play ends with a dance involving him and the lady:

Go home, ye knaves, and lay crabbes ["crabapples"] in the fyre,
For my lady and I wil daunce in the myre
for veri pure joye.

This play seems to be based on a ballad version of the story. In *Robin Hood and the Friar (A)*, it is the Friar's dogs who answer his whistle. The dogs have been transformed into men in the play for obvious practical reasons, but the resulting story is slightly awkward and there remains the vestigial and superfluous allusion to the dogs at the beginning.

Following *Robin Hood and the Friar* in Copland and White is *Robin Hood and the Potter*, a fragment of some eighty lines of verse. There is no break or heading in the text, as if it were a part of the same play. The play is incomplete, but enough remains to recognize the story from the ballad of *Robin Hood and the Potter*. It opens very similarly to the play of *Robin Hood and the Friar*: Robin and Little John remark on the doings of a certain "proude potter" and set off with the intent of making him "pay passage." The Potter's boy Jack appears, hurrying with a load of pots for market in Nottingham. Robin enters again and begins to break the pots on the ground. The Potter arrives and challenges Robin to defend himself with sword and buckler. Robin summons Little John, and they prepare to do battle as the text breaks off, again without any indication or acknowledgment of its incompleteness.[45] Some version of this play may be implied in the Marprelate tract *Just Censure and Reproofe* (1589), where Anderson, the Parson of Stepney, is protrayed as an active participant in folk customs who has on occasion borne "the potter's part."[46]

The surviving Robin Hood plays are characterized by their limited dialogue, with concomitant reliance on rapid action and physical activity, especially combat. This is particularly true of *Robin Hood and the Sheriff*, which is so short of dialogue that the words must nearly have been swallowed up by the action. The language of the fifteenth-century play may be compared to the modern mummer's play in its crude simplicity, and seems to be a genuine folk play. The sixteenth-century plays show a somewhat greater degree of sophistication, and may have been the work of professional or semi-professional authors. Yet there is some reason to suppose that these plays were already old when Copland printed them. Admittedly Copland's title page calls them "a new playe for to be played in Maye games very plesaunte and full of pastyme," but such a description looks like a publisher's marketing. Both he and White print them as if they were a single play and without any apparent recognition of their incompleteness, and since they are appended to a ballad which was recognizably old, they may well have been included as a fragment of antiquarian interest, rather than as a limb of a living tradition. Certainly by Copland's day the Robin Hood game was on the decline in much or most of the country.

As with the ballads, the extant Robin Hood plays probably represent only a small fraction of the original corpus. The very fact that any survived at all, in an age from which no other genuine folk plays survive, may well be due to sheer numbers. The popularity of Robin Hood games and the ease with which such formulaic plays could be generated would also support a much larger original corpus.

Although scripted Robin Hood plays were probably widespread, it is difficult to identify instances of performance, since contemporary references to the games never specify whether a scripted text was involved. Where money is paid to players for a Robin Hood game, a scripted play can probably be inferred, as this would be the likeliest means of winning such remuneration. Similarly, in those cases where the game traveled, a scripted play was probably involved: neighbors might be willing to open their purses out of a feeling of community spirit, but people of other villages would expect some real entertainment in exchange for their donations. References to the Sheriff of Nottingham, as in the Paston letters and in the Yeovil games in 1572–73, might also imply scripted plays.

The scripted performances may in many cases have been associated with morris dancing, an entertainment often appearing in the records in conjunction with the Robin Hood games. In the play of *Robin Hood and the Friar*, the action appears to lead directly into a dance, presumably some sort of morris. The Kingston-on-Thames records from 1515 onward frequently include the costs relating to morris dancers under the expenses for Robin Hood. There are also numerous references to payments made for shoes for Robin Hood and his men, which suggests that they may have done some dancing as well. Later in the century, the author of the Marprelate tracts linked the two, writing of "the sommer lord with his Maie game, or Robin Hood with his morrice dance."[47] Dancing was a common companion of drama in this period, and we may suppose that many Robin Hood plays, like *Robin Hood and the Friar*, had a dance to round off the action.

Later urban versions of the Robin Hood games may sometimes have taken the form of presentational tableaux. This is certainly the case with the May game in London in 1558: with its multiple displays and "spechys rond a-bowt London," it is more suggestive of the civic pageant than of the communal folk play, presaging official pageants based on Robin Hood in the seventeenth century.

In some cases these sorts of presentational entertainments may have taken place within the context of a quite different sort of play-acting in which the primary interaction was not among the players, but between the players and the audience. Participatory Robin Hood games are harder to document, since they were by definition ephemeral activities. Happily, there does survive a court record offering a reasonably substantial description of one such game, occurring in Westonzoyland in 1607. John Cornish, a parishioner of Puritan inclinations, lodged a complaint against the activities of Robert Wolfall, the parish priest:

Mr William Wolfall, beinge the Sonn of Mr Robert Wolfall, and beinge elected and chosen to be the Robin Hoode, as they call it, at Weston for their parishe Alle, Robert Woolfall by the consent, good will & free disposition of himselfe, was taken by his said sonn, Mr William Wolfall, and preferred to the highest Roome ["place"] in the Stockes, as the mann most worthye of such a place, And diverse other moore imprisoned with him in the Stockes; and their fyne and Ransome, for the deliverye out of the Stockes, was each man Severallye to take his twoe pottes of Stronge Alle, and to drynke of the same; ffor soe was Mr Wolfalls decree, he begining first, being Cheife Actor of that Comedye; and everye manne holding his legg in the Stockes duringe the tyme they weare drinking their ij pottes of stronge alle.

Many of the references to Robin Hood games are likely to represent comparable sorts of play-acting. It may probably be inferred wherever Robin Hood figures in conjunction with characters not belonging to his legend, as at Walsall where he is found in the company of the Abbot of Marham, or at Melton Mowbray and Woodstock, where he appears in addition to the Lord of the festival. In such cases, he may have stood as the captain of a costumed band, interacting with the audience in a manner comparable to that illustrated in Westonzoyland. In other cases, including Westonzoyland, Robin appears to serve as the chief presider over the festivities. This was presumably the case in those instances where the festival is named after the outlaw—as in the "Robin Hood's Revel" and "Robin Hood's Ale" at Croscombe and Tintinhull in Somerset and Bridport in Dorset, and the "ale & gatheringe" made by "Willyam Downham beyinge Robyn Hoode & Water Holwill lytle John" in Woodbury in 1573. In Chudleigh in 1561 Robin Hood and Little John appear to be in charge of the festivities, to judge by the "Count of Robyn Hodde." At Yeovil in 1572 Robin seems to have been responsible for preparations for the feast, as he is reimbursed for the cost of canvas for tablecloths and paid for providing drink for the bell ringers on Ascension Day. All of the clear English examples of Robin's presidence over the festival come from the West; he also seems commonly to have supervised the festivities in Scotland.

Where Robin Hood presides over the festival, he would seem to have served as a kind of *animateur* for the festivities, as in Edinburgh in 1518 where it is specified that Little John's role is "to mak sportis and jocositeis in the toun." Many of the amusements doubtless drew on the tradition of misrule, in which the presider parodies governmental and legal customs by promulgating mock laws and imposing mock punishments. Misrule of this sort is illustrated in the Westonzoyland case mentioned above, where William Wolfall as Robin Hood is the master of ceremonies for the festivities: he is expected by the community to

instigate activities suitable to the festive setting, and the members of the
community are in turn expected to comply with his commands. Wolfall enacts
Robin's role as a parodic authority figure, subjecting leading community figures
to the treatment normally meted out to minor troublemakers—imprisonment by
one leg in the stocks was a common means of punishing and restraining the
drunk and disorderly, adding irony to the hefty fine of tossing back two pots of
ale.

Another category of participatory activities in the Robin Hood games,
evidently peculiar to Scotland, involves ceremonies relating to citizenship. In
numerous instances in Edinburgh, Perth, Peebles, and Dumfries, Robin Hood is
involved in admitting people to the status of burgess of the town, and often
collects the fee required of the new citizen.[48] Records of these activities most
commonly place them between April and June, indicating a connection with
Robin's May festival activities; a few instances seem to happen later in the year,
which suggests that some responsibilities of the post of Robin Hood might
continue after the festival itself was over. In Aberdeen and Ayr, Robin Hood
presides over a procession of the citizens, apparently serving as an expression of
communal identity as well as a display of the civic status of the participants.[49]
Similar processions may have occurred in other towns, as suggested by one
early sixteenth-century poem celebrating the custom:

> 3e noble Merchaundis everilkane,
> Address 3ow furth with bow and flane,
>   In lusty grene lufraye;
> And folow furth on Robyn Hude,
> With hartis coragiouss and gud,
> And thocht that wretchis wald ga wod,
>   Of worschipe hald the way.[50]

Such processions were probably linked to the May festival, although in
Aberdeen in 1518 we find the parade displaced to the feast day of the town's
patron saint. These burghal ceremonies clearly involved direct interaction
between the characters and public, and in the processions the distinction was
nullified by the inclusion of the citizens in the game as the outlaw's followers.

The burghal ceremonies were peculiar to Scotland, but another of Robin's
activities—the sponsorship of archery—is found in both countries. In England
archery had been the object of royal encouragement since the thirteenth century,
and Robin Hood was particularly suited to be its patron—probably one of the
reasons for Robin's long success as a figure in May festivals was his value as a
promoter of this officially sanctioned sport. This aspect of the Robin Hood
games is evoked by Richard Robinson in his pamphlet encouraging the
maintenance of English bowmanship:

And, heare because of Archery I do by penne explane
The use, the proffet, and the praise, to England by the same,
My self remembreth of a childe in Contreye native mine:
A *May* game was of *Robyn-hood* and of his traine that time [*marg. note:*
    "1553"]
To traine up young men, stripplings and eche other younger childe
In shooting, yearely this with solempne feast was by the Guylde,
Or Brother hood of Townsmen done, with sport, with joy, and love
To proffet which in present tyme, and afterward did prove.[51]

Perhaps the earliest reference to Robin's patronage of archery comes from Exeter, where in 1508–9 an "arrow of St. Edmund" was repaired "for Robin Hood"; the arrow was presumably some sort of an archery prize. There is mention in Chagford of a silver arrow in 1587–88, which may be another example of the same; significantly, the reward offered for the shooting contest in the *Gest* is a silver arrow [st. 285]. The May game of Henry VIII in 1515 involved a display of archery. There are a number of instances where bows and arrows are mentioned, although whether as instruments of actual archery or as mere costume accessories is unclear. In Kingston-on-Thames in 1508–9 and 1509–10, expenses for Robin Hood include five or six "brode arovys." Other examples may be found in Yeovil in 1572–73 and 1577–78, and in Wells in 1607. Archery was particularly a part of English national mythology, but Robin sometimes sponsored it in Scotland as well, as in Dundee in 1521, where he was in charge of building archery butts.[52]

Probably even more important than Robin's fostering of archery was his role as a fund-raiser. Much of the evidence for the Robin Hood games in England is from the receipts of money raised by Robin and his followers. "Gathering" is mentioned in the records of Thame, Reading, Chudleigh, Woodbury, and Yeovil. "Robin Hood's money" or "Robin Hood's reckons" are found in Croscombe, Bridport, St. Columb Major, Melton Mowbray, and Henley. The defendants in the Willenhall case of 1498 declared that the purpose of the games was to gather money for the churches. In some instances the outlaws sold livery badges, as in Reading in 1501–2 and Kingston in 1522–23 and 1536–37; the activity recalls the final fit of the *Gest*, where Robin gives livery to the king. The gathering was not always in cash: the Reading records indicate that some parishioners donated malt or wheat instead, presumably for later resale in the form of ale and bread. Robin also raised money directly through the sale of beer,[53] and where there is an allusion to Robin Hood holding an ale, as at Tintinhull, the same may probably be inferred.

Fundraising was in all likelihood an integral part of the scripted Robin Hood play, to judge by its frequent inclusion in other forms of folk drama. It was probably also the impetus behind traveling Robin Hood games, which seem to have been a common feature of the tradition. The example of Robert Marshal of

Wednesbury, who brought a Robin Hood game to nearby Willenhall in 1498, is an early case; others are the tour from Mawgan to St. Breock in 1592, St. Columb Minor to St. Ives in 1588, Cleeve Prior to Tewkesbury in 1519, Colyton to Honiton in 1572, Cleeve to Crowle in 1531, Worcester to Battenhall in 1529, Ombursley to Battenhall in 1535, Henley to Reading in 1505, Finchamstead to Reading in 1506, Kingston to Croydon in 1514–15, and Hythe to New Romney in 1533. Most of these itinerant Robin Hood games involved distances under fifteen miles, but those in St. Breock and St. Ives had travelled around forty miles, a two-day journey on foot.

By whatever means, the funds involved could be very substantial. The money raised in Yeovil in 1575–76 amounted to a very respectable £18 3s. 10d., roughly three times the annual wages of a journeyman craftsman. Yet not all monetary returns can be measured so simply. The games, by attracting large audiences from outside of the community, could not only enhance the community's prestige, but draw money into the local economy, especially when the numbers could reach the 1500 to 2000 paying participants who seem to have attended some of the games at Kingston.[54] Games in smaller towns further from the country's centers of population were presumably not so heavily attended, but the numbers would still have been significant to the smaller economy. Fund-raising is not well attested for the Scottish games, except insofar as Robin was involved in collecting the fees from new citizens; apparently gathering was not a function of the civic games (which appear to have been subsidized by governmental funds), although there may have been gathering by subcommunal games, not recorded in the written record.

STRUCTURES OF THE GAMES

Our knowledge of the Robin Hood games consists primarily of discontiguous scraps of information, in contrast with the substantial texts of the ballads, yet this need not be a severe handicap in understanding the games. Even with the ballads, it is the structures rather than the narrative that dominate. This is even truer of the games, since the diminished role of text relative to context leaves the structures as the principal vehicle for carrying meaning.

The Robin Hood games were not structurally independent entities. They were incorporated into already existing practices, and it is to these practices that we must look to find the frameworks that shaped the games. While there survive few substantial descriptions of Robin Hood games, there are a number of narrative accounts of the sorts of festivities in which they took place. One of these is the Elizabethan Puritan Phillip Stubbes's oft-quoted invective against the May game (1583):

Against *May*, *Whitsonday*, or other time, all the yung men and maides, older men and wives, run gadding overnight to the woods, groves, hils, & mountains, where they spend all the night in plesant pastimes; & in the morning they return, bringing with them birch & branches of trees, to deck their assemblies withall. . . . But the chiefiest jewel they bring from thence is their May-pole. . . . they straw the ground rounde about, binde green boughes about it, set up sommer haules, bowers, and arbors hard by it; And then fall they to daunce about it, like as the heathen people did at the dedication of the Idols, wherof this is a perfect pattern, or rather the thing it self. I have heard it credibly reported (and that *viva voce*) by men of great gravite and reputation, that of fortie, threescore, or a hundred maides going to the wood over night, there have scarsely the third part of them returned again undefiled.

Stubbes also offers this vigorous description of a church ale:

First, all the wilde-heds of the Parish, conventing togither, chuse them a Graund-Captain (of all mischeefe) whome they innoble with the title of "my Lord of Mis-rule," and him they crowne with great solemnitie, and adopt for their king. This king anointed chuseth forth twentie, fortie, threescore or a hundred lustie Guttes, like to him self, to waighte uppon his lordly Maiestie, and to guarde his noble person. Then, everie one of these his men, he investeth with his liveries of green, yellow, or some other light wanton colour; And as though that were not (baudie) gaudie enough, I should say, they bedecke them selves with scarfs, ribons & laces hanged all over with golde rings, precious stones, & other jewels; this doon, they tye about either leg xx. or xl, bels, with rich handkercheifs in their hands, and sometimes laid a crosse ouer their shoulders & necks, borrowed for the most parte of their pretie Mopsies & looving Besses, for bussing them in the dark. Thus al things set in order, then have they their Hobby-horses, dragons & other Antiques, togither with their baudie Pipers and thundering Drummers to strike up the devils daunce withall. Then marche these heathen company towards the Church and Church-yard, their pipers pipeing, their drummers thundring, their stumps dauncing, their bels jyngling, their handkerchefs swinging about their heds like madmen, their hobbie horses and other monsters skirmishing amongst the route: & in this sorte they go to the Church (I say) & into the Church (though the Minister be at praier or preaching), dancing & swinging [t]heir handkerchiefs over their heds in the Church, like devils incarnate, with such a confuse noise, that no man can hear his own voice. Then, the foolish people they looke, they stare, they laugh, they fleer, & mount upon fourmes and pewes to see these goodly pageants solem[ni]zed in this sort. Then, after this, about the Church they goe againe and again, & so foorth into the church-yard, where they have commonly their Sommer-haules, their bowers, arbors, & banqueting houses set up, wherin they feast, banquet & daunce al that day & (peradventature) all the night too. And thus these terrestriall furies spend the Sabaoth day.

They have also certain papers, wherin is painted some bablerie or other of Imagery woork, & these they call "my Lord of mis-rules badges"; these they give to every one that wil giue money for them to maintaine them in their hethenrie, divelrie, whordome, drunkennes, pride, and what not. And who will not be buxom to them, and give them money for these their deuil[i]sh cognizances, they are mocked & flouted at not a little. And so assoted are some, that they not only give them monie to maintain their abhomination withall, but also weare their badges & cognizances in their hats or caps openly.[55]

A more sympathetic account of church ales appears in Richard Carew's *The Survey of Cornwall* (1602):

For the Church-ale, two young men of the parish are yerely chosen by their last foregoers, to be Wardens, who deviding the task, make collection among the parishioners, of whatsoever provision it pleaseth them voluntarily to bestow. This they imploy in brewing, baking, & other acates, against Whitsontide; upon which Holydayes, the neighbours meet at the Church house, and there merily feed on their owne victuals, contributing some petty portion to the stock, which by many smalls, groweth to a meetly greatnes; for there is entertayned a kinde of emulation betweene these Wardens, who by his graciousnes in gathering, and good husbandry in expending, can best advance the Churches profit. Besides, the neighbour parishes at those times lovingly visit one another, and this way frankely spend their money together. The afternoones are consumed in such exercises, as olde and yong folke (having leysoure) doe accustomably weare out the time withall.[56]

While these accounts cannot be taken as authoritative descriptions of all May festivals in this period, or even as reliable representations of any single festival, their details are consistent with what is known from documentary sources, and they offer a useful point of orientation from which to understand the settings in which the Robin Hood games were enacted.

May festivals were communal observations that fulfilled several functions. At an obvious practical level, they could generate funds for the parochial or civic community. This was particularly a feature of the parish-sponsored games in England, where the money was often earmarked for the physical maintenance or improvement of the parish church; it is less prominent in Scottish contexts. At a personal level, the festivals offered the commoner an opportunity for recreation in an age before weekends and vacations. One reason why they commonly fell in May and June was that this season was relatively undemanding for country folk, coming after the spring planting but before the hay harvest. The full significance of the recreative role of the festivals can easily be lost today. The modern mythology of the individual life is teleologically oriented, organized according to ideals of personal advancement. In the premodern world, stability rather than change was the accepted normal pattern of life: people expected to live out their lives in the social and economic state of their parents. In such a context, cyclicality rather than linear development was the pattern by which people interpreted their lives. Festivals, as periodically recurring opportunities for self-indulgence, were cardinal points that imparted shape and meaning to a person's life: it has been said that the peasant lived in recollection of the last festival and in anticipation of the next.[57]

Finally, May festivals provided an occasion for the ongoing work of creating the community itself. On working days, the need to focus on practical labor limited the opportunities for the sorts of social and cultural interactions by which a community is defined and maintained. Festivals were occasions for intense cultural transactions, during which the community could talk to itself and exercise its cultural resources. Just as the festivals were cardinal points in the lives of the individual participants, so too they were cardinal points in the life of the community as a whole.

The personally and communally re-creative functions of the festival were made possible by the creation of a festive space set apart from the ordinary world, notionally distinguished as a time in which the structures and strictures of ordinary life were in some way suspended. Ordinary space was transformed visually into festive space through decorations; ordinary people were transformed into festive characters through costumes and role-playing; ordinary labors were banned in favor of extraordinary spectacles and entertainments. Customary thrift and propriety gave way to indulgence and license: food and drink was consumed freely, men dressed in women's clothing, and a certain amount of sexual license seems to have been expected, at least in verbal forms (and, in Stubbes's view, in physical forms as well).[58] Even the most fundamental concepts of order were in some way set aside, as evidenced by the recurring themes of misrule and unreason.

These festive elements were not peculiar to the May festival. Christmas, the other principal occasion in the festive calendar, shared many of these features, although it focused on families and friends rather than on the community as a whole, for the obvious practical reason that Christmas celebrations had to take place indoors and therefore involved smaller groups. The subcommunal May game likewise realized some of the functions of the communal festivity, albeit in a more particularized form: it was doubtless an important ritual moment for the participants, and an occasion for the negotiation of the cultural identity of the subgroup within itself and relative to the community at large.

The modern view of traditional festivals tends to see them as fixed ritual observances, changing little over time, perpetuated by a conservative and unimaginative peasantry. This perception is conditioned by the history of folk festivals in the nineteenth century, a period when they were in decline, and genuinely lacked dynamism. Such was not true of the premodern festival, which was a demonstrably dynamic tradition. It was, in fact, a living language: rather than being a fixed set of observances, it was a process by which the community used its cultural vocabulary to express itself. Most of these expressions were necessarily conservative in that they reflected social and cultural continuity in a society where change was comparatively slow, but the festival was also quite able to express new ideas as the occasion demanded.[59]

It is in this light that we should see the Robin Hood games. The festival tradition drew its vocabulary from other aspects of popular culture, and the Robin Hood legend, as a prominent component of that culture, was open to borrowing in this way. Where the Robin Hood narratives can be seen as a language of their own, the Robin Hood games were one iconic idiom within the ritual language of the traditional festivities into which they were incorporated, and they were to a greater or lesser degree interchangeable and cooperative with other idioms in that language.

Robin Hood's inclusion in the communal discourse of the festival brought the themes and structures that dominated his legend into the festival context. His enduring and pervasive popularity as a May festival figure is testament to the legend's fundamental compatibility with the festival setting. This compatibility manifests itself in some obvious superficial respects. Robin was particularly suitable as a vehicle for festive entertainment. The legend was already a well-established form of popular entertainment and was full of elements readily adaptable into the festival context, such as costumes and disguises, physical contests, and combats. As a highway robber, Robin was also admirably qualified for the practical task of gathering money; in many instances the outlaws in the ballads collect a sort of good-natured tribute that their impersonators probably emulated in the festival context. The thinly veiled violence of having parochial donations collected by a uniformed band of armed and possibly tipsy young men, which might seem inappropriate to modern tastes, is wholly consistent with the tenor of popular culture in the period.[60] Robin's association with archery was a double advantage, allowing him to serve as patron for a participatory form of entertainment, as well as associating him with England's only officially sanctioned sport.

Even more important were the structural resonances between the legend and the festival context. Both the May festival and the Robin Hood ballads involved an "other" space cut off from the ordinary world, marginal with respect to the world outside, yet centralized from its own internal perspective. The festival space was even made to resemble the forest through the bowers, arbors, and other greenery that adorned it. Within the festival space, as in the outlaws' forest, social norms were negated. In both contexts, Robin enacts unlaw or misrule by setting aside the normal social system in favor of mock social structures and parodic legal requirements. In this respect, Robin Hood may be better compared with the Lord of Misrule than with the Summer Lord. As the patron of the festivities he did not merely preside over the occasion, but did so in a manner that evoked the unlaw of his own legend and assimilated it with the tradition of festive misrule: significantly he is paired with the Abbot of Marham in Wednesbury and takes the place of the Abbot of Narent in Edinburgh. This would also provide a framework for understanding his appearance in addition to the Summer Lord at Woodstock and Kingston. Nonetheless, in both the festivals and the ballads, this unmaking of order coexists with the construction of a genuine alternative order, expressed in the ballads in the idea of yeomanry, and in the festival as communal identity.

The theme of community is most overt in the Scottish towns where the citizenry are required to costume themselves and attend upon the outlaw, and where new citizens are admitted by the agency of Robin Hood, likening admission to the liberties of the town to joining the fellowship of the outlaw band, as happens in so many of the ballads. The analogy between an urban middling class and forest outlaws may at first seem incongruous. Perhaps some element of urban pastoralism was involved, but more important is an underlying similarity between the Robin Hood myth and that of the premodern town. The towns were analogous to the greenwood of the ballads in that they were semi-independent localities whose citizens enjoyed special freedoms and were subject to no overlord save the king himself; ironically, although the Robin Hood ballads consistently contrast the worlds of the forest and the town, Robin's world was a particularly effective icon for civic self-identity.

The Robin Hood games enjoyed prolonged and widespread popularity, lasting from the early fifteenth to the mid-seventeenth century, and appearing in most regions of England, as well as Lowland Scotland. During this period, it would seem that they were an extremely familiar phenomenon, so much so that they were regarded as one of the characteristic manifestations of popular culture. Eventually the games died out, but their legacy was profound and permanent. Although Robin Hood games did not prove as enduring as morris dancing or mumming, no other literary figure can claim to have achieved such a prominent place in folk drama and ritual (with the possible exception of St. George, who is not strictly a literary figure in the same sense as Robin Hood), nor has any literary tradition been so deeply influenced by dramatic interpretations.

The principal structural effect of the Robin Hood games on their context was the manner in which they homologized Robin Hood's world with the community that enacted the games. Robin Hood's participation in the festivals brought elements of the ballad tradition into the ritual life of the participants, giving visible, audible, and tangible form to its structures. The homology would have been most comprehensive in those cases where Robin Hood presided over the festivities as a whole, transforming the entire community into his outlaw band. A particularized version of the same transformation took place for those who took part in subcommunal Robin Hood games.

At the same time, the May festival and the Robin Hood games shaped the Robin Hood tradition in ways that have proved far more enduring than the games themselves. Some of these influences are immediately obvious, such as the introduction of the characters of Friar Tuck and Maid Marian. The games also transmitted to the legend the priorities imposed by the festival context, making the legend more intensely visual, dramatic, and ritualistic. Already in the *Gest*, we can see some hints that Robin Hood games might be at work on the legend: the disguises, the vivid dialogue, the sword-and-buckler fight between Little John and the Cook, and especially the grand entrance of Robin Hood into Nottingham, accompanied by his followers and the king, all clad in his livery of green. The games strengthened the sensuous character of the legend, its colors, shapes, sounds, and actions: disguises and combats, dialogue and costumes were emphasized, while explicit social commentary or intricate legal situations were set aside. Robin's depredations as an outlaw were de-emphasized in favor of fellowly sorts of tributes. The pastoralism of the ballads was reinforced, as was the sense of camaraderie and community. The strongly masculine character of the ballads merged with the established tradition of youth groups. Perhaps most important of all, the games reinforced the perception of Robin Hood as a present rather than a historical figure. They stressed the episodic and hence timeless and cyclical aspects of the legend: each year Robin Hood returned to town, reborn to experience another adventure. This fortified the legend against any tendency to biographize and helped consign stories of the outlaw's origin and death to the margins of the tradition.

By the end of the seventeenth century, the Robin Hood games had entirely disappeared. The passing of so prominent an element of popular folk life must be considered a major event in Anglophone cultural history; as the next chapter will show, it was part of a broader pattern of transition in the legend as a whole, reflecting the profound cultural changes at work during the early modern period. Yet Robin Hood as a dramatic figure has never left our cultural arena. The persistent popularity of dramatic interpretations of the legend is one of its most interesting features, and it may well be that the success of Robin Hood as a hero of film and television in the media age may be traced to the transformation of the legend in the late Middle Ages toward a dramatically oriented storytelling tradition.

NOTES

1. The text refers to *pecuniae . . . provenientes ante hoc tempus de Robynhode, puellis tripudiantibus, communi cervisia ecclesiæ, et hujus modi*. Scholars have persistently misread the Latin, seeing in *tempus de Robynhode* a "Time of Robin Hood." The correct interpretation is "moneys . . . coming before this time from Robin Hood, dancing girls, the church's common ale, and so on."

2. W. Wraghton, pseud. [William Turner], *The Rescuynge of the Romishe Fox, Other Wyse Called the Examination of the Hunter Deuised by Steuen Gardiner* (Bonn: L. Mylius, 1545), sig. G2r.

3. Wolfall was in fact rather well known to the legal system for his sexual indiscretions [G. R. Quaife, *Wanton Wenches and Wayward Wives. Peasants and Illicit Sex in Early Seventeenth-Century England* (London: Croom Helm, 1979), 148, 150–51, 183–84].

4. Robert Plot, *A Natural History of Staffordshire* (Oxford: printed at the Theater, 1686), 434; Christina Hole, *English Traditional Customs* (London: B. T. Batsford, 1975), 95.

5. Michael J. Preston, "The Robin Hood Folk Plays of South-Central England," *Comparative Drama* 10 (1976), 91–100; R. J. E. Tiddy, *The Mummers' Play* (Oxford: Clarendon Press, 1923), 209–13, 248–53.

6. David Wiles, *The Early Plays of Robin Hood* (Woodbridge, Suffolk: D. S. Brewer, 1981), 3.

7. Richard Barber and Juliet Barker, *Tournaments* (New York: Weidenfeld and Nicholson, 1989), 38–39, 58, 116, 124, 207.

8. *REED: Somerset*, 355.

9. Cf. Reading 1503–4.

10. Cf. Perth 1545, Dumfries 1534, 1536.

11. See Appendix A under Scotland.

12. Examples include Braunton, Bristol, Yeovil 1568–69, Kingston, Chudleigh, Exeter, Woodbury, Croscrombe, Ombursley, Woodstock, Edinburgh, Aberdeen, Dumfries, Ayr, Dalkeith, Haddington, and Kelso.

13. Other examples include St. Breock, Stratton, Melton Mowbray, Wells, Croscombe, Cleeve, Kingston, Ashburton, Chagford, and Braunton.

14. Yeovil 1572–73, Caister 1569–72, Linton 1610, Brandsby 1615.

15. *REED: Somerset*, 412.

16. J. C. Holt, *Robin Hood*, 2nd ed. (London, Thames and Hudson, 1989), 148, 161; Wiles, *Early Plays of Robin Hood*, 25–26.

17. *Calendar of the Patent Rolls Preserved in the Public Record Office. Henry V*, vol. 2, A.D. 1416–1422 (London: HMSO, 1911), 1.84.

18. *Ibid.*, 2.141.

19. *Calendar of the Patent Rolls Preserved in the Public Record Office. Henry VI*, vol. 2, A.D. 1429–1436 (London: HMSO, 1907), 10.

20. David Underdown, *Revel, Riot, and Rebellion. Popular Politics and Culture in England 1603–1660* (Oxford: Clarendon Press, 1986), 111. For the use of festive forms by rebels, cf. Sandra Billington, *Mock Kings in Medieval Society and Renaissance Drama* (Oxford: Clarendon Press, 1991), 15 ff.

21. R. B. Dobson and J. Taylor, *Rymes of Robyn Hood*, 2nd ed. (Gloucester: Alan Sutton, 1989), 158–64.

22. Melissa M. Furrow, ed., *Ten Fifteenth-Century Comic Poems*, Garland Medieval Texts 13 (New York and London: Garland, 1985), 235–69.

23. Some forests, like Inglewood, appear repeatedly in medieval romances, but Sherwood is not among them. When Sherwood features in the later "King Incognito" ballad of *King Henry and the Miller of Mansfield*, it is unmistakably an allusion to the Robin Hood legend [Margaret Spufford, *Small Books and Pleasant Histories* (London: Methuen, 1981), 222].

24. Wiles, *Early Plays of Robin Hood*, 22–25, 69.

25. John Skelton, *Magnificence*, ll. 355–58, in *The Complete English Poems*, ed. John Scattergood (Harmondsworth: Penguin, 1983), 150.

26. Michael Drayton, *The Second Part, or a Continuance of Poly-Olbion* (London: I. Marriott, I. Grismand, T. Dewe, 1622), 122. An example of a mock sermon on thieves dating to c. 1573 is printed in Thomas Wright and J. O. Halliwell-Phillips, *Reliquiæ Antiquæ* (London: J. R. Smith, 1845), 2.111–12.

27. Thomas Nashe, *The Works of Thomas Nashe*, ed. Ronald B. McKerrow (Oxford: Oxford University Press, 1966), 1.83.

28. Alexander Barclay, *The Eclogues of Alexander Barclay*, ed. John Cawood, EETS o.s. 175 (London: Oxford University Press, 1928), 166 (4.721).

29. *Merie Tales of the Mad Men of Gotam*, ed. Stanley J. Kahrl, Renaissance English Texts Society (Evanston: Northwestern University Press, 1963), 1.

30. Cf. Natalie Zemon Davis, *Society and Culture in Early Modern France* (Stanford: Stanford University Press, 1975), 104 ff.

31. Richard Niccols, *London's Artillery, Briefly Containing the Noble Practise of that Wothie* [sic] *Societie* (London: T. Creede and B. Allsopp for W. Welby, 1616), 87.

32. E. Hobhouse, ed., *Church Warden's Accounts of Croscombe, Pilton, Yatton, Tintinhull, Morebath, and St. Michaels Bath*, Somerset Record Society 4 (London: Somerset Record Society, 1890), 4, 9, 14.

33. James D. Stokes, "Robin Hood and the Churchwardens in Yeovil," *Medieval and Renaissance Drama in England* 3 (1986), 4, 21n.14.

34. Stokes, "Robin Hood," 2–3, 23n.22; John Goodchild, "Elizabethan Yeovil as Recorded in Churchwardens' Accounts," *Proceedings of the Somersetshire Archaeological and Natural History Society* 88 (1943), 60.

35. We do not know the exact mechanism by which Robin Hood would be chosen; James Stokes has suggested that in Yeovil the choice may have been in the hands of the churchwardens [Stokes, "Robin Hood," 5].

36. Cf. Woodbury 1540–41, Kingston 1515.

37. Cf. Edinburgh 1518, Dumfries 1570.

38. Cf. Farway 1567, Melton Mowbray 1534, Ayr 1544–45.

39. Cf. London 1559, Wells 1607.

40. Dobson and Taylor, *Rymes*, 203–4.

41. W. W. Greg, ed., *Malone Society Collections* 1:2 (Oxford: Oxford University Press, 1908).

42. David Wiles has suggested that the latter part may be a completely independent play. In Wiles's interpretation, the contest between Robin and the knight is a complete play; the second play opens with Robin and most of his followers in custody: Little John and Tuck plan a rescue, but they are captured too; when the Sheriff has Robin Hood brought forth to be executed, there is some visual ruse whereby the tables are turned and the Sheriff and his followers imprisoned [Wiles, *Early Plays of Robin Hood*, 33 ff.]. On the whole, the traditional interpretation still has the most merit: Wiles's reading leaves both plays with rather limp endings—in contrast with the vigorous conclusion of the play of *Robin Hood and the Friar*. The similarity of the second part to events in the ballad version would tend to confirm the unity of this text.

43. Sydney Anglo, "An Early Tudor Programme for Plays and Other Demonstrations against the Pope," *Journal of the Warburg and Courtauld Institute* 20 (1957), 179.

44. Dobson and Taylor, *Rymes*, 208, 215. A video of this play has been produced by the Poculi Ludique Societas at the University of Toronto under the title *Robin Hood and the Friar* (Toronto, Ont.: University of Toronto Media Centre, 1983).

45. Steven Knight has recently argued that this play is complete as printed [Knight, *Robin Hood. A Complete Study of the English Outlaw* (Oxford and Cambridge, Mass.: Blackwell, 1994), 103]. As with Wiles's reinterpretation of the play of *Robin Hood and the Sheriff*, the idea is unconvincing, and reflects the tendency among scholars to see the surviving evidence on the legend as essentially complete. Admittedly the play would be a great deal longer than *Robin Hood and the Friar* if the rest of the ballad story were included, but even if one does not believe in the ability of folk performers to sustain so long a piece, one would expect at least the usual ending of the "sportful combat" story in which the combatants are reconciled and the stranger invited to join Robin Hood's band.

46. *The Just Censure and Reproofe*, in *The Marprelate Tracts 1588, 1589*, ed. William Pierce (London: A. Constable and Co., 1908), 369–70.

47. See Appendix A under Halstead (Essex).

48. Edinburgh 1492, 1494, 1499, 1500; Perth 1545; Peebles 1555; Dumfries 1534, 1536.

49. Aberdeen 1508, 1517, Ayr 1550.

50. *Ane Littil Interlud of the Droichis*, ll. 137 ff., in *The Poems of William Dunbar* (Edinburgh and London: W. Blackwood and Sons, 1893), 92; "The Maner of the Crying of ane Playe," in *The Asloan Manuscript*, ed. W A. Craigie (Edinburgh, London: W.

Blackwood and sons, 1925), 149–54. The poem is no longer thought to be the work of Dunbar.

51. R. Robinson, *The Ancient Order, Society and Unitie Laudable of Prince Arthur, and His Knightly Armory of the Round Table, With a Threefold Assertion Frendly in Fauour and Furtherance of English Archery at this Day* (London: John Wolfe, 1583), sig. L4b.

52. At Wells in 1607 the Robin Hood game appears in conjunction with the "Drumme and ensigne, shott & other munition" that were assembled in the same place. Given Robin Hood's association with young men, martial sports, and archery, the association with pike-and-shot drill is easy to understand; it might have figured in other Robin Hood games, but it was probably marginal to the tradition as a whole. Pike-and-shot training did not become an integral part of militia activities until the formation of the trained bands in 1573, at a time when the Robin Hood games were on the decline. The Wells example itself stands at the border between traditional Robin Hood games and officialized Robin Hood pageants, and even in this case the degree of connection between Robin Hood and the military display is uncertain.

53. Cf. Chagford 1563–64, Exeter 1553–54, Chudleigh 1561, Woodbury 1576.

54. Sally-Beth McLean, "King Games and Robin Hood: Play and Profit at Kingston upon Thames," *Fifteenth-Century Studies* 13:213 (1988), 309.

55. Phillip Stubbes, *Phillip Stubbes' Anatomy of Abuses*, ed. F. J. Furnivall (London: Trübner and Co., 1877–79), 147–49.

56. Richard Carew, *The Survey of Cornwall* (London: S. Stafford for J. Jaggard, 1602), 69–71.

57. Peter Burke, *Popular Culture in Early Modern Europe* (New York: Harper, 1978), 179.

58. On sexual license in May festivals, see Quaife, *Wanton Wenches*, 84–86.

59. For examples of the ways in which this language could be used in response to current events, see N. J. O'Conor, *Godes Peace and the Queenes* (Cambridge, Mass.: Harvard University Press, 1934), pt. 6.; see also the full description of the Wells May Game of 1607 in *REED: Somerset*, 709–28.

60. On coerciveness in the May festival, see Stokes, "Robin Hood," 6; Wiles, *Early Plays of Robin Hood*, 14–15.

3

Rather a Merry than a Mischievous Thief

There was ... a Minister ... who understanding what great disorders there were commonly at these Church Ales upon the Saboth day, required his flock ... that they should not assemble the people together to offende God by theyr ungodly behaviours. ... Certaine of them went to the Justices to desire licence for the commyng together of the people. ... There were (by the Justices report) 36 whiche offred up unto hym theyr names ... to testifie agaynst the Minister, that where he complayned of disorder, they to the contrary affirmed that there was no disorder at all. And yet it was manifest that the same Sabboth day was shamefully prophaned, with bulbeatings, boulynges, drunkennes, dauncynges, and such lyke, in so much as men could not keepe theyr servantes from lyinge out of theyr owne houses the same Sabboth day at night.

—William Kethe, *A Sermon Made at Blandford Forum* (1571)

The sixteenth and seventeenth centuries were an age of profound social transformation in the English-speaking world, and the Robin Hood tradition, as a pre-eminent and ubiquitous feature of English-speaking culture, found itself in the front line of the process of change: the same forces that were at work on society at large can be seen reshaping the legend of Robin Hood. In 1500, the legend was still essentially medieval in character, but by the end of the seventeenth century, almost all of the principal transformations that define the modern Robin Hood legend had taken place; most importantly from the point of view of this study, the tradition had been displaced from a position of intimate interaction with its social context to one more remote from the lives of its audience.

Overall, the process of change in the Robin Hood legend in the early modern period can be perceived in three overlapping stages: an officially sanctioned syncretism prevalent in the sixteenth century, cultural fragmentation in the sixteenth and seventeenth centuries, and the ascendancy of commercial versions of the legend in the seventeenth century.

Official policy in Tudor England encouraged the use of the intellectual and artistic tools of the Renaissance to construct an inclusive English national identity from the sometimes conflicting cultural resources inherited from the past; this Renaissance syncretism incorporated the traditional figure of Robin Hood into a vision of order informed by contemporary scholarship and aesthetics. Among scholars, the syncretistic spirit manifested itself in antiquarian efforts to find a place for the outlaw in the Englishman's study of his own nation. Various authors began to include Robin in the histories and topographies they were creating for England, although it was the Scots whose enthusiasm for the legend initially led the way. Walter Bower and Alexander of Wyntoun had already offered historicizing versions of Robin Hood in the fifteenth century, placing him in the reign of Henry III; John Bellenden inserted an adaptation of Bower's account of Robin Hood into his translation of Hector Boece's *Historia Scotorum* (1536). Their countryman John Major's *Historia Britanniæ* (1521) assigned Robin to the reign of Richard I, an interpretation that was to prove particularly influential on English authors.

Most of the first examples of English scholarly interest in Robin Hood were topographically oriented. John Leland recorded in his *Itinerary* [c. 1540] that "Along the lift hond a iii miles of betwixt Milburne and Feribridge I saw the wooddi and famose forest of Barnesdale, wher they say Robyn Hudde lyvid like an owtlaw";[1] his *Collectanea* included a reference to *Kirkley monasterium . . . ubi Ro: Hood nobilis ille exlex sepultus* ["The monastery of Kirkley . . . where the noble outlaw Robin Hood is buried"].[2] Leland's work remained unpublished until the early eighteenth century, but a number of scholars had access to his work in manuscript, and his description of the outlaw as "noble" may have had some part in the invention of an aristocratic Robin Hood.

The second edition of William Camden's *Britannia* (1587) mentioned Robin Hood in passing, with reference to

Sinus . . . quem a nominatissimo exlege Roberto Hoode *Robyn Hoods Bay* vocamus; Illum enim (*Richardo Primo* regnante) floruisse author est *I. Maior* Scotus, a quo prædonum principis & prædonis mitissimi elogio honestatur.[3]

A bay . . . which of that outlaw *Robert Hood*, so much talked of, wee call *Robin Hoods Bay*. For hee (as John *Major* the Scotishman writeth) flourished in the reigne of Richard the First; and the said Author setteth him out with this commendation, that hee was in deede an Arch-robber, but the gentellest theefe that ever was.[4]

Camden added a note on the outlaw's tomb in the 1594 edition; the passage was expanded in the edition of 1600:

His relictis *Kirkley* quondam virginum sacrarum sedem, & *Roberti Hoodi* decantatissimi prædonis [1600: prædonis honestissimi, & igitur decantatissimi,] tumulum præterlapsus *Wakefeldiam* alluit [1600: *Calderus* petit *Dewsborrough*].[5]

Calder now leaving these places behind him, and having passed by *Kirkley*, an house in times past of religious Nunne[s], and the tome of *Robin Hood* that right good and honest Robber (in which regard he is so much spoken of) goeth to *Dewsborrough*.[6]

Among English historians, John Stow, in his *Summary of English Chronicles* (1565), was the first to mention Robin Hood. His description of the outlaw was essentially a translation of Major, although he expanded Robin Hood's targets from *abbatum bonis* ["the goods of abbots"] to "abbeys and the houses of ryche Carles."[7] Richard Grafton's *Chronicle at Large* (1568) was influenced by Stow, but went well beyond the information offered by any previous historian:

About this tyme, as sayth John Major, in his Chronicle of Scotland, there were many robbers and outlawes in England, among the which number, he specially noteth Robert Hood, whom we now call Robyn Hood, and little John, who were famous theves; they continued in woodes, mountaynes, and forestes, spoilyng and robbing, namely such as were riche. Murders commonly they did none except it were by the provocation of such as resisted them in their rifelynges and spoyles. And the sayd Maior sayth, that the aforesaid Robyn Hood had at his rule and commaundement an hundreth tall yomen, which were mightie men and exceedyng good archers, and they were mainteyned by such spoyles as came to their handes: And he sayth moreover, that those hundreth were such picked men, and of such force, that foure hundreth men, whosoever they were, durst never set upon them. And one thing was much commended in him, that he would suffer no woman to be opresed, violated, or other wise abused. The poorer sort of people he favoured, and would in no wise suffer their goodes to be touched or spoyled, but relieved and ayded them with such goodes as hee gate from the riche, which he spared not, namely the riche priestes, fat Abbotes, and the houses of the riche Carles. And although his theft and rapyne was to be contemned, yet the aforesayd Aucthor prayseth him, and sayth that among the number of theeves, he was worthie the name of the most gentle theefe.

But in an olde and auncient Pamphlet I finde this written of the sayd Robert Hood. This man (sayth he) discended of a noble parentage: or rather beyng of a base stock and linage, was for his manhoode and chivalry advanced to the noble dignity of an Erle, excelling principally in Archery, or shootyng, his manly courage agreeyng thereunto; But afterwardes he so prodigally exceeded in charges and expences, that he fell into great debt, by reason wherof, so many actions and sutes were commenced against him, whereunto he aunswered not, that by order of lawe he was outlawed, and then for a lewde shift, as his last refuge, gathered together a company of Roysters and Cutters, and practised roberyes and spoyling of the kinges subiects, and occupied and frequented the Forestes of wilde Countries. The which beyng certefyed to the King, and he beyng greatly offended therwith, caused his proclamation to be made that whosoever would bryng him quick or dead, the king would geve him a great summe of money, as by the records in the Exchequer is to be seene; But of this promise, no man enioyed any benefite. For the sayd Robert Hood, beyng afterward troubled with sicknesse, came to a certein Nonry in Yorkshire called Bircklies, where desiryng to be let blood, he was betrayed & bled to death. After whose death the Prioresse of the same place caused him to be buried by the high way side, where he had used to rob and spoyled those that passed that way... And the cause why she buryed him there was for that the common passengers and travailers knowyng and seeyng him ther buryyed, might more safely and without feare take their jorneys that way, which they durst not do in the life of the sayd outlawes. And at eyther ende of the sayde Tombe was erected a crosse of stone, which is to be seene there at this present.

Gerardus Marcator in his Cosmographie and discription of England, sayth that in a towne or village called little Moravie in Scotland, there are kept the bones of a great and mightie man, which was called little John, among the which bones, the huckle bone or hip bone was of such largenesse, as witnesseth Boethus, that he thrust his arme through the whole thereofe, and the same bone being conferred to the other partes of his body, did declare the man to be xiiij foote long.[8]

Grafton's version of the outlaw constitutes a significant change of course: no longer relying solely on the traditional authorities, he introduces local folklore and a mysterious "auncient pamphlet." There has been some conjecture as to the identity and even the existence of this latter source.[9] If it did exist, its aristocratic version of Robin Hood might have been influenced by Leland's characterization of the outlaw as *nobilis*. Robin's fall through prodigality recalls the last fit of the *Gest*, in which Robin Hood spends himself to ruin at court. In general, the information attributed to the pamphlet is suggestive of the content of the Sloane life and Dodsworth's seventeenth-century account of the outlaw, perhaps indicating that it too was a manuscript biography assembled by an antiquarian with an interest in the legend.

Grafton's successors were apparently reluctant to follow his lead. Robin Hood appears in Raphael Holinshed's compendium *The Chronicles of Englande, Scotlande and Irelande* (1577), but only in the histories of Ireland and Scotland, reflecting the interest in the outlaw among Scottish historians. We have already seen the reference to the legend in Staniehurst's *History of Ireland*; Holinshed's *History of Scotland* follows the customary sources, placing Robin Hood under the year 1254:

In these daies (as the translator of Hector Boethius hath written) that notable and most famous outlaw Robin Hood lived, with his fellow little John, of whome are manie fables and merie jests devised and soong amongst the vulgar people. But John Major writeth that they lived (as he dooth gesse) in the daies of king Richard the first King of England, 1198.[10]

Historians may have been generally slow to embrace Grafton's version of Robin Hood, but poets and playwrights found it highly appealing.[11] The cultivation of a national literature articulating a new English mythology was very much in fashion among Elizabethan poets, and Robin Hood, as a distinctively English character, had much to offer such mythologizers, who drew variously on histories, tales, and May games for their versions of Robin Hood. Grafton's influence is evident in William Warner's *Albion's England* (1589), an eclectic compilation of legendary and historical material. In Book 5, an old northern man recalls with nostalgia the entertainments current during his youth, which included Robin Hood games in the summer and Robin Hood tales in the winter:

> At Paske begun our Morrise, and ere Penticost our May,
> Tho Roben hood, liell John, Frier Tucke, and Marian, deftly play . . .
> At Martlemasse wa turn'd a crabbe, thilke tolde of Roben hood ["Who turned a
> crabapple in the fire at Martinmas, he told of Robin Hood"].[12]

A few chapters later, an old hermit tells of the outlaw, placing him in the reign of Richard I and following Grafton in making him a "County" (earl):

> Those daies begot some mal-contents, The Principall of whome
> A County was, that with a troope of Yomandry did rome,
> Brave Archers and deliver men, since nor before so good,
> Those tooke from rich to give the poore, and manned *Robin Hood.*
> He fed them well, and lodg'd them safe in pleasant Caves and bowers,
> Oft saying to his merry men, what juster life than ours?[13]

Michael Drayton's *Poly-Olbion* (1622), a versified topography of England, also made use of Robin Hood, combining the historicized version of the outlaw, as in Warner, with material from the Robin Hood games in a pastoral and romantic spirit:

> The merry pranks he playd, would aske an age to tell,
> And the adventures strange that *Robin Hood* befell,
> When *Mansfield* many a time for *Robin* hath bin layd,
> How he hath cosned them, that him would have betrayd;
> How often he hath come to *Nottingham* disguis'd,
> And cunningly escapt, being set to be surpriz'd.
> In this our spacious Isle, I thinke there is not one,
> But he hath heard some talke of him and little *John;*
> And to the end of time, the Tales shall ne'r be done,
> Of *Scarlock, George a Greene,* and *Much* the Millers sonne,
> Of *Tuck* the merry Frier, which many a Sermon made,
> In praise of *Robin Hood,* his Out-lawes, and their Trade.
> An hundred valiant men had this brave *Robin Hood,*
> Still ready at his call, that Bow-men were right good,
> All clad in *Lincolne* Greene, with Caps of Red and Blew. . .
> A short Sword at their Belt, a Buckler scarse a span. . .
> From wealthy Abbots chests, and Churles abundant store,

What often times he tooke, he shar'd amongst the poore:
No lordly Bishop came in lusty *Robins* way,
To him before he went, but for his Passe must pay:
The Widdow in distresse he graciously reliev'd,
And remedied the wrongs of many a Virgin griev'd:
He from the husbands bed no married woman wan,
But to his Mistris deare, his loved *Marian*,
Was ever constant knowne, which wheresoere shee came,
Was soveraigne of the Woods, chiefe Lady of the Game;
Her Clothes tuck'd to the knee, and daintie braided haire,
With Bow and Quiver arm'd, shee wandred here and there
Amongst the Forrests wild; *Diana* never knew
Such pleasures, nor such *Harts*, as *Mariana* slew. [14]

In Robert Jones's *Musical Dreame* (1609), a collection of love songs for voice and lute, the pastoral-romantic mode entirely takes over:

In Sherwood livde stout Robin Hoode,
      an Archer great, none greater;
His bow & shafts were sure & good,
      yet Cupids were much beter.
Robin could shoot at many a Hart and misse,
      Cupid at first could hit a hart of his,
Hey jolly Robin, hoe jolly Robin, hey jolly Robin Hood,
love finds out me as well as the, to follow me to the green wood.

A noble thiefe was Robine Hood,
      Wise was he could deceive him,
Yet Marrian in his bravest mood,
      Could of his heart bereave him,
No greater thiefe lies hidden under skies,
      then beauty closely lodgde in womens eyes. [st. 1–2][15]

A more rustic version of the May-game Robin Hood is evoked in one of the songs in the "Round of Three Country Dances in One," collected in the Lant roll of rounds [c. 1580] and published in Thomas Ravenscroft's *Pammelia* (1609); the tune is a version of the most common melody of the seventeenth-century Robin Hood ballads. The round appears to have been popular well into the seventeenth century and illustrates the persistence of the May-game image of Robin Hood long after the games themselves had ceased to be a reality for most Englishmen:

Robin Hood, Robin Hood, said little John,
      come dance before the Queene a.
In a redde Petticote and a greene jacket,
      a white hose and a greene a.[16]

Of all the arts, none better expressed the syncretism of the Elizabethan age than the theater. We have already seen early examples of the adaptation of Robin Hood games to suit official tastes—in Henry VIII's May games of 1510 and 1515, and in the game played in London and Greenwich in 1558. The rise of commercial theater toward the end of the century created an enormous demand for new plays, and as Elizabethan playwrights were casting about for suitably patriotic themes, the attention of some naturally lit upon this traditional English hero. Robin Hood became a familiar figure in the theaters of London during the last decade of Elizabeth's reign. George Peele's *Edward I*, entered in the Stationers' Register in 1593, incorporated a Robin Hood game in which the rebel Prince Llewellyn and his followers portray the characters of the outlaw band, including Friar Tuck and Maid Marian.[17] The Stationers' Register for 1594 includes a lost "pastorall plesant Commedie of Robin Hood and Little John." Its content can only be surmised: it has been suggested, from possible allusions in Anthony Munday's subsequent Robin Hood plays, that it may have involved traditional elements drawn from the May games.[18] *George a Greene, the Pinner of Wakefield* was performed in London during the winter of 1593-94 and entered into the Stationers' Register in 1595.[19] The latter part of the play includes the story of George a Greene's encounter with Robin Hood: Marian, jealous of the fame of George's sweetheart Beatrice, pressures Robin into challenging the Pinner to a fight; the usual friendship ensues. The play includes clear verbal echoes of the ballad as found in both the Percy Folio and the broadside ballad version of the story.

The Elizabethan Robin Hood plays reached their apex with Anthony Munday's *The Downfall of Robert, Earl of Huntingdon* and *The Death of Robert, Earl of Huntingdon*, which premiered in 1598.[20] The *Downfall* is framed as a rehearsal for a revel to be presented for Henry VIII. The story is set in the days of Richard I, during the king's absence on Crusade. Robert Hood, Earl of Huntington, incurs outlawry for his debts through the machinations of his enemies, including the Prior of York (identified as Robert's uncle Gilbert Hood) and Robert's servant Warman. Robert flees to the forest, accompanied by his sweetheart, Matilda, the daughter of Lord Fitzwater, while the traitorous Warman is rewarded with the shrievehood of Nottingham. The outlawed earl gathers a band, taking the name of Robin Hood, while Matilda becomes Marian. Robert's loyal servants Little John and Much join his band; subsequent additions include a renegade friar named Tuck. Robin has Little John proclaim a code of rules for the outlaws:

> First, no man must presume to call our master
> By name of Earle, Lord, Baron, Knight, or Squire,
> But simply by the name of *Robin Hoode* . . .
> Next 'tis agreed (if therto shee agree)
> That faire *Matilda* henceforth change her name,
> And while it is the chance of *Robin Hoode*,

To live in Sherewodde a poore outlawes life,
She by maid *Marians* name be only cald . . .
Thirdly no yeoman following *Robin Hoode*
In Sherewod shall use widowe, wife, or maid,
But by true labour, lustfull thoughts expell . . .
Fourthly, no passenger with whom ye meete,
Shall yee let passe till hee with *Robin* feast,
Except a Poast, a Carrier, or such folke
As use with foode to serve the market townes . . .
Fiftly, you never shall the poore man wrong,
Nor spare a Priest, a usurer, or a clarke . . .
Lastly, you shall defend with all your power
Maids, widowes, Orphants, and distressed men. [*Downfall* ll. 1329 ff.]

A series of adventures ensues, including a scene deriving from the story of *Robin Hood and the Beggar* in which Robin disguises himself to rescue two brothers, Scarlet and Scathlock, from being hanged by the Sheriff:

Enter Warman, Scarlet, and Scathlock bound, Friar Tuck as their confessor, Officers with halberds.

Warman: Master Frier, be brief, delay no time;
Scarlet and Scathlock, never hope for life;
Here is the place of execution,
And you must answer law for what is done . . .

Enter Robin Hood, like an old man.

Robin: Where is the shrieve, kind friends? I you beseech,
With his good worship, let me have some speech.

Friar: Here is the Sheriffe, father, this is hee.

Robin: Frier, good alms, & many blessings thank thee.
Sir, you are welcome to this troublous shire;
Of this day's execution did I heare.
Scarlet and Scathlock murdered my young son,
Me have they robbed, and helplessely undone.
Revenge I would, but I am olde and dry;
Wherefore, sweete master, for saint charitie,
Since they are bound, deliver them to me,
That for my sons blood, I reveng'd may be . . .

Warman: Doe, father, what thou wilt, for they must die . . .

Robin [*Aside*]: My horne once winded, I'le unbinde my belt
Whereat the swords and bucklers are fast tied . . .

[*Aloud*] And as yee blew your horns, at my sons death,
So will I sound your knell, with my best breat[h].

*Sound his horne. . . . Enter little John, Much, Scarlet and Scathlock; Fight; The
Frier, making as if he helpt the Sheriffe, knockes down his men, crying, Keepe
the kings peace.* [*Downfall* ll. 910 ff.]

At the end of the *Downfall*, King Richard returns, and sets all to rights.

Robin: . . . The trumpet sounds, the king is now at hand:
Lords, yeomen, maids, in decent order stand . . .

All: God save King Richard, Lord preserve your Grace.

King: Thanks all, but chiefly, Huntington, to thee.
Arise poore earle, stand up, my late lost sonne,
And on thy shoulders let me rest my armes,
That have bene toyled long with heathen wars:
True pillar of my state, right Lord indeed,
Whose honour shineth in the den of need,
I am even full of joy, and full of woe:
To see thee, glad; but sad to see thee so . . .

Robin: Now please my king to enter Robin's bower,
And take such homely welcome as he finds,
It shall be reckened as my happiness.

King: With all my heart; then as combined friends,
Go we together, here all quarrels ends. [*Downfall* ll. 2695 ff.]

The first act of Munday's second play, *The Death of Robert, Earl of
Huntingdon*, relates Robert's poisoning by his uncle and a character named Sir
Doncaster; the remainder deals with King John's pursuit of Matilda and her
eventual death at the thwarted king's behest.

The Huntingdon plays derive elements from various sources. Robin's
ennoblement comes from Grafton; the figure of Matilda Fitzwater from a poem
by Michael Drayton; the choice of title may have been a tribute to Henry
Hastings, third Earl of Huntingdon, who had died just three years before and
was something of a popular hero.[21] Several incidents in the plays, including the
rescue of Scarlet and Scathlock, are borrowed from the ballads; the inclusion of
Tuck and Marian reflects the influence of the May games.

Munday's plays seem to have enjoyed some measure of contemporary
success. They were brought to court the Christmas after they premiered, and
there are indications that the plays were originally written as one, but were
revised by Henry Chettle to make the existing two plays.[22] They were
apparently not revived or reprinted, yet they were seminal texts in the

development of the legend. They added authority to Major's identification of Robin with the reigns of Richard I and John, and transformed the May-game Maid Marian into the aristocratic and historical Marian Fitzwater. Most important of all, they identified the outlaw himself as the proscribed nobleman Earl of Huntingdon, an innovation that was to become almost canonical.

While Munday's Robin Hood plays were the most ambitious, they were not the last. The Huntingdon plays were soon followed by a piece called *Look About You*, in which Robin features as the young Robert Hood, Earl of Huntingdon. The story has nothing to do with the outlaw, although the earl is sometimes addressed familiarly as "Robin Hood." The play is a farcical piece about the young earl and presupposes an audience whose understanding of the legend has been conditioned by Munday's play.[23] The following year a play entitled *Robin Hood's Penn'orths* is mentioned in Henslowe's diary; the text does not survive, and it may never have been finished.[24]

After the death of Elizabeth, the tradition of Robin Hood plays represented by Munday all but vanishes. Ben Jonson has Robin Hood preside, like a May lord, over his pastoral *The Sad Shepherd*. The play was written in the 1630s, but left unfinished by the playwright's death in 1637.[25] It has something of a melancholy air, and reflects Jonson's awareness of the decline of the syncretic spirit in the culture of the English elite. He apologizes for subjecting his audience to matter pulled "from mere English flocks," and alludes nostalgically to the decline of old traditions:

> *Rob.* . . . To awake
> The nimble hornpipe and the tambourine,
> And mix our songs and dances in the wood,
> And each of us cut down a triumph-bough:
> Such were the rites the youthful June allow.
>
> *Cla.* They were, gay Robin; but the sourer sort
> Of shepherds now disclaim in all such sport,
> And say our flocks the while are porly fed,
> When with cush vanities the swains are led. [I.iv]

There are also a few seventeenth-century examples of Robin Hood pageants organized for public occasions. In 1615 Munday returned to the Robin Hood theme for his *Metropolis Coronata*, a civic pageant honoring the Lord Mayor of London. The piece, performed on October 30, featured a presentation by Robin Hood and his followers; the rather unlikely connection between the forest outlaw and the metropolitan setting rested on the identification of Robin, in the guise of "Robert de la Hude, sometime the noble Earle of Huntinton," as the son-in-law of Sir Henry Fitz-Alwine, the legendary first mayor of London in the time of Richard I. The brief piece is in an uninspired pastoral mode and culminates in a song praising the forest life:

What life is there like to *Robin Hood*?
        It is so pleasant a thing, a;
In merry *Shirwood* he spends his dayes,
        As pleasantly as a King, a. [26]

Robin also featured in a curious short play entitled *Robin Hood and His Crew of Soldiers*, produced in Nottingham in 1661 to celebrate the restoration of the monarchy.[27] The text implicitly associates the legendary outlaw with the rebellious activities of the previous two decades: as the play opens, Robin and his soldiers (so called, with obvious reference to the prominent role of the army in recent political events) receive a messenger from the sheriff who tells them of the king's coronation and of the sheriff's imminent arrival with armed men to reduce the outlaws to loyalty. They are appalled at the thought of submitting their liberty to the bondage of royal law, but the messenger declares that laws were made not "to enslave the Generous, but Curb the Proud and Violent," and extolls the virtues of this new king, so graced with "the true embellishments of piety and real goodnesse." The outlaws are at once converted to obedience, and the piece ends with a hearty song of loyalty to the king.

It is conceivable that Robin continued to appear during the seventeenth century as the subject of minor commercial theater aimed at popular audiences. Such evanescent performances are easily lost to the historical record, but their existence may be suggested by a reference to the outlaw as the subject of a puppet show in 1714.[28]

The rationalizing imperative in Renaissance culture inspired some of the cultural elite to bring Robin Hood into the intellectual and artistic order of the day; for others, it made the legend wholly unpalatable as being itself fundamentally disorderly. As was often the case in the cultural struggles of Tudor England, much of the conflict revolved around religious issues. Spiritually motivated distaste for the Robin Hood legend in the Middle Ages has already been seen in Chapter 1. In the sixteenth century, such opinions were given new energy by the Reformation and a new voice by the press. Religious reformers of this period, like their medieval predecessors, found in Robin Hood the epitome of all that was unregenerate about popular culture. William Roy's *Rede Me and Be Not Wroth* (1528) complains of those who oppose translating the Bible while permitting the publication of profane literature:

Their frantyke foly is so pevisshe
That they contempne in Englisshe
        To have the newe Testament.
But as for tales of Robyn hode
With other jestes nether honest nor goode
        They have none impediment. [29]

At about the same time, William Tyndale defended his translation of the Bible by condemning the alternatives:

They permit & suffer you to read Robin Hood, and Bevis of Hampton, Hercules, Hector and Troilus, with a thousand histories and fables of love and wantonness, and of ribalry, as filthy as heart can think, to corrupt the minds of youth withal, clean contrary to the doctrine of Christ & his apostles.[30]

Spiritual reformers saw the popularity of the Robin Hood legend as an abetment to impiety and spiritual impoverishment. Edward Deringe in the mid-sixteenth century commented unfavorably on past generations' taste for Robin Hood tales:

They had their spiritual enchantments in which they were bewitched—Bevis of Hampton, Guy of Warwick, Arthur of the Round Table . . . and many other of such childish folly. And yet more vanity than these, the witless devices of Gargantua, Howelglasse, Esop, Robin Hood, Adam Bell, Friar Rush, the Fools of Gotham, and a thousand such other.[31]

The character Sincerity in *The Three Ladies of London* (1584) warns of the legend's dire consequences:

> But what is he that may not on the Sabbath-day attend to hear God's word,
> But he will rather run to bowls, sit at the alehouse, than one hour afford,
> Telling a tale of Robin Hood, sitting at cards, playing at kettels
>   ["skittles"], or some other vain thing,
> That I fear God's vengeance on our heads it will bring.[32]

The reformers were predictably hostile to Robin Hood games. Beyond partaking in the inherent evils of the Robin Hood legend itself, the games fostered Sabbath-breaking since they took place on Sundays, and they encouraged sexual impropriety with their Maid Marian (who not only furnished an occasion for lewd humor, as in the play of *Robin Hood and the Friar*, but was often played by a man in violation of the biblical prohibition against cross-dressing). The extreme Protestants were especially vigorous in their condemnation of the games. One translator of Calvin's sermons in 1579 warned that "God will not have us occupied like little children in puppets or hobbie-horses, as Players and Robin Hoods."[33] The Marprelate tracts twice associate the Robin Hood games with unregenerate clergy—the priest Gliberie of Halstead in *Hay Any Work for Cooper?* is a dead ringer for Westonzoyland's Robert Wolfall:

A boy in the Church, hearing either the sommer Lord with his Maie game, or Robin Hood with his Morrice daunce going by the Church, out goes the boye. Good Gliberie, though he were in the pulpit . . . finished his matter presently, saying Ha, ye faith boie, are they there, then ha' with thee . . . and so came down and among them hee goes.[34]

Even the ecclesiastical establishment might criticize this traditional pastime. Hugh Latimer, bishop of Worcester from 1535 to 1539, learned to his chagrin that Robin Hood's besting of a bishop was not merely the stuff of ballads:

I came once my selfe to a place, ridyng on a jornay homewarde from London, and I sente worde over nyghte into the toune that I would preach there in the morninge because it was holy day . . . I thoughte I should have found a greate companye in the churche, and when I came there, the church dore was faste locked. I tarried there halfe an houer and more; at last the keye was founde, and one of the parishe commes to me and sayes, "Syr thys is a busye day wyth us, we can not heare you, it is Robyn hoodes daye. The parish are gone abrode to gather for Robyn hoode, I pray you let them not." I was fayne there to geve place to Robyn hoode; I thought my rochet shoulde have bene regarded, though I were not, but it woulde not serve, it was fayn to geve place to Robyn hoodesmen.

It is no laughynge matter my friendes, it is a wepyng matter, a heavy matter, a heavy matter, under the pretence for gatherynge for Robyn hoode, a traytoure, and a thefe, to put out a preacher, to have hys office lesse estemed, to prefer Robyn hod before the ministracion of Gods word; and al thys hath come of unpreachynge prelates. [35]

Religious disapprobation of the Robin Hood tradition is especially well documented, but there were others who disparaged the legend in secular terms. Even from the first evidence of the legend, it seems to have had a dubious literary reputation. Langland's fourteenth-century allusion hints at an association with base tastes, and Walter Bower in the fifteenth century identifies the tales as fare for the *stolidum vulgus*, the "foolish commons." The advent of Renaissance neo-classicism could only worsen Robin Hood's standing with the intelligentsia. While many educated people must have read the *Gest*, others saw in Robin Hood the quintessence of literary rubbish. Robert Braham, in the letter prefacing his edition of Lydgate's *Troy Book* (1555), uses the Robin Hood tales as the standard by which to measure inferior literature: "Caxton's recueil [i.e. his book on the Trojan wars], who so lyst wyth judgement peruse, shall rather thyncke his doynges worthye to be numbred amongest the trifelinge tales and barrayne luerdries of Robyn Hode, & Beuys of Hampton, then remaine as a monument of so worthy an history." [36] Lord Morley remarks in the Dedicatory Letter to his translation of Petrarch's *Triumphs* (c. 1555):

There be a number of that sorte . . . shall lytle set by [the Triumphs]. . . desyrynge rather to have a tale prynted of Robyn Hoode, or some other dongehyll matter. [37]

A similar attitude is evident in Nicholas Udall's translation of Erasmus's *Apothegms* (1542):

When Diogenes on a certain tyme treatyng and making a declaracion of an earnest and saige matter of Philosphie, had not one hearer that would give diligent eare unto him, he begun to sing soch another foolish song, as *Robin Hood in Barnsdale stode*, &c. and sembleed as though he would daunce withall. And when a verie great multitude of people had now gathered together and swarmed about him, he tooke tham all up for stumbling, because that to thinges foolish & servyng to no good purpose, thei came rennyng by whole flockes, and as merie as Pies, where as to serious matters . . . they neither would resort or approch.[38]

In John Rastell's *Interlude of the Four Elements* (c. 1520), the allegorical character Ignorance offers entertainment for Humanity:

> But yf thou wylt have a song that is good,
> I have one of Robyn Hode,
>   The best that ever was made.[39]

Foolish Humanity is interested, and Ignorance obliges with a nonsense song reminiscent of a burlesque found in several sixteenth- and seventeenth-century sources:

> *Humanyte*   Than begyn and care not fo[r me].
>   *Downe, downe, downe, downe, etc.*
>
> *Ygnoraunce*   *Robyn Hode in Barnysdale stode*
>   *And lent hym tyl a mapyl thystyll,*
>   *Than cam our lady and swete Saynt Andrewe,*
>   *Slepyst thou, wakyst thou Geffrey Coke?. . .*[40]

Bishop Nicholas Ridley, in condemning the "contumelious taunts, hissings, clapping of hands, and triumphs" that characterized Oxford disputations in the mid-sixteenth century, made the outlaw an adjective for idiocy: "that company of learned men, and schools which were appointed to grave men and grave matters, were contaminate and defiled by such foolish and Robinhood pastimes."[41]

As with the religious reformers, secular reformers disapproved of Robin Hood games: in their view, such public enactments of unedifying entertainments were incompatible with a well-ordered commonwealth. Sir Richard Morison urged Henry VIII to replace these pastimes with more profitable displays:

In somer comenly upon the holy daies in most places of your realm, ther be playes of Robin hoode, mayde Marian, freer Tuck, wherin besides the lewdenes and rebawdry that ther is opened to the people, disobedience also to your officers is tought, whilest these good bloodes go about to take from the shiref of Notyngham one that for offendyng the lawes shulde have suffered execution. Howmoche better is it that those plaies shulde be forbodden and deleted and others dyvysed to set forthe and declare lyvely before the peoples eies the abhomynation and wickednes of the bisshop of Rome, monkes, ffreers, nonnes, and suche like, and to declare and open to them th'obedience that your subiects by goddes and mans lawes owe unto your Maiestie.[42]

Similarly, in 1567 Sir William Pelham, lieutenant-general of the Ordinance Office, submitted to Queen Elizabeth an elaborate scheme for promoting military preparedness in the country, which included the suppression of Robin Hood plays in favor of military drill as a form of public entertainment.[43]

With such a coincidence of motives religious and secular for opposing Robin Hood games, it is hardly surprising that some officials took action against them. The earliest known instance comes from Exeter, where it would appear that problems with the games led to an order by the town council in 1509–10 that "ther shall be no riot kept in any parysh by the yong man of the same parish called Robyn hode, but oonle the Churche holyday." In 1528 the Lord Warden of the Cinque Ports, evidently worried about the possibility of public disorder and unrest, gave order to the mayors in the towns under his jurisdiction that they were not to organize or permit any "play, Robin Hood's play, watches or wakes, revels, or other such like plays whereby that any great assembly of the king's people should be made."[44] The disturbances attending the Robin Hood games at Burnley in 1579 prompted officials to restrict popular entertainments in general, although not the Robin Hood games specifically.[45]

The most determined official attack on the Robin Hood games took place in Scotland, where the ascendancy of extreme Protestantism made it possible for the goals of the religious reformers to be enacted by law. In 1555 the Scottish Parliament forbade all "convocation and assemble after the auld wickit maner of Robene Hude," and "ordainit that in all tymes cummyng na maner of persoun be chosin Robert Hude nor Lytill Johne, Abbot of unressoun, Quenis of Maii, nor otherwise, nouther in Burgh nor to landwart in ony tyme to cum."[46] The impetus behind the law was not wholly religious. Holinshed's account of the act suggests that there was a civil dimension to the decision:

In Julie was a parlement held at Edenburgh, in the which manie acts and statutes were made, right profitable (as was then thought) for the common-weale of the realme. Amongest which, to passe ouer the rest, these seeme worthie to remaine chronicled to posteritie. First, that none of the citizens (in the feasts of Whitsuntide, or anie such times, in which their hirelings are accustomed to go forth) should assemble armed, to cast forth the husbandmen after the old manner. Secondlie, that the inhabitants meeting togither, should no more assemble under a certeine colour of game, which for exercise of the bodie (as it was supposed) was holden after the example of one (I can not tell who) Robert Hood, a wild or uplandish man.[47]

Robin Hood games were an established feature of Scottish life, and popular sentiment evidently ran counter to the will of Parliament. Efforts in Edinburgh to enforce the act in 1561 led to months of rioting, and Queen Mary felt obliged to warn against any revival of the games in 1562.[48] The games persisted nonetheless. In 1577 and 1578 the General Assembly of the Church requested the king and council to forbid "All kynd of insolent playis, as King of May, Robin Hood, and sick others in the moneth of May, played either be bairnis at the schools, or other," and in 1580 the Privy Council issued a decree "dischargeing all and sindrie his majesties lieges of using of Robin Hood and other unleesum gammis." The General Assembly was still complaining about

Robin Hood games in 1591, and not without reason, since there is ample evidence of plays taking place in Scotland in the 1570s, 1580s, and 1590s, and even as late as 1610.[49]

In England there is little evidence of official efforts to suppress the Robin Hood games per se, aside from the Exeter and Cinque Ports instances mentioned already. To the degree that there was an official attack on the games, it was directed more broadly at ales and May games in general. From the reign of Elizabeth onward, there were sustained, and in the long run successful efforts by the ecclesiastical authorities to forbid revelry in churches and churchyards, although they made no effort to suppress the festivities themselves.[50] Toward the end of Elizabeth's reign, and increasingly under her successors James and Charles, regional officials issued general prohibitions of ales and May games.[51] Yet other authorities were more tolerant of such traditional observances, and some actively encouraged them: James and Charles in particular saw the assault on such traditions as a part of a dangerous Puritan movement, and repeatedly blocked the efforts of the reformers.[52] Only with the ascendancy of Parliament in the 1640s was it possible to undertake a national suppression of May festivals, and by this time the Robin Hood games were already in their final stage of decline.[53]

In Scotland the disappearance of the games might be attributed to the effects of official sanctions, but the absence of a comparable campaign in England suggests that other factors were at work. Evidence regarding the decline of the games is too thin to support more than the most tentative hypothesizing, but a few possible contributors can be suggested. One of these is the decline of the integrated traditional community. Communal Robin Hood games typically involved a large number of participants: not only were there a number of players, but a degree of audience co-operation was often required. They also presupposed the general support of the community, since they seem to have been rather elaborate undertakings requiring the use of public funds as capital. Such traditions could last only as long as the entire community could be included, and they became less viable as communities were fragmented by economic disruption and cultural division.[54]

Such an explanation is appealingly broad in scope, but on closer examination has severe limitations. Communal fragmentation was not as swift or dramatic as the disappearance of the Robin Hood games: many communities maintained or revived traditions such as the ales and May games long after the Robin Hood games were gone. Even in places where these communal traditions vanished, other subcommunal activities, such as ritual dances, lasted for centuries. Clearly other factors must be sought.

One obvious difference between the Robin Hood games and more enduring traditions such as ritual dancing is the degree of representationality. Dancing is an abstract activity, while Robin Hood games evoked specific social settings. The games were consequently more susceptible to alienation over time from the lives of the audience, and therefore especially vulnerable to the vagaries of fashion.

The decline of archery may also have played a part. One function of the Robin Hood games had been to foster the sport, and as archery waned in importance, there was doubtless less interest in the games, particularly from official quarters. It is probably no coincidence that the decline of the Robin Hood games was roughly contemporaneous with that of English military archery; at the very least, diminishing official interest in the sport left the games without an important ally. Along similar lines, communities were ceasing to use ales and May games for the purpose of fundraising: although the festivities continued in many places, they were dissociated from parish finances.[55] Since Robin Hood had been very heavily involved in gathering for the parish, the disappearance of this practice doubtless had some impact on the games.

Lastly, the disappearance of the Robin Hood game is probably related to the decline of ritual public misrule in general. While misrule lasted longer as a feature of more private celebrations, such as those at Christmas, it appears to have been receding from the May festival during the course of the sixteenth and seventeenth centuries: the Lord and Lady of the May continued as ritual figures, but the Lord of Misrule and allied characters disappear.[56] This may reflect both official interest in eliminating this disruptive element from public life and a degree of grassroots reformism. It is entirely possible that the English in general found themselves increasingly uncomfortable with the social and political implications of publicly enacting the activities of an outlaw robber. Such a development would obviously have been fatal to the communal Robin Hood games, and communal disapproval would eventually have undermined the subcommunal games as well.

BROADSIDE BALLADRY

With the decline of both the traditional Robin Hood games and the later Robin Hood stage plays, the legend came to be dominated by its balladic forms. During the sixteenth century oral balladry seems to have retained its pre-eminence in the Robin Hood tradition. Printed Robin Hood texts began to appear within about a quarter-century of the advent of printing in England, but until the latter half of the sixteenth century, printed Robin Hood balladry seems to have consisted exclusively of the *Gest*, which appeared in over a half-dozen editions between 1500 and 1600. Printing revolutionized the cost structure of written texts, but the market itself was slower to change. Literacy was still quite limited at the beginning of the early modern period: overall male illiteracy in 1500 has been estimated at 90%.[57] Since the audience for the first printed Robin Hood texts were the same elite who were reading the ballads in manuscripts in the late Middle Ages, it is hardly surprising that there was no rapid change in the kind of material circulating.

Apart from the *Gest*, no sixteenth-century printed ballad of Robin Hood survives. A ballad of "Wakefyld and agrene" was licensed in 1557–58: it presumably told the story of George a Greene's encounter with Robin Hood, and was probably not very different from the version printed in the seventeenth century.[58] A "ballett of Robyn Hod" was licensed to John Allde in 1562–63, although it may have been yet another edition of the *Gest*.[59]

After 1600, the corpus of printed Robin Hood ballads burgeoned, as the spread of literacy nourished a demand for texts created for a popular audience. Overall male illiteracy in 1640 has been estimated at 70%, suggesting a tripling of literacy rates since 1500.[60] Initially these new ballads were published as broadsides, printed on the two sides of a single sheet of paper and sold for a penny apiece.[61] The broadsides are built for the most part around quite a limited number of narrative motifs; among the twenty-five or so known to have been printed in the seventeenth century, almost half are variants on the venerable "sportful combat" theme described in Chapter 1. These are:

Robin Hood and the Pinner of Wakefield (B): This ballad recounts the traditional story of Robin's combat and friendship with George a Greene. It is probably not very different from the version mentioned in the Stationers' Register in 1557-58; there are verbal echoes in the version in the Percy Folio, and in various sixteenth-century sources. The earliest surviving printed version of this ballad is at the end of the prose chapbook *The Pinder of Wakefield*, printed in 1632; the text is slightly truncated relative to the broadside version, but generally quite close. Tune: "Robin Hood and the Pinner of Wakefield."[62]

Robin Hood and the Friar (B): This broadside tells the usual story of Robin Hood's combat with Friar Tuck (who is not actually named in the ballad). It may also be one of the more archaic of the broadside ballads: the text includes some verbal parallels to the version in the Percy Folio, and is not much shorter than that version. The earliest surviving edition dates to about 1625. Tune: ?"In Summer Time."[63]

Robin Hood and Little John: Robin Hood fights with Little John at a bridge; he is bested, and John is taken into the outlaws' band. The ballad is entered in the Stationers' Register in 1624. Tune: "Robin Hood and the Stranger."[64]

Robin Hood Newly Revived: The bulk of this broadside consists of "Robin Hood and Will Scarlett," with seven obscure stanzas at the end constituting "Robin Hood and the Scotsman." All reprints of the broadside incorporate the incoherent ending, which was even included in the prose rendering of the ballad in *The Nobel Birth*. The title, dual stories, and obscurity suggest reworking of older material. The final stanzas mention that the Scot has been faithful to "neither sire nor coz," and end with a wish for peace, which may indicate composition during the Civil Wars, after the Scots sold Charles I to Parliament in 1646. The sentiments lean toward Royalism, which might have been an incentive for obscurity if the text was published during Parliament's ascendancy. Tune: "Robin Hood and the Stranger."[65]

"Robin Hood and Will Scarlett": Robin engages in a fight with a stranger clad in red, who proves to be his cousin Gamwell; Robin takes him into his band, rechristening him Scarlett. This ballad constitutes the first and largest part of *Robin Hood Newly Revived.*[66]

"Robin Hood and the Scotsman": Robin fights a Scot. The story appears as seven obscure stanzas at the end of *Robin Hood Newly Revived*; a fuller version, in which the combatants become friends, is printed in an Irish chapbook of the late eighteenth century.[67]

Robin Hood and the Tanner: Robin fights with the famous tanner Arthur a Bland: the tanner wins, and joins the company—he turns out to be Little John's kinsman. Tune: "Robin Hood and the Stranger."[68]

Robin Hood and the Shepherd: Robin fights a shepherd, who defeats both him and Little John. Tune: "Robin Hood and Queen Katherine."[69]

Robin Hood and Maid Marian: Robin, the Earl of Huntingdon, is separated from his love Marian; while living in the forest, he meets and fights with a stranger, only to discover that it is Marian, who has come to the forest in man's attire to join him. The broadside is signed "S. S.," and has been attributed to the balladeer Samuel Sheppard, who flourished in the 1640s. Tune: "Robin Hood and the Stranger."[70]

Robin Hood and the Tinker. Robin deceives a tinker who has come with a warrant for his arrest. They fight, with the usual friendship at the end. Tune: ?"In Summer Time."[71]

Robin Hood's Delight: Robin Hood, Little John, and Scarlock meet three of King Henry's keepers. They fight, then all repair to the wine together. Tune: ?"Robin Hood and Queen Katherine."[72]

The next grouping of ballads are those in which one of the outlaws assumes a disguise and discomfits an enemy. Some of these ballads share themes with ballads in other groups:

Robin Hood and the Bishop: Robin disguises himself as an old woman to escape capture by a bishop, whom he later entraps, robs, and forces to sing him a Mass. Some form of this story evidently predates *Robin Hood and Queen Katherine*, since all versions of that tale allude to an incident in which the Bishop of Hereford was captured by Robin Hood and compelled to sing a Mass for the outlaws. An eighteenth-century ballad describes an analogous encounter with the Bishop of Hereford, but does not include the incident of the Mass. Tune: "Robin Hood and the Stranger."[73]

Little John and the Beggars (B): Little John disguises himself as a palmer and is attacked by beggars; he gives them a thrashing that makes the mute ones shout and the cripples run, and plunders £300 from them. A version of this story is in the Percy Folio; verbal parallels between the two are not very close. Tune: "Robin Hood and the Stranger."[74]

Robin Hood and the Butcher (B): Robin pays a butcher for his wares and goes into town to ply his new trade. His bargain prices attract the notice of the Sheriff, who agrees to accompany Robin to the forest to see his cattle; in the forest he is taken by the outlaws, who rob him of £300. This is a version of a ballad in the Percy Folio, but omits the fight found in the Percy version, and in general lacks close verbal parallels to it. The broadside is signed "T. R.," and has been attributed to the balladeer Thomas

Robins, which would place its composition some time around the middle of the century. Tune: "Robin Hood and the Stranger."[75]

Robin Hood's Golden Prize: Robin disguises himself as a friar. By the road he meets two priests, who refuse him alms, saying they have no money. Robin pulls them from their horses, and forces them to join him in prayer for a miracle: he then searches them and finds "good store of gold." The story is analogous to that of the mendacious monks in the *Gest*. The broadside is signed "L. P.," and has been attributed to the prolific ballad writer Lawrence Price. The ballad is entered in the Stationers' Register in 1631, which places it close to the beginning of Price's career. Tune: "Robin Hood and Queen Katherine."[76]

The Noble Fisherman, or Robin Hood's Preferment: Robin disguises himself as a sailor and sets out from Scarborough as a hand on a fishing vessel. He proves less adept with fish than with deer, but redeems himself in the eyes of the crew by defeating a ship of French marauders. Although this tale is rather unusual among Robin Hood stories, the existence of Robin Hood's Bay, north of Scarborough, as early as the 1540s suggests that such a tale might have been circulating in the sixteenth century. This ballad was entered in the Stationers' Register in 1631. Tune: "In Summer Time."[77]

The third group of ballads center on Robin's interactions with the royal household:

Renowned Robin Hood [*Robin Hood and Queen Katherine (B)*]: Robin plunders King Henry's agents and sends the money to Queen Katherine as a gift. She then engages him to shoot on her behalf in a contest with the the king's archers. The outlaws win, and the king is even more chagrined when he discovers the identity of the victors. The broadside is titled *Renowned Robin Hood*, but it parallels *Robin Hood and Queen Katherine (A)* fairly closely. Tune: "Robin Hood and Queen Katherine."[78]

Robin Hood, Will Scarlet, and Little John [*Robin Hood and Queen Katherine (C)*]: This is a third version of the story of *Robin Hood and Queen Katherine*. At the end of the ballad Robin is made Earl of Huntingdon. The text has some distinct verbal parallels with the other two versions, but is not as similar to either of them as they are to each other. Tune: "Robin Hood and the Pinner of Wakefield."[79]

Robin Hood's Chase: This is a sequel to *Robin Hood and Queen Katherine* in which the king, furious with Robin Hood, pursues him around the country. When he gives up and returns to London he finds that Robin has visited the queen in his absence. She seeks and gains the king's pardon for him. One edition bears the initials "T. R.," and the ballad has been attributed to the balladeer Thomas Robins; this would place its date in the mid-seventeenth century. Tune: "Robin Hood and the Stranger."[80]

Robin Hood, Will Scarlet, and Little John [*Robin Hood and the Prince of Aragon*]: The King is besieged in London by the Prince of Aragon. Robin, backed by Will Scarlet and Little John, fights with the Prince and his giant followers. The grateful king pardons the outlaws, and the Princess marries Scarlet, who himself is revealed to be the son of the Earl of Maxfield. The adventure is reminiscent of medieval chivalric romances. Tune: ?"Robin Hood and the Stranger."[81]

The fourth identifiable grouping of ballads focus on a rescue carried out by Robin Hood and his band:

Robin Hood and the Beggar (B): Robin fights with a doughty beggar, then exchanges clothes with him; in this disguise he rescues three brothers who were to be hanged by the Sheriff for poaching. A version of this story is used in Munday's *Downfall*, and the broadside has some verbal echoes of the Percy version. The broadside bears the initials "T. R." and has therefore been attributed to Thomas Robins, which would place its date in the mid-seventeenth century. Tune: "Robin Hood and the Stranger." [82]

Robin Hood Rescuing Will Stutly: Robin rescues his follower Stutly by force from the Sheriff's gallows. Stutly is mentioned as a member of the band in *Robin Hood and Little John* but does not appear elsewhere. Tune: "Robin Hood and Queen Katherine." [83]

Robin Hood and Allen of Dale [*Robin Hood and the Lovers (B)*]: Robin meets the disconsolate young Allen, whose love is to be married to an old knight. Robin dons the guise of a harper and gains access to the church where the wedding is to be celebrated. Once inside he blows his horn to summon his men, and calls upon the presiding bishop to marry the young couple. The bishop demurs, pointing out that the banns must be asked three times. Little John thereupon dons the bishop's vestments and asks the banns—seven times for good measure—and marries the couple. The broadside apparently derives from an older ballad, since a version of the story is incorporated into the Sloane *Life of Robin Hood*. Tune: unknown. [84]

The last three ballads are more or less biographical:

Robin Hood's Progress to Nottingham [*Robin Hood and the Foresters (B)*]: On the way to Nottingham, Robin meets fifteen foresters, who scoff at his claims to be an archer. He lays a wager with them, and wins by shooting a deer. The foresters threaten him, and Robin kills all fifteen. This story appears in the Sloane Life of Robin Hood, and the ballad leans toward archaism in style. Since Robin in the ballad is said to be fifteen years old, it was probably intended as an origin story to account for his outlawry. Tune: ?"Robin Hood and Queen Katherine." [85]

Robin Hood's Death and Burial [*Robin Hood's Death (B)*]: Robin goes with Little John to be bled by his cousin at Kirklees (apparently represented as a great hall rather than a nunnery); she bleeds him to death. Before dying, he blows his horn to summon Little John, who asks leave to destroy Kirklees. Robin forbids this, and asks John to bury him with his bow wherever his last arrow-shot lands. This broadside is entered in the Stationers' Register in 1691 but survives only in eighteenth-century copies. The text has some verbal echoes of the Percy Folio version of the story. Tune: ?"Robin Hood and Queen Katherine." [86]

Robin Hood's Birth, Breeding, Valor, and Marriage: A farcical ballad in which Robin is portrayed as the son of a forester and of the niece of the chivalric hero Guy of Warwick. He goes to visit his uncle George Gamwell of Gamwell Hall; his uncle makes Robin his heir and grants him Little John to be his page. Robin proceeds to go hunting, where he meets a shepherdess named Clorinda. He courts her, and the two are married at Titbury feast. No tune is indicated, and this ballad may not have been intended for singing. [87]

The format of the broadsides is fairly uniform, adapting a common stock of traditional resources to the new medium. Most are in the classic ballad meter of four-line stanzas alternating 4 and 3 feet to the line and riming *abcb*. Some have internal rime in the third line, and many have some sort of refrain. The ballads are typically about 20 to 40 stanzas long, divided into two parts corresponding to the two sides of the broadsheet, with extra space taken up by illustrations. This makes them shorter than the earlier oral ballads, which are generally 40 to 60 stanzas or more. Of ballads having equivalents in the Percy Folio, *Robin Hood and the Friar (B)* and perhaps *Little John and the Beggars (B)* appear to be about the same length as the Percy versions (about 40 and 25 stanzas respectively), but *Robin Hood and Queen Katherine (B)* and *Robin Hood and the Butcher (B)*, at 42 and 30 stanzas respectively, look to be only half the length of their Percy equivalents. This abridgement is evidently dictated by the physical constraints of the broadside sheet.

Almost all of the broadsides were clearly meant to be sung; the majority specify a particular tune in the heading. The tunes are drawn from a very narrow repertoire. The commonest is "Robin Hood and the Stranger," apparently used for no less than ten of the two dozen or so listed here. This tune, the only one in the repertoire that can be positively identified, represents one point of contact between the seventeenth-century broadsides and the earlier tradition. It is preserved in an early eighteenth-century source and is in fact a variant of the melody "Robin Hood" found in two music collections of the early seventeenth century, and also in the Robin Hood song incorporated into the "Round of Three Country Dances in One" collected in the Lant roll [c. 1580]. [88] "Robin Hood and Queen Katherine" accounts for another half-dozen ballads, although in this case the ascription is less certain, being based in many cases on the meter; the ballad *Robin Hood and Queen Katherine (B)* has an extra line of refrain relative to the rest, although it may still be the same melody. Two ballads are set to "Robin Hood and the Pinner of Wakefield," but the melody does not survive. [89]

The stories are constructed from a stock of traditional motifs. In addition to the major motifs already mentioned (themselves sometimes used as subordinate motifs), archery contests also recur repeatedly. All of these can be found in the premodern stories, and indeed many of the broadsides are versions of earlier tales. We have also seen that the early tales were probably more numerous than the surviving examples, and some broadsides may preserve lost tales of the premodern tradition— *The Noble Fisherman* may be one example. The surviving broadside corpus is probably fairly complete. About two dozen broadside ballads survive, some of them in a half-dozen editions or more, not to mention chapbook anthologies of the period or the even more plentiful editions of the eighteenth century. The only broadside that survives in a single edition is *Robin Hood and Queen Katherine (C)*.

The dates of composition of the ballads are generally unknown, and the question is complicated in cases where the ballad may have been circulating orally prior to publication. Once the ballads were committed to print, the texts seem to have remained fairly stable: this is true in the case of almost every surviving imprint from the sixteenth and seventeenth centuries. This suggests that seventeenth-century editions of ballads printed in the sixteenth century, such as *Robin Hood and the Pinner of Wakefield*, are probably fairly close to the lost earlier editions, a conclusion borne out in the case of *Robin Hood and the Pinner* by the close parallels between the broadside and other versions of the ballad. Some broadsides include archaisms of language and style that may similarly reflect an earlier stage in the ballad's history, although this could also be attributed to the formulaicism of the genre. Stanzas like this would not be out of place in the *Gest*:

> Robin Hood hee led about,
>> Hee shot it under hand;
> And Clifton with a bearing arrow,
>> He clave the willow wand. [*Robin Hood and Queen Katherine (B)* st. 24]

In other cases, the text shows clearly the mark of a seventeenth-century hand:

> O dastard coward, Stutly cries,
>> Thou faint-heart pesant slave,
> If ever my master do thee meet,
>> Thou shalt thy paiment have. [*Robin Hood Rescuing Will Stutly* st. 24]

A few of the broadsides are attributed to known authors: Thomas Robins (fl. c. 1650) in the case of *Robin Hood's Chase*, *Robin Hood and the Beggar*, and *Robin Hood and the Butcher*; Samuel Sheppard (fl. 1646) for *Robin Hood and Maid Marian*; and Lawrence Price (fl. ?1628–1680) in the case of *Robin Hood's Golden Prize*. Both Robins and Price were prolific balladeers; Sheppard wrote only a couple of ballads and a number of religious works.

Another prolific author who turned his hand to the legend was Martin Parker (d. ?1656), whose chapbook *True Tale of Robin Hood*, first published in 1632, enjoyed a long and successful printing career lasting as late as 1820.[90] Parker's work is a longer verse narrative printed in a chapbook of some twenty pages; the full title advertises the character of the text:

> A True Tale of Robin Hood, or, A briefe touche of the life and death of that Renowned Outlaw, Robert Earle of Huntington vulgarly called Robbin Hood, who lived and died in A. D. 1198, being the 9. yeare of the reigne of King Richard the first, commonly called Richard Cuer de Lyon. Carefully collected out of the truest Writers of our English Chronicles. And published for the satisfaction of those who desire to see Truth purged from falsehood.

The *True Tale* is generically different from the broadsides. It is 120 stanzas long, and apparently not meant to be sung; it resembles the *Gest* in its biographization of the legend. The text begins with some historical and biographic information drawn principally from Munday's Huntingdon plays. It proceeds to recount several adventures: Robin plunders the Abbot of St. Mary's and compels him to sing a Mass; he then waylays some of the king's receivers. The abbot sends a force of five hundred men against the outlaws, but they are defeated: Robin takes twelve of them prisoner, feasts them, and sends them back to the abbot with a promise that he will restore the money taken from the abbot and other victims if the abbot will intercede with the king to win the outlaws a pardon. Robin later ambushes the Bishop of Ely and his train. When Richard I returns from the crusade, Robin conveys a message to him asking for pardon. The king has it in mind to grant the request, but in the meantime sixty of Robin's men flee to Scotland in fear. The outlaw, vexed by the faithlessness of his followers, falls sick, and goes to a nunnery to be bled by a friar, with the predictable result. Parker concludes with a reference to Robin's gravestone at Kirklees, and these pious lines:

> Let us be thankefull for these times
> > Of plenty, truth, and peace,
> And leave out great and horrid crimes,
> > Lest they cause this to cease. . . .

> If any reader please to try,
> > As I direction show,
> The truth of this brave history,
> > Hee'le finde it true I know.

> And I shall thinke my labour well
> > Bestowed, to purpose good,
> When 't shall be sayd that I did tell
> > True tales of Robbin Hood. [st. 116 ff.]

Parker's version of Robin Hood is deliberately and explicitly historicizing, as he indicates in the title. Much of it is drawn from Munday, but some parts can be traced to the historians:

> One hundred men in all he got,
> > With whom (the story says)
> Three hundred common men durst not
> > Hold combat any waies. [st. 12]

Other material is taken from the ballads, as when Robin compels the Abbot of St. Mary's to recite a Mass as in *Robin Hood and the Bishop* [st. 25], or when he robs the king's receivers as in *Robin Hood and Queen Katherine* [st. 33].

Also published in 1632 was the prose chapbook *The Pinder of Wakefield*, a lively and eclectic work that fills out George a Greene's story with innumerable jests, songs, riddles, and other entertainments. The latter part of the chapbook retells the familiar story of the Pinner's encounter with Robin Hood. Robin's part in the book is fairly small, but the text is of interest as an imaginative interpretation of the Robin Hood legend for a popular audience. It develops the theme of fellowship in considerable detail, and is noteworthy both for its emphatically plebeian perspective and for its lack of overt antagonism to the social hierarchy.[91]

In the mid-seventeenth century, chapbook publications began to play a much larger role in the legend. *Robin Hood's Garland*, a chapbook compilation of ballads, appears in the Stationers' Register in 1660. This edition does not survive, but a prose version entitled *The Nobel Birth and Gallant Atchievements of that Remarkable Outlaw Robin Hood* (1662) includes prose renderings of eleven broadside ballads: *Robin Hood's Delight*, *Robin Hood and the Foresters*, *Robin Hood and the Tanner*, *Robin Hood and the Butcher*, *Robin Hood and the Beggar*, *Robin Hood Revived*, *Robin Hood and the Bishop*, *Robin Hood and Queen Katherine (B)*, *Robin Hood and the Friar*, *The Noble Fisherman*, and *Robin Hood's Chase*. It begins with a short introduction overviewing Robin's life (in which he is said to be the Earl of Huntingdon but set in the reign of Henry VIII) and ends with a brief mention of Robin's pardon and his subsequent peaceful life.[92] The earliest surviving version of the *Garland* dates to 1663; it includes the same stories as *The Nobel Birth*, with the addition of *Robin Hood and Queen Katherine (C)*, *Robin Hood's Golden Prize*, *Robin Hood and the Pinner of Wakefield*, *Robin Hood Rescuing Will Stutly*, *Robin Hood and the Shepherd*, and *Little John and the Beggars*; it does not include the introductory and concluding material of *The Nobel Birth*. The *Garland* was reprinted in several editions before 1700 and remained in print through the eighteenth and early nineteenth centuries, with various changes to the repertoire.[93]

By the end of the seventeenth century, the broadsides and chapbooks had come to dominate the Robin Hood legend. Not only were they overwhelmingly the most common form of written Robin Hood text, but they eventually supplanted the premodern ballads in the oral tradition. Already by the end of the sixteenth century the printed ballad of *Robin Hood and the Pinner of Wakefield* may have entered the oral repertoire, to judge by the numerous allusions in texts of the period. In the nineteenth and twentieth centuries a number of oral Robin Hood ballads derived from the broadsides were collected by folklorists: *Robin Hood and Little John* in Quenington, Gloucestershire, in the early twentieth century; *Robin Hood and the Shepherd* in Ireland around 1900; *Robin Hood and the Tanner* and *Robin Hood and Little John* in Virginia and Kentucky in the nineteenth century; *Robin Hood and Little John* in Illinois in 1908; *Robin Hood and the Prince of Aragon* and *Robin Hood Rescuing Three Squires* in Maine in 1927 and 1928.[94] Similarly, when folklorists of the nineteenth century found

Robin Hood as a character in several mumming plays, it was in a form obviously shaped by the commercial ballads.[95]

The blending of folk tradition with commercial creation even extended into the domain of Robin Hood places: the seventeenth century affords the earliest known evidence of the Robin Hood tourist industry. Richard Brathwaite in the early seventeenth century mentions paying a halfpenny for a drink at Robin Hood's well.[96] Another traveler in 1634 took a drink at Robin Hood's well and sat in Robin Hood's "rocky Chaire of Ceremony," where he was "dignify'd with the Order of Knighthood, and sworne to observe his Lawes"; he paid his "Fealtie fee" of 4d. to the "Lady of the Fountaine," but lacked time to "stay to heare our Charge."[97] James Brome recorded a similar visit to the well and chair at the end of the century.[98]

TRANSFORMATIONS OF THE LEGEND

Both the syncretism of the sixteenth century and the commercialization of the seventeenth tended to reshape the Robin Hood legend in ways that affected its underlying structures as outlined in Chapter 1. The cultural elite who took an interest in the legend in the sixteenth century found it full of obscurities and inconsistencies. There was no fully articulated and authoritative story of his origin, the membership of his band varied from one version to another, and the tales lacked an identifiable historic context. Such uncertainties were compatible with medieval popular culture, but they did not agree with the imperative for order and clarity predominant in the official culture of Renaissance England. Throughout the sixteenth century, there was a trend toward the establishment of a full and coherent biography of Robin Hood fixed in a specific historical setting; the process reached its apex in Munday's Huntingdon plays, which essentially offered a complete biography of the outlaw set in the reigns of Richard and John.

These changes to the legend constituted part of a general pattern by which the chaotic figure of the medieval Robin Hood was assimilated into the social and cultural order. The medieval Robin Hood lacked any social connection to the outside world, and his status as a yeoman disagreed with the expectations of a society in which the aristocracy were supposed to lead and the commonality to follow. Grafton introduced a new interpretation, in which the outlaw was either a nobleman or a commoner raised into the aristocracy; this innovation was eagerly accepted by subsequent authors. The Earl of Huntingdon, even as an outlaw, had a clear relationship to the social order; at the same time, Robin's ennoblement helped to reinterpret his outlawry as a temporary state having a clear beginning and end. In the new versions, the earl was outlawed for debt and ultimately pardoned by the king—in contrast with the medieval legend, the outlaw did not return to the greenwood after his pardon. This reinterpretation of Robin Hood as a temporarily outlawed aristocrat not only furnished Robin a clear place in society, but also legitimized his lawlessness from the perspective of official culture by recasting his outlawry and criminal activities as the result of specific abuses of the social system by unjust individuals. As an *ab initio* outlaw, Robin stood in complete opposition to the social hierarchy, but as a wronged nobleman he could actually support the social order while standing outside of it, and his position as a leader of armed followers was made more appropriate within the terms of the official social framework. At the same time, the new arrangement replaced the rough camaraderie of the medieval outlaw band with a hierarchized structure of which the earl was now unmistakably the head.

Robin's new relationship to the social order was reflected in his dealings with the king, transformed in the modernized legend from the ambivalent attitude of the premodern tradition to one of straightforward loyalty. The new Robin Hood acted against the misdeeds of royal agents while maintaining his devotion to the king, who ultimately restored him to favor and to his lost rank. The relationship between outlaw and monarch was also affected by the historicization of the legend, since the king was changed from an unspecified and unassuming Edward into a dynamic and heroic Richard I. The choice of Richard was particularly felicitous from the point of view of official culture since Robin Hood could now resist royal officials without implicitly challenging the king, whose absence on a crusade explains the corruption of society in England.

These changes in Robin's social position, by regularizing him within the hierarchy, made him fundamentally less threatening to the official social order. The dangerousness of the medieval outlaw was also mitigated by the introduction of an element of romance. Robin had no female companion in the medieval tradition, and even in the play of *Robin Hood and the Friar*, the Lady figure is associated with Tuck. By the late sixteenth century, Elizabethan authors had incorporated Maid Marian into the story as Robin's sweetheart. The new Robin Hood was no longer the informal head of a youth gang, but a fully domesticated aristocrat with servants, a fiancée, and the prospects of family life.

Not surprisingly, these changes went hand in hand with efforts to tone down his depredations as a robber. The medieval ballads had been quite forthright about Robin's life of violence and theft, but the Tudor syncretists emphasized his political motives and idyllic forest life. Deeds like Robin's disfiguration of his opponent's severed head in *Robin Hood and Guy of Gisburn* and the casual murder of the monk and his page in *Robin Hood and the Monk* were alien to the rusticating martyr of the Huntingdon plays. The diminishment of Robin Hood's dangerousness reaches an extreme with his transformation into the trivial young lordling of *Looke About You*.

The historicization of Robin Hood also helped to make him less threatening by embalming him in the past, although this development was due to external circumstances as well as to the efforts of the syncretists. Real changes in the world of the audience distanced the fictive world of Robin Hood from its social context. The longbow was ceasing to be a tool for either combat or hunting, outlawry was no longer a normal means of law enforcement, friars and abbots were long extinct in England, and the forests were not so deep and mysterious as once they had been. The displacement of Robin Hood from a vague narrative past to a specific historical setting at the far end of the Middle Ages further alienated him from the contemporary world. Robin's distance from his seventeenth-century audience is reflected in a nostalgic song in the Percy Folio:

> In old times past, when merry men
>   did merry makers make . . .
> good Robin Hood was liui[n]ge then,
>   which now is quite fforgot
> & soe was ffaire Mayd Marryan,
>   a pretty wench, god wott.[99]

Through these changes, the dangerous, chaotic, imminent outlaw of the medieval tradition was reinterpreted as a character unthreatening, orderly, and remote. Such a view of Robin Hood is evoked strikingly in Thomas Fuller's *Worthies of Old England* (1662):

Camden calls him *praedonem mitissimum*, the gentlest thief that ever was; and know, reader, he is entered into our catalogue not for his thievery, but for his gentleness. . . . One may wonder, how he escaped the hand of justice, dying in his bed, for ought is found to the contrary; but it was because he was rather a merry than a mischeivous thief, complimenting pasengers out of their purses; never murdering any but deer, and this popular robber feasted the vicinage with his venison. He played his prankes in the reign of King Richard the First. [100]

The withdrawal of elite interest in the legend and the commercialization of the ballads in some respects further diminished the seriousness of the tradition by displacing it from its former position of integration with its social context. The legend was increasingly marginalized relative to society at large. The premodern Robin Hood legend had occupied a focal position in the cultural life of England as a ubiquitous and prominent feature of folk culture. Even in the sixteenth century, texts like the *Gest* and Munday's Huntingdon plays demonstrate that the legend was still appreciated by a diverse audience who were willing to approach it with some measure of seriousness. During the seventeenth century the tradition was pushed toward the fringes: no longer seen as worthy of the interest of the cultural elite, it vanished from public celebrations and theaters, to be transmitted instead through cheap printed broadsides and chapbooks, perhaps even puppet shows, for the consumption of those of inferior social and cultural standing.

At the same time, the tradition was being alienated from its own audience. Where the medieval legend had been the ongoing public creation of an oral folk culture, the new print medium shifted the locus of production from the public to the commercial sphere. As the legend came under the hegemony of a smaller body of professional creators, the public at large fell into the role of consumer and lost the intimate relationship with the legend that had characterized the early Robin Hood tradition. This process is especially vivid in the case of Robin Hood drama: where Robin Hood has once been interpreted by the community in folk drama for its own consumption, the newer versions of Robin Hood drama were created by professional players for a commercial audience.

The commercial creators who gained new authority over the legend in the seventeenth century shared much of the social and cultural background of the syncretists, and in many respects their ballads continued to perpetuate the priorities of official culture. Parker's *True Tale* in particular presents a historicized and socially elevated version of the outlaw; like the syncretists, he downplays the violence of the tradition:

> But to speak true of Robin Hood,
>   And wrong him not a jot,
> He never would shed any mans blood,
>   That him invaded not. [st. 73]

Similar trends can be seen in many of the broadside ballads, which commonly portray Robin as a quaint, even trivial figure, engaged in countless minor escapades but never really challenging established authority. The largest subgroup among the broadsides are based on the "sportful combat" motif, in which Robin's status as an outlaw hardly figures at all. At the end of *Robin Hood's Delight* the outlaws and the agents of the Forest Laws repair to the tavern together:

> So away they went to Nottingham,
>   With sack to make amends;
> For three days they the red wine did chase,
>   And drank themselves good friends. [st. 24]

In *Robin Hood's Birth*, as in *Look About You*, Robin is not portrayed as an outlaw at all, but as a jovial member of the landholding class whose primary concerns are dynasty and household. In some cases Robin actively assists the established authorities. Aside from his service to the queen in *Robin Hood and Queen Katherine*, he rescues the royal family in *Robin Hood and the Prince of Aragon*, and in *The Noble Fisherman* he helps protect English shipping from French marauders. In *Little John and the Beggars*, Little John directs his energies against sturdy beggars, a task more appropriate to a constable or justice of the peace than a forest outlaw.

When Robin attacks authority figures, his victims are usually clerical, and therefore marginal as representatives of official order in Protestant England. Monks and abbots, as Catholic figures, were fair game, while priests and bishops were subject to varying treatment even from within the privileged classes. Parker takes pain to specify that Robin's hostility was directed against ecclesiastical rather than civil authorities:

He wished well unto the king,
    And prayed still for his health,
And never practis'd any thing
    Against the common-wealth.

Only because he was undone
    By th'cruel clergy then,
All means that he could think upon,
    To vex such kind of men,

He enterpriz'd with hateful spleen;
    For which he was to blame,
For fault of some to wreak his teen
    On all that by him came. [st. 68 ff.]

Robin's loyalty to the king can be seen in his eagerness for a royal pardon, a factor that comes into play in *Robin Hood and the Prince of Aragon* [st. 51] and *Robin Hood's Chase*; in Parker's *True Tale* he goes to considerable effort to solicit the king's forgiveness [st. 49, 80].

As with the syncretists, the commercial balladeers sometimes evoke the temporal remoteness of Robin Hood. This element is emphasized in *Robin Hood and the Beggar*:

In elder times, when merriment was,
    And archery was holden good,
There was an outlaw, as many do know
    Which men called Robin Hood. [st. 2]

The implications of Robin's historicity are made explicit in Parker's *True Tale*:

A thing impossible to us
    This story seem to be,
None dares be now so venturous,
    But times are chang'd we see.

We that live in these later days,
    Of civil government,
If need be, have an hundred ways,
    Such outlaws to prevent.

In those days men more barbarous were,
    And lived less in awe;
Now (god be thanked) people fear
    More to offend the law. [st. 108–10]

For all these reasons, the commercial balladeers' Robin Hood often appeared as unthreatening as he did in antiquarian versions of the legend. *The Nobel Birth* echoes Fuller's conclusions on Robin Hood with an ending that the medieval hero would doubtless have considered humiliating:

Robin Hood dismissed all his idel companions, and betaking himself of a civil course of life, he did keepe a gallante house, and had over all the country, the love of the rich, and the prayers of the poor. [101]

In the medieval legends of Robin Hood, the forces of authority repeatedly attempt various shifts and stratagems to capture Robin Hood; many times he is actually within their grasp; yet in the end he always escapes to the greenwood again. In some measure, the same may be said of the legend itself in the early modern period. Diverse powerful forces were at work to co-opt or vitiate the outlaw here, yet they were never fully successful.

The withdrawal of elite interest from the legend, while it deprived the tradition of some of its former strength, also frustrated the process of officialization. As such totalizing genres as chronicles and plays ceded place to the multiple voices of the commercial ballads, the trend toward order was reversed. The ballads were short and proliferate, fragmenting the vision of the syncretists into kaleidoscopic perspectives, not always congruent, sometimes explicitly contradictory. Robin Hood's earldom is mentioned only in Parker, *Robin Hood and Maid Marian*, and *The Nobel Birth*; it seems to be implicitly contradicted in *Robin Hood and the Foresters*, with its unaristocratic explanation of Robin's origin. The names of his followers vary: Scarlett is Scadlock in some ballads, Much appears as Midge or even Nick. [102] Figures such as Friar Tuck and Maid Marian, well known as characters in the tradition, appear only in the ballads relating to their fight with Robin Hood. Even the historical setting in the reign of Richard I, one of the most successful innovations of the sixteenth century, is found only in Parker and *Robin Hood and Queen Katherine (C)*: every other commercial ballad that names the king identifies him as Henry VIII. Most of the ballads have no specific chronological setting, but take place in a vague past under the auspices of an anonymous king—in which they resemble the *Gest* more than Munday's version of the legend.

The multiple voices of the ballads allow for the priorities emphasized in some texts to be negated in others. Where some ballads ignore or downplay Robin's lawlessness, in others it cannot be denied, as in *Robin Hood and the Foresters*, *Robin Hood and the Butcher*, *Robin Hood and the Beggar*, and *Robin Hood Rescuing Will Stutly*, where the outlaw is in direct and violent conflict with the civil authorities. Even within individual ballads multiple perspectives emerge. Martin Parker stresses the outlaw's loyalty to the king, yet Robin plunders the king's receivers and prompts the monarch on several occasions to hire bounty hunters. In *Robin Hood and Queen Katherine* and *Robin Hood's Chase* his treatment of King Henry is humiliating: in the former he steals the king's money and sends it to the queen, deceives him with an alias, and defeats his archers causing him to lose his wager; in the latter he leads the king a chase up and down the length of England, and visits the queen during the king's absence from London. The sexual innuendo is unmistakable: indeed, Robin Hood proposes to visit Katherine on the grounds that "It may be she wants our company,/ Which makes the king so us chase" [st. 17].

Even when Robin Hood does not directly challenge the social hierarchy, his actions sometimes express a more subtle denial of hierarchical principles. In the ballads on the "sportful combat" theme, the hierarchy is simply ignored: the environment preserves the plebeian spirit of the medieval tradition, dominated by self-confident, assertive, even violent, commoners. In some tales the official hierarchy is present but irrelevant: in *Robin Hood and the Pinner of Wakefield* and *Robin Hood's Delight* the outlaws contend with plebeian representatives of official authority, yet the conflict is personal, and Robin's adversaries seem more inclined to prove their own virility than to enforce the official order. In *Robin Hood and the Lovers*, the outlaws carry out a characteristically plebeian enactment of popular values: in an action recalling the traditional charivari, they express the popular disapproval of an inappropriate marriage and forcibly assert their own values on the aged knight and bishop. While Robin's attacks on ecclesiastical figures are generally sanctioned within the terms of English culture of the period, they do challenge one of the pillars of social authority. The implicit irreverence is made overt in *Robin Hood and the Lovers* when Little John parodies the asking of the banns, a custom that was not merely a religious ceremony, but society's principal means of preventing unlawful marriages.

The plurality of voices among the broadside ballads naturally undermined any attempts at officialization, yet some of the same contradictions can also be identified among the Tudor syncretists themselves. Grafton's history offers no less than three alternative accounts of Robin Hood: first the traditional version in which he is implicitly a yeoman, then two others in which he is a nobleman or a commoner elevated to the aristocracy. Munday emphasizes his protagonist's passivity, but Robin directly resists civil authority by rescuing Scarlett and Scadlock from the gallows. Although this scene is just a small part of the play, Munday's Earl of Huntingdon is generally overshadowed by Robin Hood. The self-denying, even feckless aristocrat who forgives his persecutors is a much less compelling figure than the bold outlaw who beguiles the Sheriff of Nottingham. For contemporary audiences, the play was clearly about Robin Hood rather than the Earl of Huntingdon: the piece is mentioned eight times in Henslowe's diaries, seven times as "Robin Hood" or "Robert Hood," and once as "The Downfall of Earl Huntingdon, surnamed Robin Hood."[103]

The predominance of Robin Hood over the Earl reflects the underlying strength of the legend's medieval structures in the face of persistent efforts to reshape them. The forest, outlawry, and yeomanry continued to dominate the legend even when they had ostensibly been marginalized. In the new versions of the legend, Robin's outlawry, his inhabitation of the forest, and his adoption of a yeomanly life were all portrayed as temporary circumstances, yet the hero was familiar principally as Robin Hood, the outlaw who inhabited Sherwood with his yeomanly band; the biographic context remained marginal to the legend as a whole. The same is still true today, when Robin's aristocratic origin is if anything a more canonical part of the legend than it was in 1700. Time has proven that the outlaw is the real character: the Earl of Huntingdon is just one of many aliases for Robin Hood.

NOTES

1. John Leland, *The Itinerary of John Leland*, ed. Lucy Toulmin Smith (London: G. Bell and sons, 1908), 4.13.

2. John Leland, *De Rebus Britannicis Collecteana* (Oxonii: e Theatro Sheldoniano, 1715), 1.54

3. William Camden, *Britannia* (London: R. Newbery, 1587), 484.

4. William Camden, *Britain, Or a Chorographicall Description of the Most Flourishing Kingdomes, England, Scotland, and Ireland, and the Ilands Adjoyning, out of the Depth of Antiquitie*, transl. Philemon Holland (London: George Bishop and John Norton, 1610), 718c.

5. Camden, *Britannia* (London: George Bishop, 1594), 532; Camden, *Britannia* (London: George Bishop, 1600), 615.

6. Camden, *Britain* (1610), 693a

7. John Stow, *A Summarie of Our Englysh Chronicles* (London: Thomas Marshe, 1566), fol. 71r–71v. Stow's *Annales of England* (1592) repeats the same material [John Stow, *The Annales of England* (London: R. Newbery, 1592), sig. P2].

8. Richard Grafton, *Grafton's Chronicle* (London: printed for J. Johnson, 1809), 1.221–22.

9. Malcolm Nelson, *The Robin Hood Tradition in the English Renaissance*, Salzburg Studies in English Literature (Salzburg: Institut für Englische Sprache und Literatur, 1973), 33–35; John Bellamy, *Robin Hood: An Historical Enquiry* (London: Croom Helm, 1985), 3; Stephen Knight, *Robin Hood. A Complete Study of the English Outlaw* (Oxford and Cambridge, Mass.: Blackwell, 1994), 40–42.

10. Raphael Holinshed, *The History of Scotland* (London: H. Bynneman for J. Harrison, 1577), 202a.

11. For examples of authors influenced by Grafton, see Richard Robinson, *Ancient Order of Prince Arthur* (London: J. Wolfe, 1583), sig. L4b; William Martyn, *The Historie and Lives of the Kings of England* (London: R. Young, 1642), 42.

12. William Warner, *Albion's England* (London: G. Potter, 1602), p. 121 (5.25).

13. Warner, *Albion's England*, p. 132 (5.27).

14. Drayton, pp. 122–23 (26th Song).

15. Robert Jones, *A Musicall Dreame* (London: W. Barley, 1609), Cantus 19.

16. Thomas Ravenscroft, *Pammelia* (London: William Barley, 1609), sig. F1v; Jill Vlasto, "An Elizabethan Anthology of Rounds," *Musical Quarterly* 40 (1954), 229, 234.

17. *SR(A)* 2.301; George Peele, *The Chronicle of King Edward the First* (Chicago: Adams Press, 1974).

18. *SR(A)* 2.649; Nelson, *The Robin Hood Tradition*, 114–16.

19. *A Pleasant Conceyted Comedie of George a Greene the Pinner of Wakefield. As it was sundry times acted by the servants of the right Honourable the Earle of Sussex* (London: Cuthbert Burby, 1599); *SR(A)* 2.295; Phillip Henslowe, *Henslowe's Diary*, ed. R. A. Foakes and R. T. Rickert (Cambridge: Cambridge University Press, 1961), 20 Roughly contemporary with the Sloane life is a manuscript account of George a Greene; the text, which was printed in revised form as a chapbook in the eighteenth century, corresponds closely to the Elizabethan play, from which it evidently derives [*The Pinder of Wakefield*, ed. E. A. Horsman, English Reprints Series 12 (Liverpool: Liverpool University Press, 1956), viii; William J. Thoms, *Early English Prose Romances* (London: Nattali and Bond, 1858), 188–94, 201–5, 208–15].

20. *SR(A)* 3.176 (1600); Anthony Munday, *The Huntingdon Plays. A Critical Edition of* The Downfall *and* The Death of Robert, Earl of Huntingdon, ed. John Carney Meagher (New York and London: Garland, 1980).

21. Meagher, *The Huntingdon Plays*, 53 ff.; Claire Cross, *The Puritan Earl. The Life of Henry Hastings, 3rd Earl of Huntingdon 1536–1595* (London and Melbourne: Macmillan; New York: St. Martin's Press, 1966).

22. Nelson, *The Robin Hood Tradition*, 127.

23. *A Pleasant Commodie Called Looke About You*, ed. Richard S. M. Hirsch (New York and London: Garland, 1980). The play was first published in 1600.

24. Henslowe, *Henslowe's Diary*, 125.

25. Ben Jonson, *The Sad Shepherd* (Cambridge: Cambridge University Press, 1929).

26. Anthony Munday, *Metropolis Coronata* (London: George Purslowe, 1615), sig. C3.

27. R. B. Dobson and J. Taylor, *Rymes of Robin Hood*, 2nd ed. (Gloucester: Alan Sutton, 1989), 237–42; Wing 1626 (1661).

28. George Speaight, *History of the English Puppet Theatre*, 2nd ed. (London: Robert Hale, 1990), 309.

29. [William Roy], *Rede Me* (Strassburg, 1528; rpt. Amsterdam: Da Capo Press, 1972), sig. Dve.

30. William Tyndale, *The Works of William Tyndale*, ed. G. E. Duffield (Appleford, Berks.: Sutton Court Press, 1964), 331. The author of *I playne Piers which can not flatter* felt similarly: "You allowe . . . *legenda aurea*, Roben Hoode, Beuys, & Gower, & al bagage besyd . . . But Gods word ye may not abyde." [*I playne Piers which can not flatter* (London: ?N. Hill, ?1550), sig. E.iii.2].

31. *Works* (1614), cited in J. O. W. Haweis, *Sketches of the Reformation and Elizabethan Age Taken from the Contemporary Pulpit* (London: William Pickering, 1845), 148.

32. *The Three Ladies of London* (1584), in W. Carew *A Select Collection of Old English Plays* (London: Reeves and Turner, 1874), 6.287.

33. Laurence Tomson, *Calvin's Sermons on the Epistles to Timothie and Titus* (London: H. Middleton for G. Bishop and T. Woodcock, 1579), 23a.

34. See Appendix A under Halstead (Essex); see also *The Marprelate Tracts 1588, 1589*, ed. William Pierce (London: A. Constable and Co., 1908), 369–70.

35. Hugh Latimer, *Seven Sermons Before Edward VI*, ed. Edward Arber (London: n.p., 1869), 173–74. Latimer's route from London to Worcester would have taken him through Oxfordshire and Gloucestershire—prime country for the Robin Hood games.

36. Robert Braham, "To the Reader," in *The Auncient Histories and onely trewe and syncere Cronicle of the warres betwixte the Grecians and the Troyans ... by John Lydgate* (London: T. Marsh, 1555), sig. A2.

37. Henry Parker, Lord Morley, *Lord Morley's* Tryumphes of Fraunces Petrarcke, ed. D. D. Carnicelli (Cambridge, Mass.: Harvard University Press, 1971), 77.

38 Nicholas Udall, trans., *The Apothegmes of Erasmus* (Boston, Lincs.: R. Roberts, 1877), 83–84.

39. John Rastell, *The Four Elements*, ll. 1388–90, in *Three Rastell Plays*, ed. Richard Axton (Cambridge: D. S. Brewer; Totowa, N.J.: Rowman and Littlefield, 1979), 67.

40. Rastell, *The Four Elements*, ll. 1394 ff.; cf. Ravenscroft, *Pammelia*, 31; Vlasto, "An Elizabethan Anthology," 225.

41. Nicholas Ridley, *The Works of Nicholas Ridley*, ed. Henry Christmas, Parker Society 39 (Cambridge: Cambridge University Press, 1841), 304.

42. Sydney Anglo, "An Early Tudor Programme for Plays and Other Demonstrations against the Pope," *Journal of the Warburg and Courtauld Institute* 20 (1957), 179.

43. Lindsay Boynton, *The Elizabethan Militia. 1588–1638* (London: Routledge and Kegan Paul, 1967), 59.

44. See Appendix A under Kent/Sussex.

45. Ronald Hutton, *The Rise and Fall of Merry England: The Ritual Year, 1400–1700* (Oxford and New York: Oxford University Press, 1994), 140.

46. See Appendix A under Scotland.

47. Raphael Holinshed, *History of Scotland*, 358b.

48. On the riots, see 160-61 and Appendix B.

49. See Appendix A under Scotland.

50. Hutton, *The Rise and Fall of Merry England*, 127.

51. *Ibid.*, 139–40, 157, 189.

52. *Ibid.*, 168–69, 191.

53. *Ibid.*, 207.

54. Cf. David Underdown, *Revel, Riot, and Rebellion. Popular Politics and Culture in England 1603–1660* (Oxford: Clarendon Press, 1985), 50.

55. Hutton, *The Rise and Fall of Merry England*, 229.

56. *Ibid.*, 242 ff.; Sandra Billington, *Mock Kings in Medieval Society and Renaissance Drama* (Oxford: Clarendon Press, 1991), 36 ff.

57. David Cressy, *Literacy and the Social Order* (Cambridge: Cambridge University Press, 1980), 176.

58. *SR(A)* 1.76.

59. *SR(A)* 1.204.

60. Cressy, *Literacy and the Social Order*, 176.

61. Marjorie Plant, *The English Book Trade* (London: G. Allen and Unwin, 1939), 220, 241.

62. *The Roxburghe Ballads*, ed. Charles Hindley (London: Reeves and Turner, 1837–74), 8.530–32; Child #124; Wing J895 (1689–92), 895A (1658–64), 896 (1663–74), 896A (1674–79), 897 (1690), 897A (1693); *SR(B)* 2.498 (1675).

63. Child #123; *Roxburghe Ballads* 8.521–25; *STC* 13686.5 (c. 1625); Wing R1629A (1663–74).

64. Child #125; *Roxburghe Ballads* 8.504–8; *SR(A)* 4.120 (1624), 4.481 (1640); Wing R1627 (1680–85).

65. *Roxburghe Ballads* 2.426–31; *The Euing Collection of English Broadside Ballads in the Library of the University of Glasgow* (Glasgow: University of Glasgow Publications, 1971), #305; Wing R1633 (?1673), 1633A (1682–1700), 1633B (1684–86), 1633C (1700); Thoms, *Early English Prose Romances*, 126.

66. Child #128; Wing R1630C (?1700).

67. Child #130. The later version is printed in Child.

68. Child #126; *Roxburghe Ballads* 8.502–3; *Euing Ballads* #304; *SR(B)* 2.123 (1657); Wing R1630D (1657), 1630E (1681–84), 1630F (1684–86), 1631 (?1695), 1631A (?1700).

69. Child #135; *Roxburghe Ballads* 8.490–92; Wing R1630 (1685), 1630A (?1685), 1630B (1685).

70. Child #150; Wing vol. 3, p. 244 (1653). The broadside has a cross-reference in Wing, but no actual entry.

71. Child #127; *Roxburghe Ballads* 8.527–30; Wing ?N775A (1641–60), 774 (?1680).

72. Child #136; Wing R1635A (1655), 1636 (1685).

73. Child #143; *Roxburghe Ballads* 2.448–53; *Euing Ballads* #303. *SR(B)* 2.35 (1656); Wing R1628 (?1650), 1628A (1674–79), 1628B (1684–86), 1628C (?1695), 1628D (?1700).

74. Child #142B; *Roxburghe Ballads* 8.496–99; *SR(B)* 2.133, 137, 142 (1657); Wing L2551 (?1670), L2551A (1657).

75. Child #122; *Roxburghe Ballads* 8.535–37; *SR(B)* 2.133, 137 (1657); Wing R1657D (?1660), 1657E (1684–86).

76. Child #147; *Roxburghe Ballads* 8.508–11; *SR(A)* 4.254 (1631); *SR(B)* 2.62 (1656); Wing P3382A (?1650), 3382B (1674–79), 3382C (1688–89).

77. Child #148; *Roxburghe Ballads* 8.486–89; *Euing Ballads* #301, 302; *SR(A)* 4.254 (1631); Wing N1205A (?1650), 1205B (1658–64), 1205C (1663–74), 1205D (1674–79), 1206 (1686–88), 1207 (?1690).

78. Child #145B; *Roxburghe Ballads* 2.418–25; *Euing Ballads* #300; *SR(B)* 2.35 (1656), 499 (1675); *STC* 13693 (c. 1630); Wing 1039C (?1656), 1039D (1663–74), 1309E (1681–84), 1309F (?1700).

79. Child #145C.

80. Child #146; *Roxburghe Ballads* 8.511–14; Wing R1657F (1663–65), 1657G (1674–79), 1657H (1688–89).

81. Child #129; *Roxburghe Ballads* 2.432–40; Wing R1633D (?1700), R1633E (n. d.).

82. Child #133; *Roxburghe Ballads* 8.515–20; *SR(B)* 2.35 (1656); Wing R1657A (c. 1660), 1657B (1663–64), 1657C (1684–86).

83. Child #141; *Euing Ballads* #307; Wing R1632 (1680–85), 1643D (?1700), 1643E (?1700).

84. Child #138; *Roxburghe Ballads* 8.492–96; *Euing Ballads* #299; Wing R1624A (1674–79), 1624B (1681), 1624C (1682–1700), 1625 (?1695); Thoms, *Early English Prose Romances*, 126.

85. Child #139; *Roxburghe Ballads* 8.499–501; *Euing Ballads* #306; *SR(B)* 2.43 (1656), 499 (1675); Wing R1641A (1656), 1642 (1663–74), 1643 (1680–85), 1643A (1684–86), 1643B (?1700), 1643C (?1700); Thoms, *Early English Prose Romances*, 124–25.

86. Child #120; *Roxburghe Ballads* 8.*540; *SR(B)* 3.393 (1691).

87. Child #149; *Roxburghe Ballads* 2.440–48. Wing R1633F (1681–84).

88. Claude M. Simpson, *The British Broadside Ballad and Its Music* (New Brunswick, N.J.: Rutgers University Press, 1966), 608–11. The melody is probably the one alluded to in William Webbe's *Discourse of English Poetrie* (London: Robert Walley, 1586), sig. D1r: "Many such can frame an Alehouse song of five or sixe score verses, hobbling uppon some tune of a Northen Jygge or Robyn hoode."

89. Simpson, *The British Broadside Ballad*, 374. The name "In Summer Time" refers to two distinct tunes, since it is used for a four-foot line in *The Noble Fisherman* and for lines alternating 4 and 3 feet in *Robin Hood and the Tinker*.

90. Child #154; *SR(A)* 4.273 (1632), 308 (1633); *STC* 19274.5 (?1632), 19275 (?1632); Wing P447 (1686), 447A (1700).

91. *The Pinder of Wakefield*, ed. Horsman; *STC* 11213 (1632); *SR(A)* 4.271 (1632).

92. Wing 1201 (1662), 1202 (1678), 1203 (1685), 1203a (c. 1690), 1203b (1700); Thoms, *Early English Prose Romances*, 523–46; *SR(B)* 8.111 (1682).

93. *SR(B)* 2.248 (1660); Wing R1637 (1663), 1638 (1670), 1638A (?1684–86); 3rd ed.: Wing 1639 (1689), 1640 (?1670–80).

94. Dobson and Taylor, *Rymes*, 165 ff.; E. L. Wilson and H. S. V. Jones, "Robin Hood and Little John," *Journal of American Folklore* 23 (1910): 432–34; Arthur Kyle Davis, *Traditional Ballads of Virginia* (Charlottesville: University Press of Virginia, 1929), 393; Louise Pound, "American Text of 'Robin Hood and Little John,'" *American Speech* 2 (1927), 75; Alfred Williams, *Folk-Songs of the Upper Thames* (London: Duckworth and Co., 1923), 296; Phillips Barry, Fannie Hardy Eckstorm, and Mary Winslow Smyth, *British Ballads from Maine* (New Haven: Yale University Press, 1929), 233–40, 240–42, 461.

95. R. J. E. Tiddy, *The Mummers' Play* (Oxford: Clarendon Press, 1923), 209–13, 248–53.

96. Richard Brathwaite, *Barnabees Journall* (London: J. Haviland, 1638), sig. S1r.

97. *A Relation of a Short Survey of 26 Counties, Observed in a seven weeks Journey begun on August 11, 1634*, ed. L. G. Wickham Legg (London: F. E. Robinson and Co., 1904), 13.

98. James Brome, *Travels Over England, Scotland and Wales* (London: Abel Roper, 1700), 85.

99. John W. Hales and Frederick J. Furnivall, eds., *Bishop Percy's Folio Manuscript* (London: Trübner, 1868), 3.120.

100. Thomas Fuller, *The Worthies of England*, ed. John Freeman (London: G. Allen and Unwin, 1952), 451.

101. Thoms, *Early English Prose Romances*, 123.

102. Much is Nick in *Robin Hood and the Lovers*, Midge in *Robin Hood and the Friar* and *Robin Hood and Queen Katherine (B)*; Scarlet is Scadlock in *Robin Hood and the Friar*, *Robin Hood and the Tinker*, and *Robin Hood and the Prince of Aragon*, Scarlet in *Robin Hood and the Pinner of Wakefield*, *Robin Hood Revived*, and *Robin Hood's Golden Prize*, Scarlock in *Robin Hood's Delight*.

103. Henslowe, *Henslowe's Diary*, 83, 84, 99.

4

Vain Tales of Robin Hood

I knew a very wise man so much of Sir Chr–'s sentiment that he believed if a man were permitted to make all the ballads, he need not care who should make the laws of a nation.

 —Andrew Fletcher of Saltoun, "An Account of a Conversation Concerning a
      Right to Regulation of Governments" (1703)

The audience of the early Robin Hood stories might well have expressed surprise—if not outright derision—at the very idea of looking for meaning in the legend. A "tale of Robin Hood" was proverbially false, foolish, or idle; according to a maxim first attested in Heywood's *Dialogue* (1546), "Tales of Robyn hoode are good among fooles."[1] Variations on this phrase occur in a great variety of contexts, from William Robertson's *Phraseologia Generalis* (1681), which glosses *Aniles fabulae* ["old wives' tales"] as "*Nifles and trifles*; *Vain tales of* Robin Hood,"[2] to Whitlock's account of the negotiations in 1644 between Charles I and Parliament during the Civil War:

The Committee who carried the Propositions of Peace to Oxford, had the King's Answer sealed up and sent to them. They . . . made an Address to His Majesty, that they might know what his Answer was . . . to which His Majesty replied, "What is that to you, who are but to carry what I send, and if I will send the song of Robin Hood and Little John you must carry it?" To which the Commissioners onely said, that the business about which they came . . . was of somewhat more consequence than that Song.[3]

At their most superficial level, the stories of Robin Hood are mere entertainments, characterized by escapism and shallow wish-fulfillment. Storytelling is an escapist activity by nature, and the more so in any narrative where individuals are empowered to a degree well beyond what the audience expect in their own lives, and where the audience's sense of justice is at first offended and then vindicated. Escapism has a low reputation among literary sophisticates, and this may well be one reason behind the scholarly community's neglect of Robin Hood.

Yet we should not allow ourselves to be deceived by appearances. Since at least the fourteenth century, the Robin Hood legend has enjoyed very wide currency; it has been employed in a remarkable variety of contexts, and has lasted undiminished to the present day. No literary tradition so pervasive and enduring can be considered trivial. If it did not fulfill some important function, it would scarcely have enjoyed such popularity, and the very fact of such frequent retelling must have had some impact on those who transmitted it. We may reasonably hypothesize that some rather more significant transactions underlie the escapist surface of the legend.

The task of interpreting the Robin Hood tradition is complex, not least because of the enormous span of time involved. The bulk of this chapter will focus on the structures of the early tradition, with some remarks at the end on the effect of transformations in the legend in the sixteenth and seventeenth centuries.

ROBIN HOOD IN THE PREMODERN WORLD

The traditional interpretation of the medieval Robin Hood legend was expressed by Maurice Keen's articles and book in the 1950s and 60s, which characterize the tales as "an expression of peasant discontent": "their theme is the righting of wrongs inflicted by a harsh system and unjust men."[4] As Keen described it, the ballads offer "a closer understanding of the attitude of the oppressed classes in medieval England. They reveal the indignation of the peasant at the system . . . and they show, at the same time, the limit of the peasant's outlook."[5] Eric Hobsbawm has likewise argued that "Robin Hood was and is essentially a peasant rebelling against landlords, usurers, and other representatives of . . . 'the conspiracy of the rich.'"[6]

J. C. Holt's gentrification of the Robin Hood legend opened the way for a new look at the legend as an medium to uphold rather than challenge the social order.[7] T. H. Aston finds in the ballads a "basic acceptance of the existing social framework," and Bernard Capp sees Robin Hood as "far from a rebel."[8] The debate surrounding the social significance of the Robin Hood tradition is just one skirmish in a broader conflict between those who seek forms of primitive radicalism in the popular culture of this period and those who believe that this culture ultimately served the interests of the social hierarchy.

As previous scholars have implicitly recognized, a literary tradition so engaged in social issues calls for a social interpretation. Yet from the outset we should guard against the assumptions inherent in any talk of "the existing social framework." In practice, a social body is not a stable hierarchy of relationships but a marketplace in which power transactions are continually negotiated. While no social model can be analytically useful without some simplification, we must at least allow for a rudimentary dialectic by distinguishing between the official social order, as defined by the privileged classes, and a popular social order, as realized in the practice of ordinary people.

The concept of a popular social order is both a valid and useful analytical tool. It is too easy to slip into the habit of representing the commons merely in relation to the social hierarchy as defined by the church and aristocracy, either acquiescing in it, or resisting it through verbal protest or physical action. This mode of thought is particularly common among medievalists, in part because medieval commoners never enter the written record except through the mediation of the privileged classes, giving the impression that their world existed entirely within the framework of the official order. The result is a fundamentally authoritarian view of society and culture.

The existence of a popular social order is a necessary consequence of the realities of commoners' daily lives. The quotidian social practices of ordinary people transpired in a context in which they themselves were almost the only participants. They had regular dealings with the official social order and were certainly subject to its influence, but almost all of their daily interactions were with others of their own class: they were necessarily the repositories and practitioners of their own social order. Their practices might be informed by the official structures, but could never be entirely governed by them.

The inclusion of a popular social order in the equation substantially changes the way in which we look at popular culture. Within this interpretative framework, popular culture is transformed from a means by which the commons positioned themselves relative to an exterior social order, to a vehicle for articulating their own social beliefs and practices. Every society needs a culture in order to communicate with itself, as suggested by Clifford Geertz's definition of the word:

The term culture . . . denotes an historically transmitted pattern of meanings embodied in symbols, a system of inherited conceptions expressed in symbolic forms by means of which men communicate, perpetuate, and develop their knowledge about and attitudes towards life. [9]

Culture is by definition an ordering force, a tool whereby the chaos of human experience is reduced to comprehensible form through selection, rationalization, and structuring. In seeking to interpret any cultural phenomenon, the most useful initial line of approach is to investigate what sort of order it creates. While the Robin Hood tradition may have upheld or subverted the official social order, this was not its primary function: it relates firstly to the social and cultural order of the people who created and transmitted it, and only secondarily to exterior orders.

The Robin Hood tradition appears in a new light when interpreted as a cultural phenomenon in this way. Premodern popular culture was preideological, in that its structures were not the abstract ideologies of theology or law, but the concrete symbologies of custom and myth: it operates at the level of sign rather than concept. In such a cultural context, the values of the society are not ultimately separable from the language in which these values are expressed.[10] The Robin Hood tradition was one of this culture's most extensive, pervasive, and characteristic manifestations. Both as an expression of this culture and as one of the obvious means by which the culture perpetuated itself, the legend takes on tremendous significance. A tale of Robin Hood, far from being a nifle or trifle, has the potential to be as significant as a biblical narrative or a parliamentary law.

As has been consistently emphasized in this study, the most useful reading of so variegated a folkloric phenomenon as the Robin Hood tradition is one that is founded on the legend's structures. At the structural core of the legend is a nonsocietal space doubly determined by the greenwood and outlawry, standing in opposition to the social world of law outside the greenwood. This opposition is present throughout the early tales. Apart from a few marginal biographical stories, the premodern Robin Hood stories consistently follow a single narrative structure: *status quo in the nonsocietal space—interpenetration of nonsocietal space and societal space—return to status quo in the nonsocietal space.*

Interpretations of Robin Hood's greenwood have focused heavily on the Forest Laws and royal ownership of the forest. These elements are present in the legend, yet they are not ultimately a structural feature. Robin is undeniably a bold poacher of venison, and doubtless his violation of the Forest Laws colored the audience response to his adventures, yet his infringement of the royal prerogative is very rarely highlighted in the ballads. Only once in the *Gest* does King Edward mention his royal rights, and then because Robin has been poaching his deer from Plumpton Park in Lancashire, not Sherwood Forest. In fact, Barnsdale is mentioned as often as Sherwood in the early legend, and Barnsdale was not a royal forest at all.

The significance of Robin's greenwood is not legal but practical. In the Middle Ages and early modern period, forested areas were places where the official social order was comparatively weak and unable to assert itself. Forest dwellers were among the most independent of England's inhabitants, and the forest was indeed a place where a thief or outlaw might live for years in defiance of all authority.[11] In the ballads, the historical freedom of the forest is made mythically absolute. Here the usual societal relationships do not necessarily operate. The yeoman, who in the outside world is supposed to be subservient to ecclesiastic and aristocratic authorities, is free to act as their equal or superior. Theft and poaching, activities severely sanctioned in the external world, can be freely practiced. The strictures that govern the exterior world cannot be enforced within the bounds of the greenwood.

This reading of Robin Hood's greenwood is corroborated by the similar role played by his outlawry. Historically, outlawry meant expulsion from society to a position outside of the protection of the law, but this early version of outlawry is hardly operative in surviving versions of the legend. Somewhat more relevant is the practice in the fourteenth and fifteenth centuries of outlawing any accused person who failed to answer to the legal system.[12] Although the actual circumstances of his outlawry do not seem to have been well defined, the governmental authorities in the legend obviously regard Robin Hood as a fugitive from the law, and their hostility toward him in many cases catalyzes the action of the tales. At its most fundamental level, however, Robin's outlawry is akin his inhabitation of the greenwood, since it places him outside the strictures of societal space. The importance of this aspect of outlawry is emphasized at the end of the *Gest*: Robin forsakes his place at court not because of any antipathy toward the king, but because he prefers the free life of the outlaw.

From the perspective of the legend, the nonsocietal space created by the greenwood and outlawry serves to free its inhabitants from objective constraints. This freedom is not defined solely in relation to the official order, as represented by the laws and civil authorities: the outlaws are equally untrammeled by ties of kinship or romance, even by basic economic necessity, since they are able to live comfortably by hunting deer and rich travelers. As an environment cut off from all constraints of the ordinary world, the greenwood-outlawry locus at the center of the Robin Hood legend is a ludic space. Play may be understood as a circumscribed activity, transpiring within a context somehow cut off from the ordinary world, neither constrained by its structures nor undertaken with the purpose of affecting it.[13] The dissociation of play from the external world bestows on it an enormous potential power. In the realm of undifferentiated activity, the range of possibilities is restricted by anterior realities and expected outcomes. Play, to the degree that it is dissevered from these externalities, creates a greater freedom within its own circumscribed space—it is a realm of possibilities.

This ludic dimension in the legend is particularly overt in the Robin Hood games, where the structures of the legend are assimilated to those of the festival context. In the games, the opposition between Robin Hood's nonsocietal space and the exterior world is aligned with that between the festival space and quotidian space. The space of the festival, like the outlaws' greenwood, is cut off from the ordinary world. The constraints of quotidian life are suspended: people engage in activities normally forbidden and take on roles and functions contrary to their usual place in society.

The ludic aspect of the legend manifests itself in a particularly pure form in the invocation of the outlaw as an icon of illogic. Robin Hood figures recurrently in nonsensical verse of the fifteenth and sixteenth centuries, as in the following example from c. 1475:

Ther were tynkerris in tarlottus, the met was fulle goode.
The sow sate one hi[e] benche, and harppyde Robyn Hoode.
The schulerde schowttyde in a schalmas, the torbot trompyde to that,
The ratton rybybyde, the fox fedylde, therto claryide the catte.[14]

[There were tinkers in tartlets, the food was full good; The sow sat on a high bench and harped about Robin Hood. The spoonbill blared away on the shawm, the turbot trumpetted along, the rat played the ribible, the fox fiddled, and the cat blew the clarion.]

Robin figures similarly in another fifteenth-century burlesque:

[The] hogge with his hornepype hyed hym belyve,
And dansyd on the downghyll, whyle all thei dey lastyd,
With Magot and Margory and Malyn hur sysstur.
The prest into the place pryce for to wynne;
Kene men of combar comen belyve,
For to mote of mychewhat more then a lytull,
How Reynall and Robyn Hod runnon at the gleyve.[15]

[The hog with his horn-pipe hurried quickly, and danced on the dunghill, while all the day lasted, with Madge and Margery and Malkyn her sister. They pressed into the place to win the prize; keen men of Cumbria came quickly, to discuss various things more than a little, how Reynold and Robin Hood ran for the prize.]

The conclusion of a fifteenth-century satiric carol on women similarly invokes the outlaw's name as representing elusiveness and contrariety:

He that made this songe full good
Came of the north and of the sothern blode
And somewhat kyne to Robyn Hode.[16]

It is probably in this light that we should interpret the obscure use of the expression "Robin Hood in Barnsdale stood" as a legal formula. The phrase is first cited by a judge of the Court of Common Pleas in 1428:

Annuite porte par un Abbe vers un Parson: Et connta qe labbe et ses predecessors avoyent este seisis de x. s. de rent del Eglise de B. a prendre par les mains le person de temps dont il ny ad memory. *Paston*: Le Dean de Pauls come en droit de sa Eglise de Pauls ad este seisi de xl. s. issant de meme leglise et vous avez este seissis de x. s. parcel de meme cele xl. s. de temps etc. Sans ceo qe vous avez este seisis de x. s. en le maner come vous avez suppose par vostre bref etc. Prest etc. *Rolf*: Robin Hood en Barnesdale stode. Sans ceo qe vous avez este seisis etc., car vostre ple est tant a purpos.[17]

[Case of an annuity brought by an Abbot against a Parson: And he stated that the Abbot and his predecessors had held 10s. of rent from the church of B., to take from the hands of the parson since time out of mind. [*Sergeant-at-Law William*] *Paston*: "The dean of Pauls by right of his church has held 40s. coming from the same church and you have held 10s. share of the same 40s. since time etc.; without your having held 10s. in the manner claimed in your writ. Ready [to aver it]." [*?Sergeant-at-Law*] *Rolf*: "Robin Hood in Barnsdale stood; without your having held etc., for your plea is so to the purpose."]

A similar use appears in a case in 1608:

Trespas, for breaking plaintiffs close, &c. *Plea, Liberum tenementum* of sir John Tyndall, and justification as his servant. . . . Adjudged against plaintiff, on the ground of the replication being bad. . . . He should have stated sir Johns seisin . . . which is not done here; *mes tout un come il ust replie* "Robin Whood in Barnwood stood, absque hoc q. def. p. commandement sir John."[18]

The latter case is somewhat clarified by a jurist in the late eighteenth century: "The court said, you might as well say, by way of inducement to a traverse, *Robin Hood in Barnwood stood.*"[19] In both cases, the expression "Robin Hood in Barnsdale stood" is used to imply that that introductory statement to a denial ("inducement to a traverse" in legal parlance) is inadequate or irrelevant. As in the burlesques, Robin Hood represents the *non sequitur*, the paradox, the negation of normal intellectual structures.

The ludic element in the legend was not invariably so chaotic. While play is independent of exterior constraints, it may be structured by internal ludic constraints, often in the form of roles or rules. Such internally constrained play may usefully be termed a game.[20] In fact, a game may be said to reproduce schematically the processes of the exterior world by substituting exterior constraints with artificial constraints of its own. These constraints allow the game to act as a kind of model relative to the exterior world, which may emulate it or explore alternatives. At the same time they actuate dynamic processes within the ludic world, which are among the principal strategies by which the participants are engrossed in the ludic activity.

The Robin Hood tradition makes extensive use of game structures to organize and motivate the ludic world. Explicit game playing in the form of wagers and contests of skill or strength is common within the tradition, and the enunciation of rules is a recurrent theme in many versions.[21] The tradition also involves role-playing, which likewise creates actuating game structures: Robin Hood, in playing the lord of the anti-society, is motivated to engage in activities suitable to a legendary sovereign (receiving guests, demonstration of piety, collection of tolls); in other cases an outlaw may play the role of a potter, butcher, or beggar.

The entire narrative structure follows that of a game. The tales begin in a state of order, but with an element of tension emanating from the opposition of two antagonistic forces. This tension is released as the conflict is enacted, and at the end, order is reestablished with the victory of the protagonists; yet the action is ludic rather than historical, since the situation always returns to the original status quo. The Sheriff, like a chess king, dies repeatedly, but he is always available for a rematch in another tale. The *agon* is played out, but in a world seen from the perspective of the circumscribed ludic space, the entire process is a game, and no actual change is involved.

Game structures are also evident in the Robin Hood games. As the outlaws create games in the greenwood, so the May game celebrants create structures through role-playing and rituals, as in the Westonzoyland games, where the action of confining several citizens in the stocks and requiring them to pay a fine is motivated by Robin's role as ruler of the day; there is even literal game playing in the enactment of archery contests.

This use of the game structure in the Robin Hood tradition fulfills a number of important functions. It is a primary reason for the generative quality of the Robin Hood tradition. As the rules of chess can generate an infinite number of matches, so those of the Robin Hood legend can generate an unlimited number of tales. Also, by creating structure within the ludic space, the game creates order within the chaotic world of the forest, helping to fulfill the basic ordering imperative of culture. Finally, the game structure's tensioned and engrossing character elicits a personal emotional investment on the part of the audience. By involvement in the game, the audience is induced to subscribe to the rules according to which the game is played.

The ludic space of the Robin Hood legend has abundant parallels in other literature of the period. What distinguishes the Robin Hood legend from comparable narrative traditions is that the ludic space occupies the central position, the fixed point at which the tales begin and end, while societal space is marginalized. The same reversal applies in the Robin Hood games: the festive space is centralized, certainly within its own temporal boundaries, and indeed within the life of the celebrants as a whole. Ritual inversion—"the world turned upside down"—is a much-discussed feature of popular culture in this period. In this case, however, we see what might better be described as "the world turned inside out."

The reversed polarity of the Robin Hood tradition relates to a fundamental contradiction within the human experience. In any society there exists an inevitable conflict between the structures of the society, which by nature objectify individuals, and the inherently subjective nature of human perception, will, and action. The objective structure of society perpetuates itself through the transmission of ideological patterns through cultural media. At the same time, it suppresses dangerous forms of subjectivity through sanctions. Subjectivity responds by expressing itself in contexts less subject to sanction. Play fulfills a vital function in this respect, since as a circumscribed activity, it can provide a socially acceptable context for the expression of subjectivity.

The world of Robin Hood, by reversing the usual polarity between the elements listed above, reverses the subject-object relationship in a manner reflecting the inherent subjectivity of the human experience. Within the world of Robin Hood, individuals and behavior normally objectified and marginalized by external social structures are subjectified and centralized. The individual is freed from the objectifying domination of social norms and is actually given power over them. The inhabitants of Robin Hood's world can violate the hierarchical order by adopting social roles other than their own, and can even reverse normal societal relationships; they may steal from the rich or poach the king's deer; they may use violence at will. Normally objectified, marginalized, and dominated, they become central and dominant.

The analogy between the outlaws' world and individual subjectivity is strengthened by the similarities between the forest's occupants and the legend's audience. The protagonists of the tradition are emphatically common men. Robin and his band are yeoman, ordinary people with whom the audience can immediately identify; they are not even particularly remarkable as individuals. This aspect of the legend is especially evident in those ballads where Robin meets a tradesman or craftsman who bests him in combat and is admitted into the band: Robin's adversary in these stories is an obvious figure for the audience. The homologization is strongest of all in the Robin Hood games, where the audience themselves are cast as the inhabitants of Robin's outlaw world.

The fundamental subjectivity of perspective in the Robin Hood tradition is congruent with the individual human experience, but at odds with the ordering imperative of culture, and the centralization of play in Robin Hood's world conflicts with the need for order at its structural center. The use of games creates temporary orders within the ludic space, but to find a more permanent and pervasive order, we must look deeper into the tradition to its ritualistic component.

The ritualism of the Robin Hood tales is manifested in many ways, including their ahistoricity and repetition, unvaried seasonal setting, and the uniform clothing of the outlaws; the ritual element is unmistakable in the Robin Hood games. There are close affinities between play and ritual, as remarked upon by Huizinga;[22] such affinities are also evident in Catherine Bell's definition of ritualization, a dynamic category which she prefers to the static term "ritual":

Ritualization is a way of acting that is designed and orchestrated to distinguish and privilege what is being done in comparison to other, usually more quotidian activities. [23]

The kinship between play and ritual is evident in the word "distinguish." Ritual is a form of play in that it is differentiated from the normal world. The special feature of this form of play is the element of privilege—the ritualized activity is not merely differentiated, but is attributed some particular importance. Bell's account of some of the differentiating strategies used to impart this sense of privilege has obvious resonances in the Robin Hood tradition:

Theoretically, these activities may differentiate themselves by a variety of features; in practice, some general tendencies are obvious. For example, these activities may use a delineated and structured space to which access is restricted; a special periodicity for the occurrence and internal orchestration of the activities; restricted codes of communication to heighten the formality of movement and speech; distinct and specialized personnel; objects, texts, and dress designated for use in these activities alone; verbal and gestural combinations that evoke or purport to be the way things have always been done; . . . and the involvement of a particular constituency not necessarily assembled for any other activities. [24]

The recognition of a ritual dimension in the Robin Hood legend offers a commanding vantage point from which to explore the deeper transactions underlying the tradition. This ritual dimension makes the tradition by definition a privileged form of discourse and suggests that it played a significant part in the lives of the people who transmitted it. At the same time, ritual is an ordering force *par excellence*, and we may reasonably expect that by applying interpretative strategies appropriate to the study of ritual, we may gain insight into the nature of order in the legend. Again, Bell offers a useful framework for understanding the workings of ritual:

Through the production of series of oppositions and the orchestration of these series into dominant and latent schemes, ritualization . . . catches up into itself all the experienced and conventional conflicts and oppositions of social life, juxtaposing and homologizing them into a loose and provisional systematicity. . . . This orchestrated deferral of signification never yields a definitive answer, a final meaning, or a single act—there is no point of arrival but a constant invocation of new terms to continue the validation and coherence of the older terms. [25]

The basic opposition in the Robin Hood tradition is between the ludic space of Robin Hood's world (the forest/outlawry or the festival) and the societal space outside. Each of these poles is overdetermined, comprising a series of homologized oppositions, here divided thematically into two clusters:

(a)
Ludic world/exterior world
Greenwood/outside the greenwood
Outlawry/law
Festival space/quotidian space
Games/laws
Freedom/restriction
Theft and poaching/property laws
Independence of society/societal ties
Disguises and roles/fixed social positions

(b)
Homogeneity/heterogeneity
Social and economic equality/social and economic hierarchy
Yeomanry/social classes
Fellowship/distinctions of rank
Uniform clothing/nonuniform clothing
Uniform standard of living/diverse standards of living
Young men/diverse ages and genders

In the Robin Hood tradition, the first series of oppositions, specifically relevant to the ludic space/societal space polarity, are aligned with a second series relating to uniformity and diversity. The latter bear a suggestive resemblance to the scheme of oppositions between liminality and the status system identified by Victor Turner in his study of rites of passage among various African communities:

Homogeneity/heterogeneity
Communitas/structure
Equality/inequality
Anonymity/systems of nomenclature
Absence of property/property
Absence of status/status
Nakedness or uniform clothing/distinctions of clothing
Sexual continence/sexuality. . .
Absence of rank/distinctions of rank. . .
Suspension of kinship rights and obligations/kinship rights and obligations[26]

In each case, the second element represents the usual social norm, and the first the situation of the initiates during the ritual. Turner explains these contrasts as based on an opposition ·between social hierarchy and a principle he calls "communitas":

It is as though there are here two major "models" for human interrelatedness, juxtaposed and alternating. The first is of a society as a structured, differentiated, and often hierarchical system of politico-legal-economic positions with many types of evaluation, separating men in terms of "more" or "less." The second, which emerges recognizably in the liminal period, is of society as an unstructured or rudimentarily structured and relatively undifferentiated *comitatus*, community, or even communion of equal individuals who submit together to the general authority of the ritual elders.[27]

The Robin Hood tradition agrees with Turner's scheme very closely in the oppositions relating to communitas and hierarchy. In the Robin Hood tradition these oppositions are homologized with those between ludic space and societal space. The analogy between communitas and the freedom of the ludic space is not inherently strong. It is hinted at in Turner's scheme with the inclusion of "suspension of kinship rights and obligations," but the emphasis on the collectivity in communitas would seem at odds with the idea of individual freedom. Here the framework created by the scheme of opposition comes into play: while the first elements under (a) and (b) do not correspond closely, the second elements do, lending an intuitive logic to the homology.

The Robin Hood tradition mediates between the conflicting imperatives of subjectivism and order through the principle of homogeneity. The inhabitants of Robin's world are mutually undifferentiated. In the ballads, they are all outlaws, all young men, all yeomen, all clad in green. In the games, various devices evoke the same idea: people dress alike, wear livery badges, are placed together in the stocks. By this means, the individual is homologized with the group. Individual subjectivities do not create disorder because all subjectivities are one. The order in the Robin Hood tradition is thus fundamentally syncretic, based not on distinction and differentiation, but on unification.

It is in this context that we can best understand the idea of yeomanry as it appears in the legend. Yeomanry is emphatically a communally oriented concept, emphasizing fellowship and equality. As manifested in the Robin Hood legend, it is also an organizing force particularly compatible with the ludic perspective of the tradition. Yeomanry constitutes a set of conventions established within the ludic space to guide the actions of its inhabitants. It contrasts significantly with the laws operating outside the ludic space: where laws are imposed from above and enforced externally, the values represented by yeomanry are more analogous to the rules of a game, existing internally and enforced by common consent of the participants. Its ludic quality is highlighted by the actual game playing it often involves in the form of contests of physical strength and skill.

This understanding of the inner workings of the tradition offers a position from which to assess its interactions with contemporary social orders. One of the foremost controversies in the study of popular culture in this period has been whether ritualized contraventions of social norms ultimately constitute agents of order or of disorder. The debate has a very long pedigree. A critique of the Feast of Fools drafted by the Faculty of Theology at Paris in 1444 summarized the position of its defenders as follows:

Nos ita joco et non serio facimus, sicut consuetum est ab antiquo, ut fatuitas nobis innata semel in anno effluat et evaporetur. Nonne utres et dolia vini sæpius rumperentur, si spiraculum ipsorum interdum non laxaretur? Nos quidem utres veteres sumus et dolia semirupta.[28]

[We do these things in jest and not seriously, as is the ancient custom, so that our innate foolishness may once a year flow out and evaporate. Do not wineskins and barrels very often burst, if their tap is not occasionally loosened? We are indeed old wineskins and bursting barrels.]

The Duke of Newcastle, advising Charles II to foster traditional pastimes, similarly stressed their contribution to the social order:

Maye games, Moris Danses, the Lords off the Maye, & Ladye off the Maye, the foole— & the Hobye Horse muste nott bee forgotten. —Also the whitson Lorde & Ladye. . . . The devirtismentes will amuse the peoples thaughts, & keepe them In harmles action, which will free your Majestie frome faction & Rebellion.[29]

Many modern scholars have also concluded that ritual disorder reinforces the social order. Some, like the contemporaries cited above, see them as providing a distraction or safety valve.[30] Others have argued that the inversion of hierarchy reaffirms the hierarchical principle itself.[31] Turner suggests that communitas and hierarchy must exist in a certain state of balance, and that rituals of communitas exist specifically for the purpose of creating this equilibrium.[32] In contrast are the views of those who find in ritual disorder some form of genuine challenge to the principle of hierarchy.[33]

Here the distinction between the official order and the popular order comes into play. The spirit of communitas evoked in the tradition may have promoted the interests of the hierarchy in many respects, yet it was not ultimately oriented toward those interests. It was a means by which the popular social order was made functional—for any society whose culture does not create some viable form of social order cannot survive—and it must principally be understood in relation to the needs of that order.

Communitas was a crucial feature of the social life of the commons in premodern England—it is no coincidence that "commons" and "communitas" derive from the same etymological root. The members of traditional communities, whether rural villages or urban boroughs, operated in a milieu that was predicated on a strong sense of communal identity, consistently emphasizing the interests of the collectivity over those of the individual. This sense of community was not only a major feature of the commons' mental world, but an essential element in the socioeconomic system: open-field agriculture in particular required an intimate degree of communal co-operation, and even industry and commerce were highly communalized activities compared to their modern counterparts. The collective identity and functioning of Robin's outlaw band provided a model for similar structures in real life; in fact, it imbued such structures with meaning by providing a mythological correlative, while the Robin Hood games enacted this myth in tangible ritual form.

The Robin Hood tradition may even claim to be the definitive social myth of the premodern commoner. It centralizes and privileges the world of the yeomanry. It expresses a coherent and comprehensive cultural vision, based on the principle of communitas and expressed in the language of yeomanry, with its attendant symbologies. In doing so, it imparts meaning to the commoner's world, providing an extensive network of terms to validate the popular social order. We have already seen the similarities between the Arthurian and Robin Hood traditions: there is every reason to suppose that Robin Hood played a similar role in constructing the identity of the commons as Arthur did for the aristocracy.

The actual interpretation of the world of the ballads into the values and practices of the audience was doubtless complex. Catherine Bell observes that the success of ritualized activities often lies in their amenability to divergent interpretation:

Ritualized activities specifically do *not* promote belief or conviction. On the contrary, ritualized practices afford a great diversity of interpretation in exchange for little more than consent to the form of the activities.[34]

Yet perhaps Bell overstates her case. While ritualized activities may allow some interpretational latitude, they must play some part in shaping human beliefs. If culture were unable to create at least some measure of shared values in a society, social life would hardly be possible. Indeed, Bell's argument presupposes a greater division between symbol and belief than is necessarily the case. Even in the modern world, people will often entertain a passionate conviction rooted entirely in symbolism. This was even more true in the context of premodern society, where ideology manifests itself principally in symbological form, and where cultural values are not ultimately separable from the symbologies by which they are expressed. Specific connections between cultural phenomena and social practices are difficult to prove conclusively, but the demonstrable correspondences between the social vision of the Robin Hood legend and the social life of its transmitters suggest that a genuine interrelation existed between them.

The Robin Hood tradition was in some respects particularly well equipped to serve as a normative force in ordering the world of the premodern commons. Through the game structure of the tradition, the audience is impelled to subscribe to the values of communitas within the context of the game; through the ritualistic and repetitive nature of the tradition, these values could become structuring principles in the audience's mental world. Perhaps even more important, by associating the values of communitas with the subjectivity of the individual, the tradition endows the former with an enormous base of power, linking it to the matrix from which all action ultimately issues. Of course, many other forces were at work in shaping popular values and practices, and we should not overestimate the significance of Robin Hood within this intricate sociocultural web, yet among the cultural traditions of the premodern commons, the Robin Hood legend must have been one of the most significant.

Although the Robin Hood tradition helped to foster order in the traditional communities of its audience, it was not necessarily the same sort of order that might have been envisioned by the official hierarchy or by a modern interpreter of the legend. Modern culture, like official culture in the premodern period, characteristically seeks to reject, suppress, or marginalize contradictions to its own order. Ludic activities, disorderly by nature in that they are free of the constraints of the objective order, are pushed toward the fringe of the cultural world, to leisure activities, to childhood. By contrast, premodern popular culture sought to incorporate rather than discriminate, protecting itself from disorderly elements by integrating them into its cultural network. Overall, this was an ordering process, but where modern order is abstract, discriminatory, and subordinative, premodern order was organic, syncretic, and coordinative.

The process is illustrated in Clifford Geertz's classic analysis of the traditional Balinese practice of cockfighting. Geertz begins with a fundamental paradox. Balinese culture, he says, emphasizes civility and gentleness, and deplores conflict and violence; among the Balinese bestial or animalistic behavior is considered profoundly shameful. At the same time, one of their foremost public entertainments is cockfighting, in which the forces they most eschew are vividly enacted. In Geertz's view, these two contraries are directly related: he argues that the Balinese use the ritual of the cockfight as a means of finding a place in their culture for these universal but potentially destructive forces, without actually putting their society at risk. As Geertz suggests, play can serve as a means by which people may not only incorporate potent, chaotic, even destructive elemental forces into their world, but also harness them and imbue them with meaning in their cultural order.[35]

It is precisely this process that can be seen at work in the premodern Robin Hood tradition. Within the context of Robin Hood's ludic space, the usual connections between things are loosened, allowing new associations to be made. Universal but dangerous forces such as interpersonal violence and subjective rejection of the objective order can become agents of social harmony. Robin fights with a tinker or peddlar or potter, and Robert Woolfall as Robin Hood imprisons his father the vicar in the stocks. Both violate the constraints of the objective order, yet in doing so they create a sense of communitas vital to the operation of premodern society. By incorporating these forces, premodern culture creates a structure at once profoundly dynamic and yet generally stable. A comparison may be drawn between the Robin Hood tradition and the youth groups that were a common feature of traditional European communities—a phenomenon strongly reminiscent of Robin Hood's outlaw band, as we have seen. Natalie Davis has characterized these youth groups as the "raucous voice" of the "conscience of the community."[36] Such groups harnessed the potentially disruptive energies of the young males of a community, incorporating them as useful contributors to the social order. In like manner, the Robin Hood tradition harnessed potentially destructive energies—lawlessness, disorder, violence—in ways that made them contributors to the popular social order.

The harness was not necessarily perfect. By choosing to harness these energies, rather than suppress them, premodern society always left open the possibility of their breaking out and becoming genuinely destructive. Geertz notes that during the Djakarta Putsch of 1965, some of the most intense violence occurred on Bali, and speculates that the tradition of the cockfight may have had something to do with it; youth groups were notorious for their propensity to get out of hand; and as we shall see, Robin Hood could also furnish an opportunity for disorder and lawlessness.

The relationship between the ethos of the Robin Hood tradition and the hierarchical order was multivalent. In times of social peace, its promotion of communitas helped keep communities socially and economically viable, a great boon to those who profited from them. In some respects the legend even legitimized the hierarchy by allowing it a place within its mythic framework, as in the roles played by the king and knight in the *Gest*. But this acceptance may not have been true acquiescence so much as a kind of cultural *realpolitik* by which popular culture dealt with the reality of the existing power structure. The degree of acceptance of the hierarchy was not necessarily very deep, as manifested by Robin's willingness to despoil the knight or abandon the king in the *Gest*. In times of social unrest, the values expressed in the Robin Hood legend could prove a means by which the commons judged the conduct of their social superiors, and the legend itself offered a model for concerted resistance, even organized violence.

The privileged classes for their part were correspondingly ambivalent in their attitude toward the ethos of the legend. To some degree they were themselves participants in popular culture, and as such shared in popular values. Official culture, however, was generally hostile to disorder in any form, and as we have seen in Chapter 3, this attitude increasingly came to determine the privileged classes' response to Robin Hood. Numerous contemporary allusions to the legend represent Robin Hood as an archetype of overt lawlessness, often in tones of contempt suggestive of latent fear. The seventeenth-century jurist Sir Edward Coke saw a direct conceptual relationship between Robin Hood and real-life robbers: "This Robin Hood . . . hath raised a name to these kind of men called Roberdesmen, his followers."[37] At the beginning of the eighteenth century Alexander Smith numbered Robin Hood among his "Most Notorious Highwaymen":

This bold robber, Robin Hood, was, some write, descended of the noble family of the earls of Huntingdon, but that is only fiction, for his birth was but very obscure, his pedigree ab origine being no higher than from poor shepherdes . . . being of a very licentious, wicked inclination, he . . . [associated himself] with several robers and outlaws.[38]

One of the earliest references to the outlaw is as the type of the lawless marauder. In 1439, when a certain John Forman was arrested in Derbyshire, a gentleman named Piers Venables assembled an armed band and forcibly released Forman from the authorities, thereafter repairing to the woods with his followers, "in manere of Insurrection . . . like as it hade be Robynhode and his meyne," as the complainants described it to Parliament; "and so they kepyn the Wodes and strange Contreays: and . . . ryde and gone as outelaws, waityng a tyme to murder, sclee, and other grete harmes in that contray do."[39] In 1612 fifteen Forest of Dean miners, angered by a monopoly on mining and firewood granted to the Earl of Pembroke in violation of their customary privileges, burned wood that had been gathered by his servants; the Earl of Northhampton characterized the rioters as "Robin Hoods" who ought to be apprehended by the local magistrates.[40]

In such cases, the term is used of people involved in very localized forms of disorder or resistance, but elsewhere it is applied to the most serious forms of treasonable rebellion. In November 1605, Robert Cecil wrote regarding the gentry who had been involved in the recent Gunpowder Plot:

Those Persons . . . have gathered themselves to a head of some fourscore or a hundred Horse, with purpose (as we conceave) to pass over Seas. . . . It is also thought fit that some Martial Men should presently repair down to those Countries where the Robin Hoods are assembled, to encourage the good and to terrifie the bad. [41]

Sir Walter Ralegh, during his trial in 1603, associated Robin with England's most notorious rebels: "Is it not strange for me to make myself Robin Hood, a Kett, or a Cade?"[42] English officials concerned with the Irish disturbances of the late sixteenth and early seventeenth centuries use the term so frequently that it seems to have been a buzzword among the authorities in Dublin and London, as when the council in Ireland discussed an uprising against some of the loyalist settlers (termed Undertakers) in 1597:

Sundry loose persons, as some of the McShees, the Lord Roche's base sons, and others, became Robin Hoods, and slew some of the Undertakers, dwelling scattered in thatched houses and remote places near to woods and fastnesses. [43]

The connection between the Robin Hood tradition and popular unruliness is most explicit in the Robin Hood games, which on several occasions afforded an opportunity to enact the legend's violent element. In 1498 a case was brought before Star Chamber as a result of an incident involving a Robin Hood game. According to the plaintiffs, certain residents of Wednesbury and Dudley in Staffordshire had been imprisoned in Walsall on charges of assault stemming from an incident during the week before Trinity Sunday. That Sunday, William Milner of Wolverhampton and Robert Marshal of Wednesbury attended Willenhall Fair in the guise of "the abbot of Marram" and "Robyn Hood," with followings said to be sixty and a hundred men respectively, "in harness after the manner of war," and "riotously assembled themselves, commanding openly that if any of the town of Walsall came therefrom, to strike them down." Not surprisingly, Marshal offered rather a different interpretation of the proceedings, describing his Robin Hood as a traditional custom used for the benefit of the local churches and protesting that he and his followers "made as gud chere unto them as they shuld do to ther lovying neyburs."[44] The exact events in Willenhall in 1498 must remain something of a mystery, but it seems at the very least that Marshal made use of the Robin Hood games as a framework within which to apply pressure on his opponents.

A similar connection between Robin Hood plays and lawless behavior seems to be implied in Fabyan's reference in 1502 to the capture of a malefactor "which had renewed many of Robin Hood's pageants, which named himself

Greenleaf." David Wiles has drawn attention to a number of minor examples of
damage to or loss of property connected with the Robin Hood games; indeed
some degree of unruliness must inevitably have arisen in an activity which
involved young bachelors, weaponry, combat, and the consumption of alcohol.[45]
We have already seen that the Exeter city council in 1509–10 felt it necessary to
forbid the youth of the city from engaging in Robin Hood games except in the
context of the official parish holiday; the Lord Warden of the Cinque Ports in
1528 ordered the mayors of the towns under his jurisdiction to prohibit Robin
Hood games "or other such like plays whereby that any great assembly of the
king's people should be made"; and in Lancashire in 1579 there were "sturres att
Brunley, aboute Robyn hoode and the May games" considered serious enough
to justify suppression of the games.

The most violent scenes in the history of the Robin Hood games come from
Edinburgh after the parliamentary ban of 1555. In April 1561 the provost and
baillies in Edinburgh had wind of imminent plans among "the prentissis and
servandis of merchanttis and craftismen and utheris within this burgh" to "mak
convocatioun and assemblie efter the auld wikit maner of Robene Hude," and
issued a proclamation "dischargeing all sic conventionis . . . and of all bering of
armour, wappinnis, striking of suesche ['drum'], sounding of trumpet, bering of
baner, standert, or anseyne ['ensign'] or lyke instrument, for sic vane
besynes."[46] The would-be revelers disregarded the authorities and not only
chose one George Durye to be their Robin Hood, but assembled with "ane
displayit handsenȝe, halbrownis, jakkis, culveringis, morriounis, twa handit
swerdis, cotis of malȝe ['mail'], and utheris wapynnis invasive" and marched
into the city. The disturbances lasted for weeks. According to John Knox, on
one occasion the city authorities confiscated some of the rioters' weapons and a
banner,

quhilk wes occasioun that thay that same nycht maid a mutinye, keippit the portis of the
towne, and intendit to have persewit some men within thair awin housses; bot that, upoun
the restitutioun of thair swerdis and enseynȝe, wes stayit. Bot yit thay ceassit nott to
molest, alsweill the inhabitantes of Edinburgh as diverse countrey men, taking frome
thame money, and threitnyng some with farder injureis.

The provost and baillies of Edinburgh, determined to make an example,
arrested a cordwainer's servant named James Killone on charges of robbery
committed during the rioting, and condemned him to hang. The leaders of the
crafts pleaded unsuccessfully with the authorities and with John Knox on
Killone's behalf, warning of dire consequences should the sentence be pursued.
Their predictions proved correct. On July 21 a riot broke out, apparently led by
the apprentices and servants of the craftsmen. The rioters destroyed the gibbet,
broke into the Tolbooth, and released Killone and the other prisoners there.
While they were trying unsuccessfully to leave the town at the lower gate, the
city authorities took refuge in the Tolbooth. As the rioters passed back up the

street, one of those in the Tolbooth fired a pistol at them, wounding one of the rioters. The angered crowd besieged the Tolbooth for several hours. The leaders of the crafts were called upon to assist the authorities, but declined; according to Knox, their response to the provost and baillies was "Thai will be Magistratis allone, latt thame reule the multitude allone." Only at nine that evening, after the intervention of the Constable of Edinburgh Castle and a promise from the city authorities not to punish the rioters, was the tumult brought to an end.[47]

The events in Edinburgh illustrate the intimate relationship between ritual and riot in the Robin Hood tradition. Even a peaceful enactment of the games might incorporate a latent element of riot, especially when they involved a significant number of armed participants, as often seems to have been the case. In Edinburgh, as in Willenhall, the games offered a context for the use of violence, whether explicit or implicit. In both cases the violence was not aimless, but a response to a political situation: as Robert Marshal's Robin Hood game was directed against the town authorities in Walsall, so in Edinburgh the games are aimed at the civic administration—not only by the rioters themselves, but by the leaders of the crafts who appear to be tacitly backing the disturbances.

It may even be argued that the use of violence is one of the most important cultural elements in the Robin Hood tradition as a whole. The violent spirit of some of the early Robin Hood ballads has often troubled scholars, but the violence in the Robin Hood tales reflects the real world of English commoners. The casual slaughter of the courier-monk and his boy in *Robin Hood and the Monk* is very much in keeping with the violence inflicted by the mobs of 1381, and historians have come to recognize that even in the absence of major national disturbances, localized violence for social or political purposes was endemic in the medieval and early modern age.[48] Violence could be an integral part of even a merry occasion: according to a popular phrase of the seventeenth century, "Tis no festival unless there be some fightings."[49]

Whether express or intimated, violence is an integral part of the social process. Violence as used by the official social order is readily recognized as ordered, whether exercised through judicial or military structures. Popular violence, as viewed from the perspective of the official order, appears chaotic, but historians in recent decades have shown that popular violence had an order of its own, dictating appropriate targets, punishments, and forms.[50] As a ritualistic myth incorporating a prominent element of violence, the Robin Hood legend was one of the means by which the commons transmitted their attitudes to violence and specifically to the acceptable contexts and means for its use. Significantly, Robin Hood's sole statement of purpose in the *Gest* focuses as much on the use of violence as on theft.

Aside from incidents stemming from the games, Robin Hood seems to have informed popular violence from behind the scenes, but in a few cases he was actively invoked. A band of yeomen and laborers blocked a road in Southacre, Norfolk, in 1441, waylaying travelers and threatening to murder Sir Robert Harsyk, and singing "We arn Robynhodesmen, war, war, war."[51] At

Whitestaunton in 1659, a reveller assaulted a watchman, identifying himself as Robin Hood before being hauled off to the authorities.[52] Robin might also stand as an emblem of violent resistance for people too powerless to enact it. The play of Robin Hood and the Sheriff in Brandsby in 1615 was performed by Catholics: the outlaw's resistance to civil authorities would have been especially signficant to this minority during the decade of severe governmental persecution that followed the Gunpowder Plot of 1605.

As an icon for resistance to authority, Robin Hood could take on a political significance beyond the localized examples mentioned so far. In 1469, the leaders of anti-Yorkist riots took the names Robin of Redesdale and Robin of Holderness; the rebel Sir Robert Umfreville called himself Robert Mendmarket.[53] The choice of names in these cases strongly suggests the influence of the Robin Hood legend; in others, Robin's own name was used. The leaders of Jack Cade's Kentish rebels in January 1450 adopted a variety of nicknames, including "King of the Fairies," "Queen of the Fairies," "the Hermit Blewbeard," and "Robin Hood."[54] In 1640, when Charles I reluctantly decided to reconvene Parliament after eleven years of autocratic rule, opponents of royal policy in Somerset formed a political grouping of Puritan and populist tendencies called the "Robins," whose candidate was to be "Robin Hood."[55] This choice of name not only associated this faction with popular values: it implicitly conveyed a belligerent spirit and intimated a willingness to defend those values by violent action if necessary.

From protesting abuses within the hierarchical framework it was not so great a step to challenging the terms of the framework itself. Robin Hood played a particularly important role in such challenges, precisely because of his marginality. Direct challenges to the official hierarchy were violently suppressed, so that resistance could only survive if it found a protected position from which to operate. Robin Hood's fictional ludic space was ideally suited to such purposes. At the most basic level, Robin could serve as an icon of willful rejection of the external order. We have already seen how in literary contexts the very name of Robin Hood was sometimes used to conjure absurdity. This absurdity sometimes had serious political undertones. A joke in *A Hundred Merry Tales*, printed in 1526, counterposes Robin Hood against official cultural norms:

A yong man of the age of xx yere, rude & unlernyd, in the time of Lent cam to his curat to be confessyd; whiche when he was of his lyfe serched & examyned coude not say his Pater noster. . . . His confessour . . . injoyned hym in penaunce to fast every fryday brede & water tyll he had his Pater noster well & suffycyently lerned. This yonge man mekely acceptyng his penaunce so departed & came home to one of his companyons & sayd to his felow, "so it is, that my gostly fader hath gyven me in penaunce to fast every fryday brede & water tyll I can say my Pater noster, therfore I pray ye teche me my Pater noster; & by my trouth I shall therfore teche the a songe of Robyn hode that shall be worth xx of it."[56]

Underneath this frivolous tale runs a real undercurrent of negation of the official cultural order: the invocation of Robin Hood deconstructs the textual hierarchy in its implication that the Paternoster is just another text, not fundamentally different from a song of Robin Hood. Such use of the legend was not restricted to fictional contexts. Thomas Randolph, the English ambassador to Mary Queen of Scots, reported to Queen Elizabeth in 1564 that "one of the Queen's chappel, a singing man, said that he believed as well a tale of Robin Hood as any word is written in the Old Testament or New."[57] The hierarchy did not take such use of the legend lightly. In 1532 a certain William Umpton, a groom of the king's hall, having been in prison a year and two months, wrote from the Tower to seek the intercession of Thomas Cromwell. Umpton explained that his situation was the result of an argument with a pardoner of St. Thomas hospital at Woodstock. The pardoner had said that St. Thomas of Canterbury died "for fifty-two points concerning the commonwealth," "which fifty-two your said orator denied, one excepted for the clergy, and that the same fifty-two points were a dance called Robin Hood." The pardoner had asked Umpton if he would compare Robin Hood with St. Thomas before the bishop of Lincoln, and Umpton in turn asked the pardoner why St. Thomas was a saint rather than Robin Hood—for which he was accused of heresy.[58]

As well as highlighting the arbitrariness of the hierarchical order, the legend embodied values and a vision that offered genuine alternatives. The outlaws' society is no mere carnivalesque parody, but a credible alternative to the official hierarchy. Real outlaws did form bands comparable to Robin's, and even law-abiding commoners enacted comparable social structures, both annually in the context of May festivals, and continually through the groupings of young bachelors in the country and journeymen and apprentices in the towns.

The specific political structure favored by the outlaws is especially significant. Although they occasionally use the conventions of feudalism, the structure of their society is not feudal. There is no intermediary between Robin, as its head, and his "subjects," and indeed their loyalty to him is contingent on his behavior toward them. These principles extend to the outlaws' interactions with King Edward. They deal with the king immediately and personally, indeed rather familiarly, and are loyal to him only as long as it suits them. As P. R. Coss has observed, the political vision of Robin Hood's world resembles that of the rebels of 1381, who proposed a commonwealth in which all Englishmen would be equal under the king.[59] The familiarity with which the outlaws deal with the monarch also savors of the Peasants' Revolt.[60] Like the rebels, the outlaws would make their monarch one of themselves. As the rebellion sheds light on the legend, so the legend may illuminate the rebellion: we may wonder whether the loyalty of the peasantry to the king in 1381 was as superficial as that of Robin Hood to his monarch.

One should not overestimate the radicalism implied in the early Robin Hood tradition. Mythic and ritualistic modes of thought operate through symbols taken directly from the cultural environment, and such symbols are so closely implicated with the status quo that they allow relatively little play with which to establish a differentiated point of perspective. Abstract modes of perception operate at the level of the concept, at one more remove from the status quo; they too are tied to the cultural order, but the extra degree of displacement accords them that much more play. The kind of radicalism possible within a premodern mode of thought is therefore quite limited relative to modern radicalism; yet within the restrictions imposed by the concretist character of premodern popular culture, the Robin Hood tradition offered an ethos and vocabulary for popular alternatives to the official hierarchy.

TRANSFORMATIONS

The processes of change in the legend in the sixteenth and seventeenth centuries inevitably brought about changes in the network of significances it embodied. These changes affected the legend diversely: some were fully successful, some had very little effect, some were largely complete by 1700, while others were only potentialities waiting for later cultural circumstances to be suitable to exploit them. Overall, the legend underwent a fragmentation of its traditional meanings, although its enduring success is a clear sign that some key structures remained viable.

Some aspects of the legend remained largely impervious to historical change, the most important of which was the basic opposition between ludic and societal space. Although outlawry and the forest were less familiar as realities in the world of the audience, we have already seen in this chapter that the concept of outlawry and the greenwood was more important than the historical reality; indeed the nonsocietal space may have served its structural purpose even better once the audience was less likely to associate it with specific social realities.

The structural centrality of the nonsocietal space also proved surprisingly unaffected by the assimilation of the legend toward a biographic pattern. With Robin's outlaw life in the greenwood framed by his life in the outside world, the ludic space might have been displaced from its central position, yet this displacement never truly penetrated the structural level. In the legend as a whole the biographic frame remained marginal to the episodic bulk of the story; even in biographized versions of the legend, the Earl of Huntingdon was overshadowed by Robin Hood. In the end, the ludic perspective was so deeply encoded into the legend that it was simply impossible to dislodge it. The centrality of Robin's outlaw status and inhabitation of the forest was embodied in his relationship to the Sheriff and to his own followers, in the image of the longbow and the concept of yeomanry, even in the very names of Robin Hood and Sherwood. The biographizing elements were by comparison thin and lacking in resonance—their weakness remains apparent in the legend today, for there is still no authoritative version of the outlaw's origin and fate. The enduring subjective and ludic perspective of the tradition meant that Robin never wholly lost his old power as an icon for defiant rejection of the imposed objective order, as demonstrated by the convicted murderer William Alcock in 1733: Alcock refused all prayers, and instead "on his way to the gallows he sang part of an old song of Robin Hood, with the chorus, Derry, derry, down."[61]

Other aspects of the tradition were affected profoundly. During the period of transition, the legend was alienated from its audience, both as the world it represented became more remote and as the modes of transmission were displaced from the public to the commercial sphere. The audience no longer interacted with the legend with the same immediacy, whether as consumers or producers, and Robin Hood could no longer carry the same sort of sociopolitical significance he had enjoyed in the early period. This diminishment of social relevance is particularly evident in the domains of community and violence. For the modern audience, Robin Hood and his band were becoming alien figures, whose sense of fellowship could only be distantly experienced. Indeed the very concept of communitas itself was losing much of its meaning with the fragmentation of the older communal social structures, while the legend's own sense of fellowship was beginning to show signs of strain with the introduction of elements of class and gender into the outlaw band. Likewise, the relevance of the legend's violent element was attenuated as the world of Robin Hood lost its resemblance to that of the audience. This change was emblematized by the demise of the bow as a feature of English life, although at least some measure of familiarity must have lingered as long as the sword and quarterstaff remained in use. By extension, the very principle of Robin Hood's resistance to the official hierarchy had less obvious relevance as the modern parties to this perennial conflict became increasingly unlike the adversaries in the legend.

While the distancing of the legend from the contemporary world was dismantling some of the legend's old meanings, it also brought the possibility of new avenues of signification. We have already seen that the early Robin Hood legend, as a mythic and ritualistic phenomenon drawing its symbologies from the real world of the audience, was itself necessarily bound up with the status quo. Only the uncoupling of the legend from the contemporary world could allow it enough distance to offer a point of perspective for social observation and comment. It is no coincidence that the next major new interpretation of the legend was that of Joseph Ritson, a man who combined an antiquarian interest in the past with a radical political perspective on the present. It may also be significant that Ritson produced his work on Robin Hood precisely at a time when English radicalism was on the decline in reaction to the excesses of revolutionary France. Once Robin was removed to a distant and unthreatening past, his legend could be used as a medium in which to win a hearing for radical perspectives in an environment hostile to radicalism—as a number of blacklisted authors who wrote for the 1950s Robin Hood television series might attest.[62] In the long run, this medieval legend could never retain the social immediacy it had enjoyed in the early centuries of its history; but what has been lost in political relevance has been recouped in mythic and ethical significance.

Indeed, Robin Hood has worn remarkably well over the years. The reasons for his long-term success are the same that ensured him so prominent a place in medieval popular culture and allowed him to weather the cultural turbulence of the sixteenth and seventeenth centuries. Among these, the hero's name has already been mentioned. As the twentieth-century media experience has shown, it can be much easier to gain and keep celebrity status if one has the right name, and Robin Hood is particularly blessed with a name at once elemental and evocative—much the same might also be said of Maid Marian, Little John, Friar Tuck, the Sheriff of Nottingham, and Sherwood itself. The names of Robin Hood and Sherwood are particularly important, since they are tied up with Robin's permanence as a forest-dwelling outlaw, a highly distinctive feature of the legend that has been crucial to its enduring vitality. The forest world of the outlaws as a ludic space stands as a permanent locus for human subjectivity, addressing a constant of human experience. At the same time, it has allowed the legend to survive over time by two Darwinian principles that apply to literature as well as species: propagation and adaptation. The ludic format of the legend is infinitely generative, allowing the creation of any number of episodic tales from the matrix of the basic scenario. Moreover, because the tales happen in a ludic space, the structures by which it is organized can change to meet the needs of the audience by altering the rules of the game. This adaptive capacity in the Robin Hood legend has been demonstrated in recent decades with the enhanced role accorded to Maid Marian in response to changing gender relations, and the introduction of non-European characters into Robin Hood's band to reflect the multicultural realities of the modern world. To survive as an outlaw, one must be elusive and versatile: after more than seven hundred years of evading authority, Robin Hood has learned these lessons well, and there is every reason to believe that he will continue lurking in the forests of our cultural world for generations to come.

NOTES

1. John Heywood, *John Heywood's* A Dialogue of Proverbs, ed. Rudolph E. Habenicht (Berkeley and Los Angeles: California University Publications, 1963), 172 (l. 2514); cf. Morris Palmer Tilley, *A Dictionary of the Proverbs in England in the Sixteenth and Seventeenth Centuries* (Ann Arbor: University of Michigan Press, 1950), T53.

2. William Robertson, *Phraseologia Generalis, or a full large and general phrase book* (Cambridge: John Hayes, 1681), 1258.

3. Sir Bulstrode Whitlocke, *Memorials of the English Affairs* (London: Nathaniel Ponder, 1682), 110.

4. Maurice Keen, *The Outlaws of Medieval Legend* (Toronto: University of Toronto Press, 1961), 145; cf. 159.

5. Maurice Keen, "Robin Hood, a Peasant Hero," *History Today* 8 (1958), 689; cf. Maurice Keen, "Robin Hood—Peasant or Gentleman?" *Past and Present* 19 (1961), 14.

6. E. B. Hobsbawm, *Social Bandits and Primitive Rebels* (Glencoe, Ill.: Free Press, 1959), 4, 13; Rodney H. Hilton, *The English Rising of 1381* (London: Lawrence and Wishart, 1950), 89, 76.

7. See the Introduction for the history of Robin Hood scholarship.

8. T. H. Aston, "Robin Hood. Communication," *Past and Present* 20 (1962), 7; Bernard Capp, "Popular Literature," in Barry Reay, ed. *Popular Culture in Seventeenth-Century England* (New York: St. Martin's Press, 1985), 211.

9. Clifford Geertz, *The Interpretation of Cultures* (New York: Basic Books, 1973), 89.

10. Cf. Claude Lévi-Strauss, *The Savage Mind* (Chicago: University of Chicago Press, 1966), 16–21.

11. Cf. David Underdown, *Revel, Riot, and Rebellion. Popular Politics and Culture in England 1603–1660* (Oxford: Clarendon Press, 1985), 34.

12. On historical outlawry, see John Bellamy, *Crime and Public Order in the Later Middle Ages* (London: Routledge and Kegan Paul, 1973), 105–6.

13. For definitions of play, cf. J. Huizinga, *Homo Ludens. A Study of the Play-Element in Culture* (Boston: Beacon Press, 1955), 13; R. Rawdon Wilson, *In Palamedes' Shadow. Explorations in Play, Game, & Narrative Theory* (Boston: Northeastern University Press, 1990), 66.

14. T. Wright and J. O. Halliwell-Phillips, *Reliquiae Antiquae* (London: J. R. Smith, 1845), 1.85. For another example see 1.81.

15. Wright and Halliwell-Phillips, *Reliquiae Antiquae*, 1.84.

16. R. L. Greene, *Early English Carols*, 2nd ed. (Oxford: Clarendon Press, 1977), #401B st. 7.

17. W. C. Bolland, *A Manual of Year Book Studies* (Cambridge: Cambridge University Press, 1925), 107. Rolf was a sergeant-at-law in 1425 [100], but his status in these proceedings cannot be determined from the published text.

18. Joseph Ritson, *Robin Hood* (London: T. Egerton, 1795), 1.lxxx.

19. *Ibid.*, 1.lxxx.

20. Cf. Wilson, *In Palamedes' Shadow*, 76 ff.

21. Cf. the *Gest* st. 11 ff.; Anthony Munday, *The Downfall of Robert Earl of Huntington*, 1330 ff., in *The Huntingdon Plays* (New York and London: Garland, 1980).

22. Huizinga, *Homo Ludens*, 5 ff.

23. Catherine Bell, *Ritual Theory, Ritual Practice* (New York and Oxford: Oxford University Press, 1992), 74.

24. *Ibid.*, 204–5.

25. *Ibid.*, 105–6.

26. Victor Turner, *The Ritual Process. Structure and Anti-Structure* (Chicago: Aldine Publishing Company, 1969), 106.

27. *Ibid.*, 96.

28. J.-P. Migne, ed., *Petri Blesensis … Opera Omnia*, Patrilogia Latina 207 (Paris: Garnier, 1904), 1.1171.

29. Sandford Strong, ed., *A Catalogue of Letters and Other Historical Documents Exhibited in the Library at Welbeck* (London: John Murray, 1903), 227.

30. Cf. Keith Thomas, "Work and Leisure in Pre-Industrial Society," *Past and Present* 29 (1964), 53–54.

31. Max Gluckman, *Custom and Conflict in Africa* (Glencoe, Ill.: Free Press, 1956), ch. 5.

32. Turner, *The Ritual Process*, 178.

33. The most famous example is Mikhail Bakhtin, *Rabelais and his World*, transl. Helene Izwolsky (Cambridge, Mass.: Massachusetts Institute of Technology Press, 1968).

34. Bell, *Ritual Theory*, 186.

35. Geertz, *The Interpretation of Cultures*, 412-53. On paradoxicality in the medieval popular mentality, see also Aron Gurevich, *Medieval Popular Culture: Problems of Belief and Perception*, transl. János M. Bak and Paul A. Hollingsworth (Cambridge: Cambridge University Press, 1988), 176.

36. Natalie Davis, *Society and Culture in Early Modern France* (Stanford: Stanford University Press, 1965), 108.

37. Sir Edward Coke, *The First Part of the Institutes ... or a comentarie upon Littleton* (London: Company of Stationers, 1648), 3.197.

38. Alexander Smith, *A Compleat History of the Lives and Robberies of the Most Notorious Highwaymen*, 5th ed. (London: S. Briscoe, 1719–20), 3.23–31.

39. *Rotuli Parliamentorum* (London: n.p., 1767–77), 5.16.

40. Roger B. Manning, *Village Revolts* (Oxford: Oxford University Press, 1988), 275–76.

41. Sir Ralph Winwood, *Memorials of Affairs of State* (London: T. Ward, 1725) 2.172–73.

42. Thomas Bayly Howell, *Cobbett's Complete Collection of State Trials* (London: R. Bagshaw, 1809), 2.11.

43. *Calendar of the Carew Manuscripts*, ed. J. S. Brewer and William Bullen (London: Longmans, Green and Co., 1869), 3.273. For other examples, see *Calendar of the State Papers Relating to Ireland of the Reign of Elizabeth 1596, July–1597, December*, ed. Ernest George Atkinson (London: HMSO, 1893), 124, 130, 232, 300, 302, 313, 474; *Calendar of the State Papers Relating to Ireland of the Reign of Elizabeth 1598, January–1599, March*, ed. Ernest George Atkinson (London: HMSO, 1895), 255, 373; *Calendar of the State Papers Relating to Ireland of the Reign of Elizabeth 1599, April–1600, February*, ed. Ernest George Atkinson (London: HMSO, 1899), 52; *Calendar of the State Papers Relating to Ireland of the Reign of Elizabeth 1600, March–October*, ed. Ernest George Atkinson (London: HMSO, 1903), 263, 390; *Calendar of the State Papers Relating to Ireland of the Reign of James I 1603–6*, ed. C. W. Russell and John P. Prendergast (London: Longman and Co., 1872), 342. Fynes Moryson similarly applies the name to Hugh McGuire, a leader in the Irish uprising of 1599 [Fynes Moryson, *An Itinerary* (London: John Beale, 1617), 2.181].

44. See Appendix A.

45. David Wiles, *The Early Plays of Robin Hood* (Woodbridge: D. S. Brewer, 1981), 15.

46. See Appendix B for the texts pertaining to this riot.

47. See Appendix B.

48. See especially Manning, *Village Revolts*.

49. Underdown, *Revel, Riot, and Rebellion*, 96.

50. Barret L. Beer, *Rebellion and Riot. Popular disorder in England during the Reign of Edward VI* (Kent, Ohio: Kent State University Press, 1982); Manning, *Village Revolts*, 53–54, 98; Davis, *Popular Culture in Early Modern France*, 154; J. A. Sharpe, *Crime in Early Modern England 1550–1750* (London and New York: Longman, 1984), 133.

51. Colin Richmond, "An Outlaw and Some Peasants: The Possible Significance of Robin Hood," *Nottingham Medieval Studies* 37 (1993), 101.

52. Underdown, *Revel, Riot, and Rebellion*, 270.

53. Richard Grafton, *A Chronicle at Large* (London: J. Johnson, 1809), 1.497.

54. I.M.W. Harvey, *Jack Cade's Rebellion of 1450* (Oxford: Clarendon Press, 1991), 65.

55. Underdown, *Revel, Riot, and Rebellion*, 135.

56. *A C mery talys* (London: J. Rastell, 1526), fol. xv–xv verso.

57. John Knox, *Works of John Knox* (Edinburgh: Wodrow Society, 1864), 2.472.

58. *Letters and Papers, Foreign and Domestic, of the Reign of Henry VIII* (London: HMSO, 1862), 5.551 (Item #1271).

59. P. R. Coss, "Aspects of Cultural Diffusion in Medieval England: The Early Romances, Local Society, and Robin Hood," *Past and Present* 108 (1985), 75–76. This was a common feature in peasant revolts, expressed also by the German rebels in early sixteenth-century Münster, who would have "No lord but the emperor" [Michael Mullett, *Popular Culture and Popular Protest in Late Medieval and Early Modern Europe* (London, New York, and Sidney: Croom Helm, 1987), 94, 104].

60. Cf. R. B. Dobson, *The Peasants Revolt of 1381* (London: Macmillan; New York: St. Martin's Press, 1970), 131, 144, 165, 195, 203, 207, 365.

61. Ritson, *Robin Hood*, 1.xciii.

62. Stephen Knight, *Robin Hood. A Complete Study of the English Outlaw* (Oxford and Cambridge, Mass.: Blackwell, 1994), 235.

Appendix A:

Robin Hood Games

WESTERN ENGLAND

Bristol

1525-26. St. Nicholas Church pays 6s. 8d. for "two pair of hosyn for Robin Hood and Lytyll John . . . and for lyning of the same" [Mark Pilkinton, *Records of Early English Drama: Bristol* (Toronto: University of Toronto Press, 1997), 37].

Cornwall

Mawgan

1591–92. See St. Breock.

St. Breock

1573–74. Parish receives income from Robin Hood and his company.
1590–91. Parish makes payment to Robin Hood of St. Columb Minor.
1591–92. Parish makes payment to Robin Hood of Mawgan [References courtesy of Evelyn Newlyn and Sally L. Joyce].

St. Columb Major

1588. Churchwardens' accounts record money received "for the lont of the Robbyn hoodes clothes" [J. Charles Cox, *Churchwardens' Accounts from the Fourteenth Century to the Close of the Seventeenth Century* (London: Methuen, 1913), 280; Jane

A. Bakere, *The Cornish Ordinalia. A Critical Study* (Cardiff: University of Wales Press, 1980), 18].

1595. Churchwardens' accounts record debts "of Robin hoodes monyes" [Bakere, *The Cornish Ordinalia*, 18].

St. Columb Minor

1587–88. See St. Ives.
1590–91. See St. Breock.

St. Ives

1583–84. Borough accounts record money received of James Pormantor for the Robin Hood.
1587–88. Money paid to the Robin Hood of St. Columb Minor [References courtesy of Evelyn Newlyn and Sally L. Joyce].

Stratton

1535–36. Parish receives 12s. 4d. from "I. Greby which was callyd Robynhode & of his felows" [Reference courtesy of Evelyn Newlyn and Sally L. Joyce].
1536. Parish receives £1 18s. 4d. from "John Marys and his company that playd Robin Hoode."
1538. Parish receives £3 10d. "of Robyn hode & of hys men."
1543. Martha Rose and Margaret Martin are paid 3s. for the "wode of Robyn Hode is howse" [N. M. & A., "'Howde Men': Robin Hood's Men," *Notes and Queries* 11 ser., no. 2 (July 2, 1910), 16].

Devon

Ashburton

1526–27. St. Andrews churchwardens' accounts record money paid for a new coat [*tunica*] for "Robyn Whode" [*REED: Devon*, 21; Alison Hanham, "Churchwarden's Accounts of Ashburton, 1479–1580," *Devon and Cornwall Record Society* New Series 15 (Torquay: Devonshire Press, 1970), 78].
1541–42. Parish pays 19s. 11d. for coats for Robin Hood and his followers [*REED: Devon*, 25; Hanham 109].

Barnstaple

1558–59. Receivers' accounts record 3s. 4d. "paid to Robart Hode for his pastime" [*REED: Devon*, 42].

Braunton

1560–61. St. Brannocks churchwardens' accounts record 2s. paid "for meat & drynke for Robyn hoode & his company" [*REED: Devon*, 52].

1561–62. St. Brannocks Church ale expenses include 12s. "payd for cloth to make Robyn hoodes Cote." Whitsun payments include 12d. "for Robyn hood & hys Company" [*REED: Devon*, 52, 310].

1563–64. 6s. 8d. paid "for litle Iohns Cote" [*REED: Devon*, 52].

Chagford

1537. Parish pays 35s. "for dowing the office of the Howde Coat" [Ethel Lega-Weekes, "'Howde Men': Robin Hood's Men at Chagford," *Notes and Queries* 11 ser. no. 1 (April 30, 1910), 346].

1554–55. St. Michael's parish accounts include "The accompte of the yongemen off the parysche of Chagfford, Iohn Northecott and other for the howde," with profits of 10s. [*REED: Devon*, 54]

1555. Parish accounts include 10s. received "of Iohn Northcutt And other Roben Howde ys Company" [*REED: Devon*, 54].

1555–56. Parish accounts include "The accompte of Robard lopass, Iohn frend, and other of the howde ys men of the parysche of Chagford," with 4s. paid for two coats [*REED: Devon*, 54].

1557–58. Parish accounts include "The accompte of Iohn Newcomb Iunior and other of the howddes men with yn the parysche of Chagfford," with profits of 24s. 4d. [*REED: Devon*, 54–55]. There is also an account from "Roberd lopas, Iohn penycott, and of other of the howdde ys men," with 6s. 8d. paid "for the howddes Cote" [*REED: Devon*, 55].

1558–59. Parish accounts include 20s. 8d. received "of Robert Lapas howdde þat yere" and 24s. 4d. received "of Iohn Newcomb Iunior & other owddes men that yere" [*REED: Devon*, 55].

1559–60. Parish income includes 5s. "of Iohn Row & other hys felowys howdesmen" [*REED: Devon*, 55].

1562. John Newcombe is paid 35s. "for dowing the office of the Howde" [Lega-Weekes, "Howde Men," 346].

1563–64. The accounts from Nicholas Peryman and "otheres of hys Companye the howdes men" includes 45s. received for ale sold that year [*REED: Devon*, 55–56].

1564. £4 9d. received "of Iohn Newcomb & other howdesmen." The accounts also mention "Iohn Newcomb beyng howde" and "Nycollas peryman & other howdes men" [*REED: Devon*, 56].

1587–88. The "Young Men's or Hoodsmen's Accounts" list assets including "the siluer arrow" [*REED: Devon*, 56].

Chudleigh

1561. St. Martins and St. Marys churchwardens' accounts include "The Count of Robyn Hodde & Litle Iohn" [*REED: Devon*, 57; see p. 64].

Colyton

1571–72. See Honiton.

Exeter

1426–27. Receivers' accounts include 20d. given to players of a Robin Hood play [*REED: Devon*, 89].

1487–88. St. Johns Bow churchwardens' accounts include 5s. received from a play called "Robyn Hode" [*REED: Devon*, 108].

1508–9. St. Johns Bow churchwardens' accounts include 4d. paid for repair of the arrow of Saint Edmund the Martyr for Robin Hood [*REED: Devon*, 118].

1509–10. City Council bans Robin Hood games except on the church holy day and holidays close to it [*REED: Devon*, 119; see p. 119].

1553–54. St. Johns Bow churchwardens' accounts include money from "Robyn whode & lytell Iohn" for the sale of ale [*REED: Devon*, 145].

Farway

1567. St. Michaels churchwardens' accounts record 5s. 6d. owing to Walter Bucknoll who was chosen as "Robert howde" but "after put owt" [*REED: Devon*, 207].

Honiton

1571–72. St. Michaels churchwardens' accounts include money paid for a pound of gunpowder "when Robarte hode of collyton came in" [*REED: Devon*, 207].

1576–77. Parish accounts include 17s. profit from Robin Hood [*REED: Devon*, 208].

Woodbury

1540–41. St. Swithins churchwardens' accounts include 8s. paid "ffor Robert Hode & lytyll Iohn Cott" and 2s. paid "ffor ther Wardyns Labor as the Custome ys" [*REED: Devon*, 284].

1573–74. Parish accounts record that "Willyam Downham beynge Robyn Hoode & Water Holwill lytle Iohn made an ale & gatheringe & brought yn redie monye, xl s" [*REED: Devon*, 285].

1574–75. Parish accounts record 20s. 10d. paid for 35 yards of canvas, and 16d. paid to Andrew Pierce "for maken of Roberte Hoodes Howse" [*REED: Devon*, 285].

1576–77. Parish accounts include 40s. "receaued of William Dounom & Water Holwill the monye that they made with ale when he was Roberte Hood &c" [*REED: Devon*, 285].

1581–82. 8s. received from William Rider for two green coats. [*REED: Devon*, 286].

Dorset

Bridport

1555. Money made for a Robin Hood Ale, and for sale of a booth.

1557–8. £7 6d. received of Robin Hood's money [References courtesy of R. C. Hays and C.E. McGee].

Netherbury

?c1567. Seventeenth-century compilation of sixteenth-century Yondover manor presentments mentions church ales at Whitsunday featuring Robin Hood and Little John, with the gentlemen of the parish as the chief participants [Reference courtesy of R. C. Hays and C.E. McGee].

Poole

1508–9. Money gathered by Robin Hood is said to be in the town box.

1509–10. Money gathered by Robin Hood and his company again in the town box.

1510–11. Robin Hood's money in the town box. [References courtesy of R. C. Hays and C.E. McGee].

Somerset

Croscombe

1476–77. St. Marys churchwardens' accounts record 40s. of "Roben Hod's recones" from Thomas Blower and John Hill; Hill was churchwarden that year [*REED: Somerset*, 86].

1481–82. 40s. 4d. collected from John Halse and Roger Morris "for Robin Hod's revel." Morris was a churchwarden that year [*REED: Somerset*, 87]. This money is designated "Roben Hode money" [*REED: Somerset*, 87].

1482–83. 33s. 4d. received of Robin Hood [*REED: Somerset*, 87].

1483–84. 23s. received of Richard Wills, who "was Robin Hood" [*REED: Somerset*, 87].

1484–85. 23s. 8d. received of Robin Hood [*REED: Somerset*, 88].

1486–87. £3 6s. 8^1/2d. received of William Windsor as Robin Hood. Windsor was a former churchwarden [*REED: Somerset*, 88].

1488–89. £3 7s. 8d. received of Robin Hood [*REED: Somerset*, 88].

1490–91. 50s. received for Robin Hood [*REED: Somerset*, 88].

1494–95. 46s. 8d. received of Robin Hood [*REED: Somerset*, 88].

1500–1. 15s. received of Robin Hood and Little John [*REED: Somerset*, 89].

1502–3. 40s. received of Robin Hood [*REED: Somerset*, 89].

1505–6. 53s. 4d. received for "the sport of Robart Hode and hys company" [*REED: Somerset*, 89].

1506–7. 43s. 4d. received for "the sport of Robart hode" [*REED: Somerset*, 89].

1507–8. 9s. 7d. presented by the churchwardens for the sport of Robin Hood [*REED: Somerset*, 90].

1509–10. £3 received of John Honythorne as Robin Hood [*REED: Somerset*, 90].

1510–11. £3 6s. 8d. received of Robin Hood [*REED: Somerset*, 90].

1511–12. 35s. 10d. received of J. Honythorn and J. Steven for Robin Hood [*REED: Somerset*, 90].

1526–27. Gifts include £4 4d. for Robin Hood [*REED: Somerset*, 90].

Glastonbury

1500. St. John Baptist churchwardens' accounts include 40s. received for Robin Hood and the parishioners. 14s. is also paid for a coat for Robin Hood, and 8d. for a pair of lined hose for Robin Hood [*REED: Somerset*, 126].

Tintinhull

1512–13. 11s. received from "Robine Hoods All" [*REED: Somerset*, 231].

Wells

1498. Corporation Act Book records inquiry to be made into the whereabouts of money coming from Robin Hood, the dancing girls, the church's public ale, and such like [*REED: Somerset*, 252].

1607. Church ale over a series of weeks includes a Robin Hood in the marketplace on May 31 (Trinity Sunday), in which Robert Prinne, a yeoman of Wells, was the Robin Hood, and Stephen Millard, a tailor of Wells, aged forty-three, was his man, carrying a bow and arrows; the displays featured drums, shot, pikes, bows and arrows, morris dances, "and other shows" [*REED: Somerset*, 321, 944]. According to a poem describing the festivities: "And Robbyn Hoodd was likewise seene/ with all his gallantes rayed in greene,/ theire arrowes were a longe Clothe yard" [*REED: Somerset*, 267].

Westonzoyland

1607. Articles charged against Robert Wolfall, minister of Weston, by John Cornishe, carpenter describe a Robin Hood Ale held on the Sunday after Ascension Day [*REED: Somerset*, 388–89; see pp. 70, 91].

Yeovil

1516–17. St. John Baptist churchwardens' accounts include 20s. presented "by Robarte Hood and by the devotion of the pepylle" [*REED: Somerset*, 405].

1519–20. £6 8^1/2d. received of Richard Hacker as Robin Hood "that be his gud prouysyon & dylygent labors and by the gud deuocion of the towne & the contrey he presentyd to god & holy church." Also a belt with silver buckle and chape and gilt bells are donated by Joan Withers, "to the intent the Sayd gyrdyll shuld too honour to god and worshyp to the sayd church and parysh when Robyn hood makyth hys besyness Or such other lyke" [*REED: Somerset*, 405].

1539–40. £12 14s. 1d. received of John Phelips as Robin Hood [*REED: Somerset*, 406].

1540–41. £8 12s. 2^1/2d. received of John Dore as Robin Hood [*REED: Somerset*, 406].

1541–42. £8 7s. 5d. received of William Short as Robin Hood [*REED: Somerset*, 406].

1544–45. £5 8s. 9^1/2d. received "Of Iohn Delagryse being R Hood this yere" [*REED: Somerset*, 406].

1545–46. £9 10d. received of John Hacker the Elder as Robin Hood [*REED: Somerset*, 406].

1551–52. £8 11s. 4d. received of Tristram Brook as Robin Hood. Also £11 12s. 5d. received of John Marchant as Robin Hood (perhaps for a previous year?) [*REED: Somerset*, 406–7].

1557–58. £13 5d. received of John Hacker as Robin Hood [*REED: Somerset*, 407].

1558–59. £11 10s. 5^1/2d. received of Lionel Harrison as Robin Hood [*REED: Somerset*, 407].

1561–62. £10 13s. and odd pence received of Reynold Harding as Robin Hood [*REED: Somerset*, 407].

1562–63. £9 18s. received of William Longye as Robin Hood [*REED: Somerset*, 407].

1563–64. £9 15s. 3^1/2d. received of John Gaylord as Robin Hood [*REED: Somerset*, 408].

1564–65. £10 5s. 8^1/4d. received of John Dennis as Robin Hood [*REED: Somerset*, 408; Goodchild 63].

1566–67. £4 8d. received from Robin Hood [*REED: Somerset*, 408].

1568–69. 2d. paid for a ribbon lace for Little John's horn [*REED: Somerset*, 409].

1569–70. £10 21^1/4d. received of John Tucker as Robin Hood [*REED: Somerset*, 409].

1572–73. £13 8s. 2^1/2d. received of William Beck as Robin Hood [*REED: Somerset*, 409]. Also 10s. 5d. paid for 12^1/2 yards of Normandy canvas delivered to Robin Hood to make two tablecloths; 4d. paid for a green silk ribbon for the Sheriff; 8d. paid to Robin Hood for drink for the bellringers on Ascension Day; and 4d. paid for feathering Robin Hood's arrows [*REED: Somerset*, 409–10].

1573–74. £16 2s. 5^1/2d. received from James Everdon as Robin Hood [*REED: Somerset*, 410].

1575–76. £17 2s. received from William Forde as Robin Hood [*REED: Somerset*, 410].

1577–78. John Dyer as Robin Hood pays the parish £18 3s. 10d. "made by kepinge the Churche ale." Dyer was a churchwarden that year. Also 6d. paid for refeathering Robin Hood's arrows [*REED: Somerset*, 410–11].

1578–79. 4d. paid "for mending Robyn Hoods bar and a new key," perhaps used for securing the substantial sums gathered in the Yeovil games [*REED: Somerset*, 411].

Wiltshire

Longleat

1562. Longleat accounts mention payment to players of a Robin Hood play in the house of Sir John Thynne [David Burnett, *Longleat. The Story of an English Country House* (London: Collins, 1978), 30].

SEVERN VALLEY AND ENVIRONS

Gloucestershire

Tewkesbury

1519. See Worcester.

Shropshire

Bridgnorth

1588–9. Chamberlain's accounts include 2s. 6d. "Paied at Roger Harleis by the commaundment of Mr. Bailiff upon them which plaied Robin Hood" [*REED: Shropshire*, 19].

Ludlow

1566–67. Bailiffs' and chamberlains' accounts include 10s. given to Robin Hood [*REED: Shropshire*, 83].

Shrewsbury

1552–53. Bailiffs' accounts include 49s. 3^1/2d. paid for painted coats and other clothing for Robin Hood, and 14s. for wine for the players [*REED: Shropshire*, 203].

Staffordshire

Wednesbury/Willenhall

1498. Star Chamber case alleges riot at Willenhall Fair on Trinity Sunday by William Milner of Wolverhampton, under the name of the Abbot of Marram, and Robert Marshal of Wednesbury, under the name of Robin Hood, with upwards of 180 armed followers. The defendants claim that the assembly was a traditional and peaceful entertainment for the purpose of gathering money for the churches [*Collections for a History of Staffordshire*, New Series 10 (London: Harrison and Sons, 1907), 1.80–82; see p. 159].

Warwickshire

Stratford-on-Avon

1622. May games with morris dancing and a Robin Hood play [David Underdown, *Revel, Riot and Rebellion. Popular Politics and Culture in England 1603–1660* (Oxford: Clarendon Press, 1985), 57].

Worcestershire

Cleeve Prior

1531. Prior William More, while at Crowle the week of July 23–29, pays 6s. 8d. "in reewardes to the tenantes of clyve pleying with Robyn Whot Mayde Marion & other" [*REED: Worcester*, 513; 338n.77; William More, *Journal of Prior William More*, ed. Ethel S. Fegan (London: Worcester Historical Society, 1913–14), 332].

Worcester (with Battenhall, Crowle and Ombursley)

1519. More, at Worcester the week of June 19–25, pays 3s. 4d. in "rewardes to Robyn whod & hys men for getheryng to tewkesbury bruge" [*REED: Worcester*, 462; More, *Journal*, 87].

1529. More, at Worcester and Battenhall the week of May 16–22 (the week leading up to Whitsun) pays 12d. in "rewardes to certen yong men of seynt Elyns þat pleyd Robyn Whod" [*REED: Worcester*, 503; More, *Journal*, 293].

1530. More, at Worcester and Battenhall the week of June 12–18 (the week following Trinity Sunday) pays 12d. "to þe box of Rybyn hood &c xij d." [*REED: Worcester*, 507; More, *Journal*, 309].

1531. See Cleeve Prior.

1535. More, at Battenhall the week of May 30–June 5 (the second week after Trinity Sunday), pays 12d. to "Robyn Whod & litle Iohn of Ombursley" [*REED: Worcester*, 529; More, *Journal*, 405].

THAMES VALLEY

Berkshire

Abingdon

1566. St. Helen's pays 18d. for setting up "Robin Hoodes bowere" [Cox, *Churchwardens' Accounts*, 284; J. Ward, "Extracts from the Church-wardens Accompts of the Parish of St. Helens in Abingdon, Berkshire," *Archaeologia* 1 (177), 16; David Wiles, *Early Plays of Robin Hood* (Woodbridge: D. S. Brewer, 1981), 64].

Finchamstead

1506. See Reading.

Reading

1498–99. The parish of St. Lawrence receives 19s. "of the gaderyng of Robyn Hod" [Charles Kerry, *A History of the Municipal Church of St. Lawrence, Reading* (Reading and Derby: Charles Kerry, 1883), 227; Cox, *Churchwardens' Accounts*, 282].

1501–2. The parish receives 6s. "of the May play callyd Robyn Hod on the fayre day"; also 6d. are paid to minstrels "at the chosyng of Robyn Hod," and 200 liveries and 100 pins are purchased for Mayday [Kerry, *History of the Municipal Church*, 227; Cox, *Churchwardens' Accounts*, 282].

1503–4. Robin Hood gathers 10 bushels of malt, 1 bushel of wheat, and 49s. in money. Also 4d. paid for bread and ale "to Robyn Hod & hys company," 5s. 4d. for a coat for Robin Hood, and another 16d. for meat and drink for Robin Hood and his company [Kerry, *History of the Municipal Church*, 227; Cox, *Churchwardens' Accounts*, 282].

1504–5. 18s. 11 ^{1}/2d. received from the gathering of Robin Hood [Reference courtesy of A.F. Johnston]. Also 6s. 7d. paid for Robin Hood's coat and hose, and 6s. for wine for "Robyn Hod of Handley & his company" [Kerry, *History of the Municipal Church*, 228; Cox, *Churchwardens' Accounts*, 283].

1505–6. £5 10s. 5d. received from Robin Hood's gathering at Whitsun; 3d. paid for ale for Robin Hood and his company [Reference courtesy of A.F. Johnston]. Also 18d. "payed for a supper to Robyn Hod & his company when he cam from ffynchamsted" [Kerry, *History of the Municipal Church*, 228; Wiles, *Early Plays*, 64].

1507–8. 17s. and odd pence received "of the gaderyng of Robyn Hod pley" [Kerry, *History of the Municipal Church*, 228; Cox, 283].

1510–11. £8 2s. 5d. received from the gathering of Robin Hood [Reference courtesy of A.F. Johnston].

Buckinghamshire

Amersham

1530. Money received "of the lad [?*read:* lades] for Robyn hode" [Wiles, *Early Plays*, 64; F. G. Lee, "Amersham Churchwardens' Accounts," *Records of Buckinghamshire* 7 (1897), 44; *The Edwardian Inventories for Buckinghamshire*, transcr. J. E. Brown, ed. F. C. Eeles, Alcuin Club Collections 9 (1908), 126].

London

1502. "Also thys yere, about Mydsomer, was taken a felowe whych hadde renewed many of Robin Hodes pagentes, which named him selfe Greneleef" [Robert Fabyan, *The New Chronicles of England and France*, ed. Henry Ellis (London: F. C. and J. Rivington, 1811), 687].

?1531–45. Stephen Gardiner, Bishop of Winchester 1531–1551, "forbad the players of london . . . to play any mo playes of Christe, but of Robin Hode and litle Johan, and of the Parlament of Byrdes and suche other trifles" [W. Wraghton, pseud. (William Turner), *The Rescuynge of the Romishe Fox Other Wyse Called the Examination of the Hunter Deuised by Steuen Gardiner* (Bonn: L. Mylius, 1545), sig G2r].

1552. Inventory includes "xv Robyne Hoodes Cottes" at Holy Trinity the Less [H. B. Walters, *London Churches at the Reformation with an Account of their Contents* (London: Society for Promoting Christian Knowledge; New York: Macmillan, 1939), 129].

1559. "The xxiiij day of June ther was a May-game . . . with a gyant, and drumes and gunes . . . and then sant Gorge and the dragon, the mores dansse, and after Robyn Hode and lytyll John, and M[aid Marian] and frere Tuke, and thay had spechys rond a-bowt London. The xxv day of June the sam May-gam whent unto <?the palace> at Grenwyche, playng a-for the Quen and the consell." [Henry Machyn, *The Diary of Henry Machyn*, ed. John Gough Nichols. Camden Society 42 (London: Printed for the Camden Society by J.B. Nichols and Sons, 1847), 201].

Oxfordshire

Enstone

1652. A Latin account of a visit by "Eric Rosekrantsii et Petrie Reedtsii" to Enstone on June 21 describes villagers celebrating games "quos sua lingua Rabben hüt vocabant" [A. Rhodes, "'Howde Men': Robin Hood's Men," *Notes and Queries* ser. 11 no. 1 (June 18, 1910), 494].

Henley-on-Thames

1499. Money in the hands of gatherers of the Robin Hood play is to be spent to buy a silver thurible for the church [P. M. Briers, "Henley Borough Records. Assembly Books i–iv, 1395–1543," *Oxfordshire Record Society* 41 (1960), 125].

1505. See Reading (Berkshire).

1520. £4 13s. 4d. collected "of Robyne Hoodys money" [P. M. Briers, "Henley Borough Records," 189].

Thame

1474–75. 26s. 9d. received of Robin Hood's Ale at Whitsun [W. P. Ellis, "The Churchwardens' Accounts of the Parish of St. Mary Thame, Commencing in the Year 1442," *Berkshire, Buckinghamshire, and Oxfordshire Archaeological Journal* 19 (1913), 22].

1496–97. 14s. profits gathered by Robin Hood at the May Ale at Whitsun.

1501–2. 20s. gathered by Robin Hood at the May Ale at Whitsun [References courtesy of A.F. Johnston].

Woodstock

1627–28. £7 7s. 1d. brought in by Robin Hood and Little John at Whitsun, in addition to £9 brought in by the Whitsun lord [Reference courtesy of A.F. Johnston].

Surrey

Croydon

1515. See Kingston-upon-Thames.

Kingston-upon-Thames

1506. 39s. gathered by Robin Hood from Whitsun to Fair Day; also 3d. paid for painting a banner for Robin Hood and 17s. paid for borrowing coats for Robin Hood and Little

John [Wiles, *Early Plays*, 68–69; Daniel Lysons, *Environs of London. I. Surrey* (London: T. Cadell and W. Davies, 1810), 166].

1508–9. Expenses for the King-Game and Robin Hood include money for a kilderkin (18 gallons) of strong beer and a kilderkin of single beer, 7 bushels of wheat, $2\,{}^1\!/2$ bushels of rye, 3 sheep, a lamb, 2 calves, 6 pigs, 3 bushels of coals and wages for the cooks; also 16d. for making a coat for Robin Hood, 18d. for food and drink for Robin Hood and his men, 4d. for the Friar's coat, 8s. for Little John's coat, and 7d. for 5 broad arrows; the income from the King-Game and Robin Hood's gathering is 4 marks (£2 13s. 8d.) [W. E. St. L. Finny, "Mediæval Games and Gaderyings at Kingston-upon-Thames," *Surrey Archaeological Collections* 44 (1936), 122–23; Lysons, *Environs of London*, 169].

1509–10. 3 marks (£2) received "for Robyn Hodes gaderyng" [Finny, "Mediæval Games," 121].

1509–10. Churchwarden's Accounts list the following "Costes of ye Kyngham and Robyn Hode":

"First paid for a pece of Kendall for Roben Hode and litell Johns cote 12s. 10d.

"Item paid for III yerdes of white for the freres cote 3s.

"Item paid for III yerds of Kendall for mayde marion is huke 2s. 4d.

"Item paid for saten of sypers for ye same huke 5d.

"Item paid to mayde marion for her labor for II yere 2s. . . .

"Item paid for II payre of glovys for Robyn Hode and Mayde maryon 4 $^1\!/2$d.

"Item for VI brode arovys 6d.

"Item paid for mete and drynke for Robyn Hode and his compeny 2s. 2d.

"Item paid to Alis Toth for mete and drynke for Robyn Hode and his company 5d.

"Item paid for II Kylderkenys of III halpeny bere for Robyn Hode and his compeny 2s. 8d. . . .

"The Recettes of ye Same Yere.

"Item receuid for gadering of ye King and Whitsontyde 19s.

"Item rec. at ye Kyngham and for ye gaderyng of Roben Hode 4 marke 20d." [Finny, "Mediæval Games," 123–25].

1509–10. 7s. 6d. paid "for half Robyn Hodes cote"; also 3s. paid for the friar's coat, 8s. 3d. for Little John's coat, and 15d. for Kendal for Robin Hood's coat [Finny, "Mediæval Games," 105].

1510–11. 4 marks received from Robin Hood's gathering; also 25s. 6d. paid "for Robyn Hodes cote and for litell Jhons cote and for ye freres cote" [Finny, "Mediæval Games," 121].

1514–15. 12s. received for Robin Hood's gathering; another 9s. 4d. received for his gathering at Croydon [Finny, "Mediæval Games," 121].

1515–16. 23s. received at Whitsun for Robin Hood's gathering; 8d. paid for a pair of shoes for Robin Hood [Finny, "Mediæval Games," 104].

1515–16. Churchwarden's accounts list "Chooses for Mores Davnsars and Roben Hod and hes Compenye: . . . Item for Roben Hod a peyer of chone 8d. . . . Item to Roben Hode for hes labor 12d. Item to leytell Jhon for hes labor 10d. Item to Freer tuk 8d. Item in mony amongest Roben Hodes men at nythe 8d." [Finny, "Mediæval Games," 115].

1517–18. 6s. 6d. received for Robin Hood's gathering [Finny, "Mediæval Games," 121].

1519–20. Churchwarden's accounts include: "Item Reseuyd of Jhon gaddysbe for Robyn Hode ye yere before past, 3s. 2d. [Finny, "Mediæval Games," 104].

"Item Resayued of the Maye game and Robyn Hode £3 12s. 4d.

"The Expenses.

"For ye Maye game and Robartte Hode:

"Furst payet for VII yerdys of satane . . . at 2s. ye yerd 14s.

"Item payett for canves to lyne ye same cottes 16d.

"Item payett for ye makyn of ye same cottes 2s.

"Item payett for III brode yerdes of rosett to make ye freers cott 3s.

"Item payett for XIIII candall cottes, beside ye gyfthe of Masters of the towne, and for ye makyng of ye same cottes 12s.

"Item payett for VIII payers of schewes for ye morris daunsers, ye freer and made maryen at VIIId ye payer 5s. 4d." [Finny, "Mediæval Games," 117–18].

1520–21. 8s. received for Robin Hood's gathering at Whitsun [Finny, "Mediæval Games," 104].

1521–22. 8s. ^{1}/2d. received for Robin Hood's gathering [Finny, "Mediæval Games," 121].

1522–23. Churchwarden's accounts include: "Res. for ye gaderyng of Robyn Hode 46s. 8d.

"Pd. for the hyre of 20 hattes for Robin Hode 16d.

"Pd. for a hatt that was lost 10d.

"Pd. for 1500 of leveres for Robyn Hode 5s.

"Pd. for 4 estrygge fethers for Robyn Hode 20d.

"Pd. for 2 peyre of shone for Robyn Hode and lytell Jhon 21d." [Finny, "Mediæval Games," 121].

1523–24. 45s. 4d. received for the gathering of Robin Hood [Finny, "Mediæval Games," 121].

1524–25. £3 10s. 5d. profits received from the King Game and Robin Hood; also 12s. 6d. paid for 6^1/4 yards of satin for Robin Hood's coats [Finny, "Mediæval Games," 122].

1525–26. 20s. received for Robin Hood's gathering [Finny, "Mediæval Games," 122].

1526–27. 31s. 2d. received for Robin Hood's gathering [Finny, "Mediæval Games," 122].

1527–28. 12s. received for Robin Hood's gathering [Finny, "Mediæval Games," 122].

1528–29. 15s. 4d. received for Robin Hood's gathering at Whitsun [Finny, "Mediæval Games," 122].

1529–30. 26s. 8d. received for Robin Hood's gathering; also 2d. paid for mending Robin Hood's coats [Finny, "Mediæval Games," 122].

1530–31. 20s. 6d. received for Robin Hood's gathering; also 3d. paid "for spungyng and brushyng of Robin Howdes cotes" [Finny, "Mediæval Games," 122].

1536–37. "Charges for Robyn Hodde" include costumes for a friar, fool, morris dancers, and Maid Marian, 6 pair of single-soled shoes and 6 pair of double-soled shoes, and 1300 livery badges [Finny, "Mediæval Games," 126; see p. 66].

1536–37. £5 6s. 8d. received for Robin Hood's gathering [Finny, "Mediæval Games," 122]; also 2s. paid for 600 "Robyn hoddes lyuereys" [Reference courtesy of Sally-Beth MacLean].

1538–39. 23s. 1d. received for Robin Hood's gathering; 7s. paid for Robin Hood's coats [Finny, "Mediæval Games," 122].

EASTERN ENGLAND

Essex

Halstead

1589. "A boy in the Church, hearing either the sommer Lord with his Maie game, or Robin Hood with his Morrice daunce going by the Church, out goes the boye. Good Gliberie, though he were in the pulpit. . . finished his matter presently, saying ha, ye faith boie, are they there, then ha with thee. . . and so came down and among them hee goes" [*Hay any work for cooper?* in *The Marprelate Tracts 1588, 1589*, ed. William Pierce (London: A. Constable and Co., 1908), 226–27].

Hertfordshire

Hexton

Early seventeenth century. Francis Taverner's history of Hexton states that "Maying feasts, with their playes of Robynhood and little Iohn" had been recently abandoned. [Peter Greenfield, "Parish Drama in Four Counties Bordering the Thames Watershed," in *English Parish Drama*, ed. Alexandra F. Johnston and Wim Hüsken (Amsterdam and Atlanta: Rodopi, 1996), 114].

Kent

Hythe

1532–33. New Romney Accounts include 4s. paid to Robin Hood players from Hythe, and 8d. in expenses on them [*Records of Plays and Players in Kent 1450–1642*, ed. Giles E. Dawson. Malone Society Collections 7 (Oxford: printed for the Malone Society by the University Press, 1965), 133].

New Romney

1533. See Hythe.

?Penshurst

1574. Payments for Robert Sidney (aged 11) and his sisters include 3s. given to those that played Robin Hood [Historical Manuscripts Commission, *Report on the Manuscripts of Lord De L'Isle and Dudley Preserved at Penshurst Palace*, ed. C. L. Kingsford (London: HMSO, 1925), 1.268].

Kent/Sussex

1528. Lord Warden of the Cinq Ports orders mayors of Sandwich, Faversham and other towns not to organize or permit any "play, Robin Hood's play, watches or wakes, revels, or other such like plays whereby that any great assembly of the king's people should be made" [Peter Clark, "Reformation and Radicalism in Kentish Towns c. 1500–1553," in *The Urban Classes, the Nobility, and the Reformation*, ed. Wolfgang J. Mommsen, Publications of the German Historical Institute London 5 (Stuttgart: Klett-Cotta, 1979), 112].

Norfolk

?Caister

1473. Sir John Paston complains of a servant whom he has kept for three years "to pleye Seynt Jorge and Robynhod and the shryff off Notyngham" [*Paston Letters and Papers of the Fifteenth Century*, ed. Norman Davis (Oxford: Oxford University Press, 1971, 1976), 1.461; see p. 63].

Yarmouth

1599. "Citty, towne, cuntry, Robin hoode and little Iohn, and who not, are industrious and carefull to squire and safe conduct him [ie. the herring] in, but in vshering him in, next to the balies of Yarmoth, they trot before all" [Thomas Nashe, *The Praise of the Red Herring* (1599), in *The Works of Thomas Nashe*, ed. Ronald B. McKerrow (Oxford: Oxford University Press, 1966), 3.186].

EAST MIDLANDS AND NORTHERN ENGLAND

Lancashire

Burnley

1580. Letter of Edmund Assheton to William Farington, 12 May: "I am sure (Righte worshippfull) youe haue not forgotten the laste yere sturres att Brunley, aboute Robyn hoode and the May games; Nowe consideringe that itt is a Cause that bringeth no good effecte, beinge Contrarie to the beste, Therfore a Numbre of the Iustices of peace herein in Sallforde hundrethe haue Consulted with the Commyssioners to suppresse those Lewde sportes tendinge to no other ende but to stirre vpp our ffrayle Natures to wantonnes" [*REED: Lancashire*, 6].

Manchester

?c1555. "It is reported & belieued that Iohn Bradford preaching in Manchester in king Edwards dayes told the people as it were by a Prophetical spirit that because they did not readily embrace the word of God the Masse should bee sayd againe in that church & the play of Robin Hood acted there which accordingly came to passe in Queen Maries reigne" [Richard Hollingworth, *Mancuniensis* [17c.], cited *REED: Lancashire*, 283].

Leicestershire

Leicester

1525. Witnesses before an episcopal visitation at Newark College testify that "touchyng Maygamys, and Robyn Hode and sanct George many tymys vseth to comme into the colledge" [A. H. Thompson, ed., *Visitations in the Diocese of Lincoln 1517–1531*, Lincoln Record Society 37 (Hereford: printed for the Lincoln Record Society by the Hereford Times, 1947), 145; see also 173].

1526. The parish of St. Leonard is owed 40s. from John Laverock for a Robin Hood play enacted for the benefit of the church [A. P. Moore, "Proceedings of the Ecclesiastical Courts in the Archdeaconry of Leicester 1516–1535," *Associated Architectural Societies' Reports and Papers* 28:1 (1905), 202].

1534. William Billar, registrar of the Archdeaconry Court of Leicester, submits a bill of expenses incurred in participation in a Robin Hood game, including 16d. for a yard and a half of Kendal, 4d. for the hire of a coat for two days, and 8d. for borrowing a sword and buckler [William Kelly, *Notices Illustrative of the Drama* (London: John Russell Smith, 1865), 61].

Melton Mowbray

1556. Townwardens' accounts include 29s. 8d. gathered by Steven Shaw and his company with "Robyn Hoods playe" over two years; also 5s. received of John Hopkins in payment of "Robyn Hoods money" [Kelly, *Notices Illustrative of the Drama*, 64]. Melton had a Lord of Misrule at Whitsun the same year [61].

1565–67. 49s. 9d. owed by John Dalderby and William Blyth for the Lord and Lady's money for 1563; also 14s. 1d. of Robin Hood's money received of John Downes [Reference courtesty of REED].

Yorkshire

Brandsby

1615. The play of Robin Hood performed in the churchyard and church, with local recusants taking the parts of Robin Hood and the Sheriff [Hugh Aveling, *Northern Catholics: The Catholic Recusants of the North Riding of Yorkshire 1558–1790* (London, Dublin, and Melbourne: Geoffrey Chapman, 1966), 289].

THE ENGLISH ROYAL COURT

1510. Henry VIII, the Earls of Essex and Wiltshire, and a number of other nobles dress as outlaws and visit the Queen and her ladies [Edward Halle, *The Union of the Two Noble ... Families York and Lancaster* (London: R. Grafton, 1548), fol. 6v; see p. 69].

1515 (May). Henry VIII, Queen Catherine and the court are entertained with an elaborate Robin Hood game officially organized for them [Halle, *Union*, fol. 56v–57r; cf. also *State Papers and Mss Relating to English Affairs Existing in the Archives and*

Collections of Venice, and in Other Libraries of Northern Italy, ed. Rawdon Brown and G. Cavendish Bentnick (London: HMSO, 1864), 2.248 (#624); see p. 69].

1559. See London (Thames Valley).

SCOTLAND

1531 (April 5). The crown pays 22s. 6d. for taffeta for "the Kingis Robene Hudis baner" [*Accounts of the Lord High Treasurer of Scotland*, Scottish Record Office (Edinburgh: H. M. General Register House, 1877), 5.432; see also 432–33].

1555. Parliament decrees "that in all tymes cummyng na maner of persound be chosin Robert Hude nor Lytill Johne, Abbot of unressoun, Quenis of Maii, nor otherwise, nouther in Burgh nor to landwart in ony tyme to cum" [*Acts of the Parliament of Scotland*, ed. Thomas Thomson, Record Commission Publications 36 (Edinburgh: Record Commission, 1814), 2.500].

1577. General Assembly resolves to ask the Regent "that his Grace wald discharge playes of Robin Hood, King of May, and sick vthers, on the Sabboth day" [*Acts and Proceedings of the General Assemblies of the Kirk of Scotland*, ed. Thomas Thomson (Edinburgh: Bannatyne Club, 1839–45), 1.388].

1578. General Assembly resolves to make "a supplicatioun to his Grace and Counsell to discharge be opin proclamation, all kynd of insolent playis as King of May, Robin Hood, and sick vthers, in the moneth of May, played either be bairnes at the schools or others" [*Acts and Proceedings of the General Assemblies*, 2.407; for another resolution to same effect see 2.410].

1592. General Assembly resolves "It is craveit . . . The acts of Parliament made for the suppressing of the enormities following may be put to executioun: . . . profaners of the Sabboth day be Robein Hoodes playis" [*Acts and Proceedings of the General Assemblies*, 2.784].

Lothian

Edinburgh

1492. Robert Coupland is made a citizen by George Martin as Robin Hood [Anna Jean Mill, *Medieval Plays in Scotland* (Edinburgh and London: W. Blackwood and Sons, 1927), 219].

1494. John Smollet and John Seton are made citizens by George Martin as Robin Hood; John Carmure is made a citizen by Andrew Bertram as Robin Hood [Mill, *Medieval Plays*, 219].

149?. William Dixon is made a citizen by Andrew Bertram as Robin Hood; James Thompson is made a citizen by Alexander Crawford as Robin Hood [Mill, *Medieval Plays*, 219].

1499 (Mar. 2). John White is made a citizen by Alexander Carkettle as Robin Hood [Mill, *Medieval Plays*, 219].

1500. Andrew Ross is made a citizen by Robin Hood; James Dun is made a citizen by William Halkston as Little John [Mill, Medieval Plays, 219].

1518. City records relate that the Abbot of Narent is now "callit Robin Huid and Little Jhone" [J. D. Marwick, ed., *Extracts from the Records of the Burgh of Edinburgh AD*

1403–1528. (Edinburgh: printed for the Scottish Burgh Records Society, 1869), 66; Mill, *Medieval Plays*, 220].

1518 (Apr. 17). Francis Bothwell submits a letter from the Earl of Arran to excuse him "fra the office of Litiljohn, to the quhilk he was chosin for this yeir." According to the letter, "Francis Boithwell your nichtbour is chosin to be Litiljohn for to mak sportis and jocositeis in the toun, the quhilk is a man to be vsit hiear and gravar materis, and als is apon his viage to pas beyond sey his neidfull erandis" [Marwick, *Extracts*, 176; Mill, *Medieval Plays*, 220].

1544 (Apr. 21, Saturday 2 weeks after Easter). The crown donates money "to Robert Hude in Edinburght" [*Accounts of the Lord High Treasurer of Scotland*, 8.282].

1547 (May). The crown pays money "to certane menstrallis of the toun, and thair Robert Hude" [*Accounts of the Lord High Treasurer of Scotland*, 9.73–74].

1547 (May 14, Saturday before Ascension). The crown pays £4 8s. "to Robert Hude of Edinburght" [*Accounts of the Lord High Treasurer of Scotland*, 9.74].

1549 (June). The crown pays £4 10s. "to Jhonne Arthure, Robene Hude of Edinburght" [*Accounts of the Lord High Treasurer of Scotland*, 9.316].

1550 (Apr.). The crown pays £3 9s. "to Robert Hude in Edinburgh" [*Accounts of the Lord High Treasurer of Scotland*, 9.393].

1561. Riots from May to August resulting from efforts to suppress Robin Hood games. See Appendix B.

1562 (Apr. 30). Queen Mary writes to the Town Council that "it is notour vnto yow that be oure act of parliament it is statute and commandit that na Robene Hudis nor Litil Jhoneis suld be chosin within oure realme, nochttheles as we are informeit ye intend to elect and cheis personis to beir sic offices this Maii approcheand, incontrair the tennour of oure said act, quha vnder colour of Robene Hudis play purpoissis to rais seditione and tumult within our said burgh, for perturbatioun of the commoun tranquilitie quhairin oure gude subjectis ar desyrous to leif; quhairfore it is oure will, and we charge yow, that on na wys ye permit nor suffer this yeir ony sic as Robene Hude or Litil Jhonne to be chosin." The proclamation enjoins "that na maner of persoun . . . tak vpoun thaime ony sic office or power as Robene Hude, Litil Jhonne, Abbat of Vnressoun or the like office . . . to mak convocatioun or beir armour, contrair the tennour . . . of the actis of parliament" [Mill, *Medieval Plays*, 223].

1562. Town treasurer's accounts include a payment for a trumpet blown at the town cross for the proclamation against Robin Hood plays [*Edinburgh Records. The Burgh Accounts*, ed. Robert Adam (Edinburgh: for the Lord Provost, Magistrates and Council, 1899), 1.367; Mill, *Medieval Plays*, 224].

1572. "Thair wes in this foirsaid moneth greit penuritie and scant of vivaris within the burgh of Edinburgh, sua that all wes at ane exceiding darth. Nochttheles the remaneris thairin abaid patientlie, and wer of good comfort, and vsit all plesouris quhilkis wer wont to be vsit in the said month of Maij in ald tymes, viz. Robin Hude and Litill Johne." [*A Diurnal of Remarkable Occurrents that have Passed within the Country of Scotland since the Death of King James the Fourth till the Year MDLXXV*, ed. Thomas Thomson. Bannatyne Club 43 (Edinburgh: Bannatyne Club, 1833), 263].

1579 (May 1). The provost, baillies, council, and deacons order a proclamation "that na inhabitant within this burgh presume to accompany any sic as ar of mynde to renew the playes of Robene Hude" [Mill, *Medieval Plays*, 224].

Cranston

1590 (May 28). Thirteen men are summoned before the Presbytery "for prophaning the sabboth with pasch playis as robene hudis abbottis vnresson etc." [Mill, *Medieval Plays*, 170].

Dirleton

1585 (May). "The King remained at Dirleton twelve dayes. There were in companie with him Arran, Sir Robert Melvill, Secretar Matlane, Phairnihirst, Colonell Stewart, and the Maister of Gray. They passid the time with the play of Robin hood" [David Calderwood, *The History of the Kirk of Scotland*, ed. Thomas Thomson (Edinburgh: Wodrow Society, 1842–49), 4.366].

Dalkeith

1582 (May 24). The Presbytery gives order for measures to suppress "abbott of vnressones playis or robene hudis" [Mill, *Medieval Plays*, 168–69].

Haddington

1588 (Dec. 4). Town authorities promise "to abolische and remoue . . . maj plaijs of roben hude, litle Iohne, abitis of vnresoun" [Mill, *Medieval Plays*, 253; cf. 254–55].

1589 (Apr. 16). Presbytery complains of "þe insolence of þe ȝouth in chasing robene hui[d and] vþer prophane playis vsit vpone the saboth day" [Mill, *Medieval Plays*, 254].

1589 (Apr. 30). "Þe ȝouth of the toun of hadingtoun" apologize for "pasche playis, abbot of onresone, robene houd & sic vþer prophane playis" [Mill, *Medieval Plays*, 254].

1589 (?September). The Presbytery resolves to ask "þat ane mair substantious act may be maid aganis peace playis, robene huid etc." [Mill, *Medieval Plays*, 255].

Lasswade

1583 (Jul. 4). George Ramsay of Lasswade is summoned by the Presbytery concerning "the prophanatione of the sabboth day with Robert hude & litill Ihone & may playis" [Mill, *Medieval Plays*, 169].

1583 (Sep. 12). John Abell "with the rest of his band prophaneris of the sabboth be Robene huidis play" are summoned by the Presbytery [Mill, *Medieval Plays*, 169].

North Sea Coast

Aberdeen

1508 (May 8). The alderman, baillies, and council ordain that all able citizens are to be prepared "with þar arrayment maid in grene and ȝalow bowis Arrowis brass And all vþer conuenient thingis according þarto" to process with Robin Hood and Little John

"all tymes convenient þarto quhen þai be Requirit be þe saidez Robyne & litile
Iohne," on pain of a 40s. fine and loss of certain privileges [Mill, *Medieval Plays*,
137].

1508 (Nov. 17). The town authorities decree that "all personis burges nichbouris and
Inhabitaris burges sonnys" are to be prepared to ride with Robin Hod and Little John,
"quhilk was callit in ȝeris bipast Abbot and priour of Bonacord," on Saint Nicholas
Day upon pain of loss of pensions and profits under the town's jurisdiction [Mill,
Medieval Plays, 137].

1517 (May 15). Certain disobedient residents who have refused to process with Robin
Hood and Little John are reproved and warned to obey the proclamation "and pas with
þe saidez Robert & Iohn all þe sondais of may & vther tymes quhen þai be warnit"
[Mill, *Medieval Plays*, 140].

1565 (May 11). One Henry Marshall "Is convickit for being in conventioun with his
colleggis in making of robin huid & litill Iohnne aganis þe act of parliament" [Mill,
Medieval Plays, 153].

1565 (May 14). The provost and baillies order a bellman to make proclamation "to all
burges men craftismen & all vtheris . . . That nane of thame tak vpone hand . . . to
convene þe quenis legis in chesing of robin huid litill Iohnne abbot of ressoune queyne
of maij or siclyk" [Mill, *Medieval Plays*, 153].

1565 (May 28). The provost reads publicly a letter from the Queen to the town that
"Certane seditious personis, craftismen, cutlaris baxteris, saidlers, swerdslipparis,
cordinaris, blaksmythis, goldsmythis, cowparis, barboris and vþeris . . . hes arrogantlie
attemptit in this instant moneth of maij to elect amangis thame selffis Robene hude
and Litil Iohnne And to mak oppine convocatioun in weirlyk maner alsweill on the
sabbaoth as vþeris prophane dayis Tending as appeiris to na thing vþer bot a plane
seditioune and wproar and witht tyme to aspure vnto farther Licentious libertie gif
thair temerarius attemptatis be nocht quiklie repressit" [Mill, *Medieval Plays*, 154].

Arbuthnot

1570. Seventeen men are accused of choosing a "Robert Hude and Abbot of Unreasoune"
[Robert Pitcairn, *Ancient Criminal Trials in Scotland from A.D. MCCCCLXXXVIII to
A.D. MDCXXIV* (Edinburgh: Maitland Club, 1833), 1.15–16; Mill, *Medieval Plays*,
24].

Dundee

1521 (Apr. 4). The provost and baillies authorize a grant of 5 marks or a citizenship to
Robin Hood for building archery butts [Mill, *Medieval Plays*, 173].

Perth

1503 (Jun. 26). The King pays 4 French crowns to Robin Hood of Perth [*Accounts of the
Lord High Treasurer of Scotland*, 2.377; Mill, *Medieval Plays*, 319].

1545 (May 16, May 21, and May 27). Robert Sibbald, Robert Meik, and Walter
Oliphant are made citizens, paying their fees to James MacBrek as Robin Hood [Mill,
Medieval Plays, 265].

St. Andrews

1575 (March 2). It is decreed that none shall "presume nor tak upon hand to violat the Sabbat day, be using of playis and gemmis publiclie as they war wont to do, contrafating the playis of Robein Huid" [Mill, *Medieval Plays*, 286].

1575. The General Assembly sends a delegation to the minister of St. Andrews "to inquir quhat is the caus that at that tyme Robin Huidis playes wes sufferit to be playit, and thairthrow prophanand the Fasting." The minister replies "concernyng the suffering of Robine Huidis playis, certane servandis and young childering plaid thame certane days . . . alwayis the kirk bayth prevatlie in thair assemblie, and I publictlie in tyme of preching dischargeit the samin as it is notoriouslie knawin, and desyrit the magistrattis to tak ordour thairwith" [*Miscellany of the Maitland Club Consisting of Original Papers and Other Documents Illustrative of the History and Literature of Scotland* (Edinburgh: Maitland Club, 1834), 1.114–15].

Southern Lowlands

Ayr

1539 and 1540. £6 13s 4d. are paid for the "Robert Hudis plais" at 5 marks each year [George S. Pryde, ed., *Ayr Burgh Accounts 1534–1624*, Scottish Historical Society 3rd ser. 28 (Edinburgh: Scottish Historical Society, 1937), 84].

1540. 5 marks are paid to William Nesbit "for robert hudis plais," and the same to Alexander Kennedy for the plays the following year [Mill, *Medieval Plays*, 165].

1543. The town pays £3 6s. 8d. "to Robert hudis play" [Mill, *Medieval Plays*, 166].

1545. Treasurer Andrew Dalzell incurred reimbursable expenses as Robin Hood [Pryde, *Ayr Burgh Accounts*, 102; Mill, *Medieval Plays*, 166].

1547. The town pays 35s. 8d. "to george dun for þe franchemennis lawingis in robert hvdis playis" [Mill, *Medieval Plays*, 166; Pryde, 100].

1548. The town pays 10 marks "quhilk suld haue bene gevin to George dun and hew montsode quhen þai wer robert hude & litle Johnn" [Mill, *Medieval Plays*, 166].

1549. William Wallace and John Campbell (a barber) apply for citizenship for their labors when they served as Robin Hood and Little John [Mill, *Medieval Plays*, 166].

1550. 5 marks paid "to Johnn Jamesone quhen he was robene hude" [Mill, *Medieval Plays*, 167].

1550. John Adam is admitted to citizenship on the condition "þat he be honestlie cled as ane honest man as efferis to ane burges man to be betueyn & sunday nixt tocum to serf robert hud" [Mill, *Medieval Plays*, 167].

1551. 40s. paid "for þe expens of four frenchemen quhen george dun wes robene hude in his hous xl s." Also 5 marks each are paid to Charles Campbell and Robert McMillan when they were Robin Hood and Little John [Mill, *Medieval Plays*, 167].

1554. 4s. 6d. paid for gunpowder "To robene hudis playis" [Mill, *Medieval Plays*, 167].

Dumbarton

Robin Hood games in Dunbarton are mentioned by Mill [*Medieval Plays*, 24], but no details are given.

Dumfries

1534 (Oct. 9). Jock Wilson and Will Thomson are made citizens by the Robin Hood and Little John who were chosen the previous Easter [Mill, *Medieval Plays*, 171].

1536 (Apr. 21). Simeon Crocket is made a citizen by Robin Hood and Little John [Mill, *Medieval Plays*, 171].

1536 (Apr. 27). Two men are to be chosen to become citizens at the hands of Robin Hood and Little John [Mill, *Medieval Plays*, 171].

1536 (Jun. 14). John Pawtonson is made a citizen by Robin Hood and Little John for 40d. [Mill 171].

1570 (Jun. 17). The town authorities authorize payment to Herbert Raning for taffetas received from him for the use of Robin Hood [Mill, *Medieval Plays*, 171].

1570 (Nov. 3). The town authorities levy a fine on Tom Trustre for his refusal at Easter to take on the office of Robin Hood and Little John [Mill, *Medieval Plays*, 172].

Linton

1610 (May 17). John Middlemest of Shairpsrig, George Davison of Hoisla, and George Ker of Linton are accused of playing the Sheriff, Little John, and Robin Hood [Mill, *Medieval Plays*, 258].

Peebles

1555 (May 6). Robert Murro is made a citizen, paying his "burges siluer" to "my lord Robene Hude" [Mill, *Medieval Plays*, 263].

Appendix B:

The Edinburgh Riots of 1561

Apr. 23, order of city authorities [cited Anna Jean Mill, *Medieval Plays in Scotland* (Edinburgh and London: W. Blackwood and Sons, 1927), 221]:

The prouest baillies and counsale vnderstanding that the prentissis and seruandis of merchanttis and craftismen and vtheris within this burgh ar of mynd vpoun Sounday nixt to mak convocatioun and assemblie efter the auld wikit maner of Robene Hude, nocht regarding the pvnishment thretnit in Goddis word vpoun the braikaris of the Saboth, nor having feir of the temporale pvnischment content in our Souerane actis vpoun the vsurparris of sic vane pastymes . . . ordanis ane proclamatioun to be maid at the foure principale pairttis of this burgh . . . dischargeing all sic conventionis . . . and of all bering of armour, wappinnis, striking of suesche, sounding of trumpet, bering of baner standert or anseyne or lyke instrument, for sic vane besynes.

Jul. 20, court record [Robert Pitcairn, *Ancient Criminal Trials in Scotland from A.D. MCCCCLXXXVIII to A.D. MDCXXIV* 3 (Edinburgh: Printed for the Maitland Club, 1833), 1.*409–10]:

The quhilk day, James Cowper, tailȝeour, come in Will for arte and parte of þe chesing of George Durye in Robert Hude, vþerwayis calland and nemmand him Lord of (In)obedience (Misrule), amangis þe Craftismen and þair seruandis, within þe burgh of Edinburgh, in þe moneth of Apryill last bypast, foreseand and assistant to him incontrair þe tennour of þe Act of Parliament. . . . Item for breking of þe Proclamatioun of þe Provest and Bailleis of Edinburghe, maid for observing of þe said Act. . . . Item for Convocatioun of our souerane ladies liegis, in cumpany with þe said George Durye, callit Lord of (In)obedience, to þe nowmer of — persones, bodin in feir (of weir), with ane displayit handsenȝe, halbrownis, jakkis, culveringis, morriounis, twa handit swerdis, cotis of malȝe, and vþeris wapynnis invasive, vpone Soneday þe xij day of Maii last bypast, in cumpanye with certane brokin men of were, betuix thre and four houris eftir none, cumand within þe burghe of Edinburghe, enterand at þe Eist Porte þairof, and passed to þe Trone þairof, quhair þai wer met be ane parte of þe Bailleis, counsale, and officiaris of þis burghe, for eschewing trouble and misordour in þe samyn: And, nochtwithstanding þe said charge, violentlie and contempnandlie passand fordward to þe said Castell-hill, and returnand againe to þe Portis of þe said burghe; vsand þe samyn be ische and entre, at þair plesour, makand plane rebellioun and inobedience aganis þe Magistratis of þe said burgh..

Aug. 8, court record [Pitcairn, *Ancient Criminal Trials*, 1.*410]: Various citizens are named for involvement with the "cheising of þe said Lord of (In)obedience, tvmult, and rysing aganis þe Magistratis of þe said burgh, be way of rebellioun and vþeris crymes . . . in þe moneth of July last bypast and August instant" and for failing to assist the city officials "vpone the xxj day of July last bypast, quhen þe seruandis and prentissis of þe Craftis . . . wer assegeand and invadand þe saidis Provest and Bailleis in þe tolbuyth of þe said burgh, be abstracting and withdrawing of þame selffis fra þe help, supporte, frething, and releving of þame."

John Knox, *The History of the Reformation in Scotland*, in *The Works of John Knox*, ed. David Laing (Edinburgh: Wodrow Society, 1864), 2.157–160:

The Papistis and Bischoppis, dissapoyntit of thair principall purpose and interpryse did yet make broillie for troubel; for the raschall multitude war stirred up to mak a Robene Hude, quhilk enormitie wes of mony yeiris left and dampnit by statute and act of Parliament. Yit wald thay nott be forbiddin, bot wald disobey and truble the Towne, especiallie upone the nycht. Quhairat the Baillies offendit, tuke fra thame some swerdis and an enseynze, quhilk wes occasioun that thay that same nycht maid a mutinye, keippit the portis of the towne, and intendit to have persewit some men within thair awin housses; bot that, upoun the restitutioun of thair swerdis and enseynze, wes stayit. Bot yit thay ceassit nott to molest, alsweill the inhabitantes of Edinburgh as diverse countrey men, taking frome thame money, and threitnyng some with farder injureis. Quhairwith the Magistratis of the towne, heychtlie offendit, tuke mair diligent heid to suche as resortit to the towne, and so apprehendit ane of the principall of that misordour, namit Gillone, a cordinare, quhome thai put to ane assisse; and being convicted, for he could not be absolved (for he wes the cheif man that spoillit Johnne Mowbray of ten crownis of the Sone), thai thocht to have execute jugement upone him, and so erected a jebbet beneath the Croce. But, quhidder it came by pactioun with the Provest and some uther, or by instigatioun of the Craftismen, quha ever haif bene bent too muche to mayntene such vanitie and rytousnes, we fullie knaw nott, but suddandlie thair did ryse a tumult; the Tolbuyth wes brokin up, and not onlie the said Gillone, quho befoir wes damnit, wes violentlie takin furth, bot also all uther malefactouris wer set at fredom; the jebbete wes pullit downe, and dispitfullie brokin, and thairefter, as the Provest and some of the Counsall assemblit to the Clerkis chalmer for consultatioun, the hail rascall multitude bandit togidder, with some knawin unhonest craftismen, and intendit invasioun of the said chalmer. Quhilk percevit, the Provest, and such as were in his cumpany, past to the Tolbuyth, suspecting nothing that thay wald haif bene sa enragit that thei wald make new persute, efter that they had obtenit thair intent. Bot thai wer suddandlie deceavit, for from the Castlehill thai come with violence, and with stanis, gunnis, and such uther weaponis as thei had, began to assault the said Tolbuyth, ran at the dure of it, quhilk that parte by stanis cast from above, and partlie by a pystoll schott by Robert Norwell, quhilk hurt ane Twedy, thai wer repulsit fra the door; but yit ceassit not thai to cast and schute in at the wyndowis, threitnyng deith to all that war within. And in verray deid the malice of the craftismen, quho were suspectit to be the occasioun of that tumult, bare na gude will to dyvers of thame that wes with the Provost.

The argumentis that the Craftis wer the caus of that uproire, besydis thair first misordour that thay haid usit befoir, in tackin Sandersoun from the exectioun of punishment, are twa. The formar, Archibald Dewar, Patrik Schange, with uther five deaconis of the craftis come to Johnne Knox, and willit him to solist the Provest and the towne to delay the executioun: quho did answer, That he haid sa oft solistit in thair favouris, that his awin conscience accusit him, that thay usit his labouris for na uther end, bot to be a patrone to thair impietie. For he haid befoir maid intercessioun for William Harlaw, James Frissall, and utheris, that wer convict of the formare tumult. Thai proudlie said that gif it was not stayit, bayth he and the Baillies suld repent it. Quhairto he answerit, He wald not hurt his concsience for ony feir of man. And sa thai departit; and the tumult (as said is) immediatlie thairefter did aryse. The secund argument is, the tumult continewit fra twa at efter none till efter aucht at nycht. The Craftismen wer requyrit to assemble them selfis togidder for deliverance of thair Provest and Baillies; bot thai past to thair foure houris penny, and in their jesting said, "Thai will be Magistratis allone, latt thame reule the multitude allone." And sa, contrair to the ayth that thai haid maid, thai denyit thair assistance, counsall, and conforte to thair Provest and Baillies; quhilk are argumentis verray probable, that the said tumult raise by thair procurement. The end heirof was, that the Provest and Baillies wer compellit to gif thair handwrittis, that thai suld never perseu ony of thame that war of that tumult, for ony cryme that wes done in that behalf. And this wes proclamet at the Croce efter nyne houris at nycht; and sa that truble quyetted. Bot the Nobilitie avowit, that thai suld not spare it; and sa a greit nomber of that factioun war absent frome the towne, till the arryvall of the Quene. The haill multitude wer haldin excommunicat, and war admittit to no participatioun of the sacramentis, unto suche tyme as thai satisfied the Magistratis, and maid humble sute unto the Kirk.

[For a derivative account of the same events, see David Calderwood, *The History of the Kirk of Scotland*, ed. Thomas Thomson (Edinburgh: Wodrow Society, 1842–49), 2.123–25.]

A Diurnal of Remarkable Occurrents that have Passed within the Country of Scotland since the Death of King James the Fourth till the Year MDLXXV, ed. Thomas Thomson. Bannatyne Club 43 (Edinburgh: Bannatyne Club, 1833), 65–66:

Vpoun the xxj day of Julij . . . Archibald Dowglas of Kilspindie, provest of Edinburgh, Dauid Symmer and Adame Foulartoun, ballies of the samyn, causit ane cordinare servand, callit James Killone, to vnderly the law in the tolbuith of Edinburgh, for the cuming in the toune of Edinburgh, and playing with Robene Hud; and for that caus thair was certane craftismenis servandis put to the horne of befoir, of the quhilk the said James Kellone wes ane; and causit the assyiss quhilk thaj had electit of thair assistaris pas thairvpone, qhua condamnit him to be hangit. And thair efter the craftismen maid greit solistatiouns at the handis of the said provest, Johne Knox minister and the ballies, to have gottin him relevit . . . quha wald doe nathing bot have him hangit. And quhen the tyme of the poore mans hanging approchit, and that the poore man wes cumand to the jibbet with the ledder vpone the quhilk the said cordinar suld have been hangit, the craftismennis childer and servandis past to armour; and first thaj howsit Alexander Guthrie, and provest and baillies, in the said Alexanderis writting buith, and syne come doune againe to the croce, and dang doun the jibbet, and brak it in pecis, and thairefter past to the tolbuith, quhilk wes then steikkeit; and quhen thay culd nocht apprehend the keis thairof, they brocht foir hamberis and dang vp the samyn tolbuith dure perforce . . . and when the said dure wes broken vp, ane part of thame past in the samyn, and nocht allanerlie brocht the said condampnit cordiner furth of the said tolbuith, bot also all the remanand presonaris being thairintill; and this done, thaj past doun the hie gait, to have past furth at the nether bow, quhilk wes then steikit, and because thaj culd nocht get furth thairat, thaj past vp the hie gait againe; and in the mene tyme the provest, ballies, and thier assistaris, being in the writting buith of Alexander Guthrie, past to the tolbuith; and in thair passing vp the said gait, they being in the tolbuyth as said is, schot furth at the said servandis ane dag, and hurt ane servand of the craftismennis. That being done, their was nathing bot tak and slay, that is, the ane pairt schotand furth and castand stanes, the vther pairt schotand hagbutis in agane; and sua the craftismennis servandis held them continewallie fra thre houris efternone quhill aucht at even, and never ane man of the toun sterit to defend thair provest and baillies. And than thaj send to the maisteris of the craftismen to caus them, gif they mycht, to stay the saidis servandis; quha purposit to stay the samen, but thaj culd nocht come to pas, but the servandis said that thaj vald have ane revenge for the man quhilk was hurt. And thairefter the provest send ane massenger to the constable of the castell to cum to astay the matter, quha came; and he, with the maistaris of the crafistmene treitit on this maner, that the provest and bailȝes sould discharge all maner of actiouns quhilk thaj had aganes the saidis craftischilder in ony tyme bygane, and chairgit all their maistaris to ressave them in service as thaj did of befoir, and promittit neuer to persew thame in tyme to cum for the samen. And this being done and proclamit, thaj skalit, and the provest and ballies come forth of the tolbuith.

[For another version of the same text, see 283–85.]

Selected Bibliography

Accounts of the Lord High Treasurer of Scotland. Scottish Record Office. Edinburgh: H. M. General Register House, 1877.

Andrew of Wyntoun. *The Orygynale Cronykil of Scotland*, ed. David Laing. Edinburgh: Edmonston and Douglas, 1872.

The Anonimalle Chronicle 1333–1381, ed. V. H. Galbraith. Publications of the University of Manchester 175. Historical Series 45. Manchester: Manchester University Press, 1927.

Arber, Edward. *A Transcript of the Registers of the Company of Stationers of London, 1554–1640*. London: privately published, 1875–94.

Aston, T. H. "Robin Hood. Communication." *Past and Present* 20 (1962): 7–9.

Atwater, N. A. *The Outlaw Tradition from Hereward the Saxon to Robin Hood*. Unpublished Brown University thesis, 1964.

Axton, Richard. "Folk Play in Tudor Interludes." In *English Drama: Forms and Development*, ed. M. Axton and R. Williams. Cambridge: Cambridge University Press, 1977, 1–23.

Bellamy, John. *Robin Hood: An Historical Enquiry*. London: Croom Helm, 1985.

Bessinger, J. B. "The Gest of Robin Hood Revisited." In *The Learned and the Lewed: Studies in Chaucer and Medieval Literature*. Cambridge, Mass.: Harvard University Press, 1974.

Bessinger, J. B., Jr. "Robin Hood: Folklore and Historiography, 1377–1500." *Tennessee Studies in Literature* 11 (1966): 61–69.

Blackstone, M. A. *Robin Hood and the Friar*. Poculi Ludique Societas Performance Texts 3. Toronto: Poculi Ludique Societas, 1981.

Bower, Walter. *Scotichronicon*. Aberdeen: Aberdeen University Press, 1987.

Burke, Peter. *Popular Culture in Early Modern Europe*. New York: Harper, 1978.

Chaucer, Geoffrey. *The Riverside Chaucer*, ed. Larry D. Benson. Boston: Houghton Mifflin, 1987.

Child, F. J. *The English and Scottish Popular Ballads*. Boston: Houghton, Mifflin, and Co., 1882–98; rpt. New York: Cooper Square, 1962.

Clawson, William Hall. *The Gest of Robin Hood*. University of Toronto Studies, Philological Series. Toronto: University of Toronto, 1909.

Coss, P. R. "Aspects of Cultural Diffusion in Medieval England: The Early Romances, Local Society, and Robin Hood." *Past and Present* 108 (1985): 35–79.

Cox, J. Charles. *Churchwardens' Accounts from the Fourteenth Century to the Close of the Seventeenth Century*. London: Methuen, 1913.

Cressy, D. *Literacy and the Social Order*. Cambridge: Cambridge University Press, 1980.

Crook, David. "Some Further Evidence Concerning the Dating of the Origins of the Legend of Robin Hood." *EHR* 99 (1984): 530–34.

Dobson, R. B., and Taylor, J. "Medieval Origins of the Robin Hood Legend: A Reassessment." *Northern History* 7 (1972): 1–30.

Dobson, R. B., and Taylor, J. "Robin Hood of Barnsdale: A Fellow Thou Has Long Sought." *Northern History* 19 (1983): 210–20.

Dobson, R. B., and Taylor, J. *Rymes of Robin Hood*. 2nd ed. Gloucester: Alan Sutton, 1989.

The Euing Collection of English Broadside Ballads in the Library of the University of Glasgow. Glasgow: University of Glasgow Publications, 1971.

Eyre, G.E.B. *A Transcript of the Registers of the Worshipful Company of Stationers from 1640–1708 A.D.* London: privately printed, 1913.

Fordun, John. *Johannis de Fordun Scotichronicon*, ed. T. Hearne. Oxford: e Theatro Sheldoniano, 1722.

Fowler, D. C. *A Literary History of the Popular Ballad*. Durham, N.C.: Duke University Press, 1968.

Gable, J. Harris. *Bibliography of Robin Hood*. University of Nebraska Studies in Language, Literature, and Criticism 17. Lincoln, Nebr.: University of Nebraska, 1939.

Geertz, Clifford. *The Interpretation of Cultures*. New York: Basic Books, 1973.

George, David. *Records of Early English Drama: Lancashire*. Toronto: University of Toronto Press, 1991.

Goodchild, John. "Elizabethan Yeovil as Recorded in Churchwardens' Accounts." *Proceedings of the Somersetshire Archaeological and Natural History Society* 88 (1943): 56–72.

Grafton, Richard. *A Chronicle at Large*. London: Printed for J. Johnson, 1809.

Gray, D. "The Robin Hood Poems." *Poetica: An International Journal of Linguistic and Literary Studies* (Tokyo) 18 (1984): 1–39.

Greene, R. L. *Early English Carols*. 2nd ed. Oxford: Clarendon Press, 1977.

Gutch, John Matthew. *A Lyttel Geste of Robin Hood*. London: Longman, Brown, Green and Longmans, 1847.

Hales, John W., and Frederick J. Furnivall, eds. *Bishop Percy's Folio Manuscript*. London: Trübner, 1868.

Hanawalt, Barbara A. "Ballads and Bandits: Fourteenth-Century Outlaws and the Robin Hood Poems." In Barbara A. Hanawalt, ed. *Chaucer's England. Literature in Historical Context*. Medieval Studies at Minnesota 4. Minneapolis: University of Minnesota Press, 1992, 154–75.

Harris, P. Valentine. *The Truth About Robin Hood*. Rev. ed. Westgate, Notts.: Linneys of Mansfield, 1973.

Harris, P. Valentine. "Who Was Robin Hood?" *Folk-Lore Quarterly* 66 (1955): 288–94.

Henslowe, William. *Henslowe's Diary*, ed. R. A. Foakes and R. T. Rickert. Cambridge: Cambridge University Press, 1961.

Hilton, Rodney H. "The Origins of Robin Hood." *Past and Present* 14 (1958): 30–44.

Hilton, Rodney H. *Peasants, Knights, and Heretics*. Cambridge: Cambridge University Press, 1976.

Hirsch, Richard. *An Introduction to the Huntingdon Plays*. Unpublished Brown University masters thesis, 1967.

Hobhouse, E., ed. *Church Warden's Accounts of Croscombe, Pilton, Yatton, Tintinhull, Morebath, and St. Michael's, Bath*. Somerset Record Society 4. London: Somerset Record Society, 1890.

Hobsbawm, E. B. *Bandits*. New York: Delacorte Press, 1969.

Hobsbawm, E. B. *Social Bandits and Primitive Rebels*. Glencoe, Ill.: Free Press, 1959.

Hodgart, M. J. C. *The Ballads*. London, New York: Hutchinson's University Library, 1950.

Holinshed, Raphael. *The First-Laste Volume of the Chronicles of England, Scotlande, and Irelande*. London: H. Bynneman for J. Harrison, 1577.

Holt, J. C. "The Origins and Audience of the Ballads of Robin Hood." *Past and Present* 18 (1960): 89–110.

Holt, J. C. *Robin Hood*. 2nd ed. London: Thames and Hudson, 1989.

Holt, J. C. "Robin Hood: Some Comments." *Past and Present* 19 (1961): 16–18.

Holt, J. C. "Robin Hood Revised." *Johns Hopkins Magazine* (February 1984): XII–XVI.

Holt, J. C., and T. Takamiya. "A New Version of A Rhyme of Robin Hood." *English Manuscript Studies* 1 (1988): 213–21.

Hutton, Ronald. *The Rise and Fall of Merry England. The Ritual Year 1400–1700*. Oxford: Oxford University Press, 1994.

Ingram, R. W., ed. *Records of Early English Drama: Coventry*. Toronto: University of Toronto Press, 1981.

Johnston, Alexandra F. "Parish Entertainments in Berkshire." In J. A. Raftis, ed. *Pathways to Medieval Peasants*. Toronto: Pontifical Institute of Medieval Studies, 1981. 335–37.

Keen, Maurice. *The Outlaws of Medieval Legend*. Toronto: University of Toronto Press, 1961; rev. ed. London: Routledge and Kegan Paul; Toronto: University of Toronto Press, 1977.

Keen, Maurice. "Robin Hood, a Peasant Hero." *History Today* 8 (1958): 684–89.

Keen, Maurice. "Robin Hood—Peasant or Gentleman?" *Past and Present* 19 (1961): 7–15.

Kennedy, D. N. "Who Was Robin Hood?" *Folk-Lore Quarterly* 66 (1955): 413–15.

Kevelson, Roberta. *Inlaws/Outlaws. A Semiotics of Systemic Interaction: "Robin Hood" and the "King's Law."* Indiana University Publications Studies in Semiotics 9. Bloomington: Indiana University Press, 1977.

Klausner, David, ed. *Records of Early English Drama: Herefordshire and Worcestershire*. Toronto: University of Toronto Press, 1990.

Knight, Stephen. *Robin Hood. A Complete Study of the English Outlaw*. Oxford and Cambridge, Mass.: Blackwell, 1994.

Knight, Stephen, and Thomas Ohlgren, eds. *Robin Hood and Other Outlaw Tales*. TEAMS Middle English Texts Series. Kalamazoo, Mich.: Medieval Institute Publications, 1997.

Lancashire, Ian. *Dramatic Texts and Records of Britain. A Chronological Topography to 1558.* Toronto: University of Toronto Press, 1984.

Lega-Weekes, Ethel. "'Howde Men': Robin Hood's Men at Chagford." *Notes and Queries* 11 ser. no. 1 (April 30, 1910): 346.

Lévi-Strauss, Claude. *The Savage Mind.* Chicago: University of Chicago Press, 1966.

MacLean, Sally-Beth. "King Games and Robin Hood: Play and Profit at Kingston-upon-Thames." *Research Opportunities in Renaissance Drama* 29 (1986–1987): 85–94.

Maddicott, J. R. "The Birth and Setting of the Ballads of Robin Hood." *EHR* 93 (1978): 276–99.

Major, John. *Historia Majoris Britanniae*, ed. R. Freebairn. Edinburgh: R. Freebairn, 1740.

Manning, Roger B. *Village Revolts.* Oxford: Oxford University Press, 1988.

Meagher. *See* Munday.

Mill, Anna Jean. *Medieval Plays in Scotland.* Edinburgh and London: W. Blackwood and Sons, 1927.

Mitchell, William Reginald. *Exploring the Robin Hood Country.* Clapham, N. Yorks.: Dalesman, 1978.

Mitchell, William Reginald. *The Haunts of Robin Hood.* Clapham, N. Yorks.: Dalesman, 1970.

Munday, Anthony. *The Huntingdon Plays. A Critical Edition of* The Downfall *and* The Death of Robert, Earl of Huntingdon. Ed. John Carney Meagher. Renaissance Drama: A Collection of Critical Editions. New York and London: Garland, 1980.

Nashe, Thomas. *The Works of Thomas Nashe.* Ed. Ronald B. McKerrow. Oxford: Oxford University Press, 1966.

Nelson, Malcolm A. *The Robin Hood Tradition in the English Renaissance.* Salzburg Studies in English Literature. Salzburg: Institut für Englische Sprache und Literatur, 1973.

Parfitt, George. "Early Robin Hood Plays: Two Fragments and a Bibliography." *Renaissance and Modern Studies* 22 (1978): 5–12.

Phillips, Graham, and Martin Keatman. *Robin Hood: The Man Behind the Myth.* London: O'Mara Books, 1995.

The Pinder of Wakefield. Ed. E. A. Horsman. English Reprints Series 12. Liverpool: Liverpool University Press, 1956.

Pitcairn, Robert. *Ancient Criminal Trials in Scotland from A.D. MCCCCLXXXVIII to A.D. MDCXXIV.* 3 vols. Edinburgh: Printed for the Maitland Club, 1833.

Pollard, A. W., and G. R. Redgrave. *A Short-Title Catalogue of Books Printed in England, Scotland, and Ireland and English Books Printed Abroad 1475–1640.* 2nd. ed., rev. W. A. Jackson, F. S. Ferguson, Katherine F. Pantzer. London: The Bibliographical Society, 1986.

Richmond, Colin. "An Outlaw and Some Peasants: The Possible Significance of Robin Hood." *Nottingham Medieval Studies* 37 (1993): 90–101.

Potter, Lois, ed. *Playing Robin Hood: The Legend as Performance in Five Centuries.* Newark, Del.: University of Delaware Press, 1998.

Ritson, Joseph. *Robin Hood: A Collection of All the Ancient Poems, Songs and Ballads Now Extant.* London: T. Egerton, 1795.

The Roxburghe Ballads, ed. Charles Hindley. London: Reeves and Turner, 1837–74.

Simeone, William E. "The May Games and the Robin Hood Legend." *Journal of American Folklore* 64 (1951): 265–74.

Simeone, William E. "Renaissance Robin Hood Plays." In *Folklore in Action: Essays for Discussion in Honor of MacEdward Leach*, ed. Horace P. Beck, 184-99. Philadelphia: The American Folklore Society, 1962.

Simeone, William E. "Robin Hood and Some Other Outlaws." *Journal of American Folklore* 71 (1958): 27–33.

Simeone, William E. "Still More about Robin Hood." *Journal of American Folklore* 65 (1952): 418–20.

Simpson, Claude M. *The British Broadside Ballad and Its Music*. New Brunswick, N.J.: Rutgers University Press, 1966.

Skelton, John. *The Complete English Poems*, ed. John Scattergood. Harmondsworth: Penguin, 1983.

Stallybrass, Peter. "'Drunk with the Cup of Liberty': Robin Hood, the Carnivalesque and the Rhetoric of Violence in Early Modern England." *Semiotica* 54 (1985): 113–45.

Steckmesser, Kent L. "Robin Hood and the American Outlaw: A Note on History and Folklore." *Journal of American Folklore* 79 (1966): 348–55.

Stokes, James D. "Robin Hood and the Churchwardens in Yeovil." *Medieval and Renaissance Drama in England* 3 (1986): 1–25.

Tardif, Richard, "The 'Mistery' of Robin Hood: A New Social Context for the Texts." In *Words and Worlds. Studies in the Social Role of Verbal Culture*, ed. Stephen Knight and S. N. Mukherjee, 130–45. Sydney Studies in Society and Culture 1. Sydney: Sydney Association for Studies in Society and Culture, 1983.

Thompson, Stith, ed. *The Motif-Index of Folk Literature*. Copenhagen: Rosenkilde and Bagger, 1955–58.

Thoms, William J. *Early English Prose Romances*. 2nd. ed. Vol. 2, *Virgilius, Robin Hood, George a Green, Tom a Lincolne*. London: Nattali and Bond, 1858.

Tiddy, R. J. E. *The Mummers' Play*. Oxford: Clarendon Press, 1923.

Underdown, David. *Revel, Riot and Rebellion. Popular Politics and Culture in England 1603–1660*. Oxford: Clarendon Press, 1985.

The Vision of William Concerning Piers the Plowman in Three Parallel Texts, ed. W. W. Skeat. London: Oxford University Press, 1886.

Vlasto, Jill. "An Elizabethan Anthology of Rounds," *Musical Quarterly* 40 (1954): 222–34.

Walker, J. W. "Robin Hood Identified." *Yorkshire Archaeological Journal* 36 (1944): 4–46.

Walker, J. W. *The True History of Robin Hood*. Wakefield: EP Publishing, 1952.

Wasson, John M. "The St. George and Robin Hood Plays in Devon." *Medieval English Theatre* 2 (1980): 66–99.

Wasson, John M., ed. *Records of Early English Drama: Devon*. Toronto: University of Toronto Press, 1986.

Wiles, David. *The Early Plays of Robin Hood*. Woodbridge, Suffolk: D. S. Brewer, 1981.

Williams, Jay. "More about Robin Hood." *Journal of American Folklore* 65 (1952): 304–5.

Wilson, R. M. *Lost Literature of Medieval England*. 2nd ed. London: Methuen, 1970.

Wing, Donald. *A Short-Title Catalogue of Books Printed in England, Scotland, Ireland, Wales and British America and of English Books Printed in Other Countries 1641–1700*, rev. John J. Morrison, Carolyn Nelson, and Matthew Seccombe. New York: Modern Language Association, 1994.

Wright, Thomas, and J. O. Halliwell-Phillips. *Reliquiae Antiquae*. London: J. R. Smith, 1845.

Index

About the Author

JEFFREY L. SINGMAN is a medievalist and former editor at *The Middle English Dictionary* project. His previous books include *Daily Life in Elizabethan England* (1995) and *Daily Life in Chaucer's England* (1995), both available from Greenwood Press.

ISBN 0-313-30101-8

9 780313 301018

EAN

90000>

HARDCOVER BAR CODE